Aspects of Fairness in Contract

Law in its Social Setting

Aspects of Fairness in Contract

Edited by
Chris Willett
School of Law, University of Warwick

First published in Great Britain 1996 by Blackstone Press Limited,
9–15 Aldine Street, London W12 8AW. Telephone 0181-740 2277

ISBN: 1 85431 602 8

British Library Cataloguing in Publication Data
A CIP catalogue record for this book is available from the British Library.

Printed by Bell & Bain Ltd, Glasgow

Contents

List of Contributors

Hugh Beale has been Professor of Law at the University of Warwick since 1987. Previously he was Lecturer at University College Wales, Aberystwyth and Lecturer and then Reader at the University of Bristol. He has also taught in the United States and in France. He is author of *Remedies for Breach of Contract* (1980) and, with Bill Bishop and Michael Furmston of *Contract, Cases and Materials* (3rd edition 1995).

William Bratton is a Professor of Law in the Cardozo Law School, New York.

Roger Brownsword is a Professor of Law at the University of Sheffield. His principal research interests lie in the fields of Common Law and Legal Theory. He is the co-author (with John N. Adams) of *Understanding Contract Law* (2nd ed. 1994), *Understanding Law* (1992), and *Key Issues in Contract* (1995); he is the co-author (with Deryck Beyleveld) of *Law as a Moral Judgement* (1986; reprinted 1994), and *Mice, Morality and Patents* (1993); and he is the co-editor (with Geriant Howells and Thomas Wilhelmsson) of *Welfarism in Contract Law* (1994). In addition to publishing numerous articles in law reviews in the UK, North America and Australia, Professor Brownsword has acted as case-note editor for the *Modern Law Review* since 1990.

Hugh Collins studied law at Oxford University and Harvard Law School, and became a Fellow of Brasenose College from 1976-1990, when he was appointed Professor of English Law at the London School of Economics. He has published works in legal theory, labour law, and contract law. His recent books include: *Justice in Dismissal* (Oxford University Press, 1992); *Law of Contract* 2nd ed. (Butterworths, 1993).

Morton Hviid is a lecturer at the Department of Economics at the University of Warwick. His research interests are Industrial organisation, game theory, and law and economics.

Ewoud Honduis (1942) read law in Leyden University and Columbia University. He was Professor of Civil Law in Leyden until his appointment in the same position in Utrecht University in 1980. He also served as Visiting Professor at the Universities of Sydney and London (Queen Mary and Westfield College). He has published a number of books on subjects such as consumer protection, European private law, precontractual liability, prescription (limitation of actions) and unfair contract terms.

Geraint Howells is a Reader in Law at the University of Sheffield. He is editor of the Consumer Law Journal and has written widely on common law and consumer law, notably *Comparative Product Liability* and *Consumer Protection* both published by Dartmouth.

Joseph McCahery was a judicial clerk for the Honorable Nathaniel R. Jones of the United States Court of Appeals for the Sixth Circuit. He teaches international economic law at the University of Warwick. He is the co-author (with Keith Ansell-Pearson) of *Machinic Postmodernism; Complexity, Technics and Regulation* (1996) and co-editor of *International Regulatory Competition and Co-ordination* (Oxford University Press, 1996) and *Corporate Control and Accountability* (Oxford University Press 1993).

Hans Micklitz is a Professor of Law of the University of Bamberg. He has researched and published extensively in the areas of European and Consumer Law. In particular he has published books (as co-author) on Consumer Law in the EC and on Federalism and Responsibility.

Thomas Wilhelmsson is Professor of civil and commercial law at the University of Helsinki since 1981. He has written books on contract law, insurance law, consumer protection, products liability, partnerships and legal theory. His books in English include: *Contract Law and European Integration* (Dartmouth 1995). He has been a Judge at the Market Court 1980-1990/

Chris Willett is a Senior lecturer at the School of Law, University of Warwick. Previously he taught at Brunel University and Oxford Brookes University. He has published widely in consumer and commercial law, his books including (with A. ODonnell) *Scottish Business Law* (2nd ed. 1996)) and *Quality and Remedies in Sale and Supply of Goods* (1996). He is also editor of another Blackstones collection on *The Citizen's Charter in the New Public Sector* (1996).

General Editor's Preface

This collection of essays on Fairness in Contract forms part of the series of books published under the auspices of the Warwick Law School's Legal Research Institute.

Law in its Social Setting aims to foster the established commitment of Warwick to the contextual study of law. The series brings together authors from other research centres in Britain and abroad to enrich debates on issues of contemporary importance in the area of legal and socio-legal studies.

This collection is intended to contribute to important debates about the different aspects of fairness in contract law.

Mike McConville
University of Warwick

Editor's Preface

This collection developed from a conference on Fairness in Contract Law, held at the University of Warwick in May 1994. It is intended to contribute to debate on various important concepts and theories associated with fairness.

Chris Willett
University of Warwick

Table of UK Statutes

Table of Statutory Instruments

Table of European Community Legislation

Table of Cases

1. Introduction

Chris Willett

INTRODUCTION – THE SCOPE OF THE COLLECTION

The collection is not driven by the search for the definitive conception of fairness, (if indeed such a conception exists). The aim, rather, is to facilitate discussion and debate on the sorts of concepts and concerns involved in various important areas where the rules might be said to be fairness oriented.

There is a chapter on fairness as it relates to quality obligations and remedies in contracts for the sale of goods (chapter 6 below). There are several chapters on the issue of unfair terms in consumer contracts (see chapters 2, 3 and 4 below). There is a chapter on the control of terms which provide for agreed remedies (see chapter 5 below), one on manufacturer's and sub-contractor's liability to those with whom they have no direct contract (see chapter 7 below), and one on norms of trust and co-operation in corporate contracts (see chapter 8 below).

The purpose of this editing essay is to introduce these topics and set them within a broader doctrinal and theoretical context. This essay is divided into three main parts. Part 1 gives a brief overview of the ways in which fairness issues might arise. The purpose of this is to show the range of different types of fairness issue that might exist and to highlight the limited scope of this collection within the larger picture. Part 2 introduces the specific chapters that follow. Part 3 discusses some theoretical themes which are typically relevant to analysis of fairness issues. These themes are discussed by reference to the topics discussed in subsequent Chapters, and also by reference to topics which are not discussed in these subsequent chapters. The purpose of this discussion is to set the scene for the subsequent chapters and to facilitate the making of theoretical connections between topics discussed here and between these and other topics.

PART 1

This part given an overview of rules that might be said to be fairness oriented. I refer to fairness here in a very broad sense. I include rules which are explicitly named as fairness rules. I also include rules where some form of fairness seems to be involved, even although it is not spoken of openly, e.g. where good faith or reasonable expectations seem to be at issue, or where for some other reason it is thought that one party's interests should be promoted or protected. As the following chapters illustrate there may well be additional ways of rationalising a good number of these rules. With this caveat in mind we will proceed to an overview of fairness rules.

One type of fairness is fairness in the pre-contractual context. So we are dealing with a situation in which the parties have had some form of contact before entering a main contract. The nature of this contact may vary enormously from case to case. However the typical scenario is that something has happened between the parties, which raises a question as to whether one of them should have some form of right or remedy against the other, despite the fact that this right or remedy cannot be grounded in the main contract. The problem is likely to have something to do with one party having raised expectations in the other, by a promise, an agreement or some pattern of behaviour. The sorts of expectatons raised could take many different forms. Party A may have thought that party B was committed only to negotiate with him to the exclusion of others. There may have been an actual 'lock out agreement' to this effect. Alternatively party B may have promised party A to hold open an offer for a certain period. In these sorts of situations the question of fairness is often expressed in terms of good faith. Any mechanisms to hold B to account tend to be thought of as being about a requirement of good faith being placed on B. An expectation of some kind has been raised by B and it would be bad faith to seek to avoid responsibility for it.

There are no chapters in this collection devoted to this type of fairness issue.[1] However I will return to pre-contractual fairness in Part 3 of this editing essay in an attempt to show connections between some of the fairness issues involved in pre-contractual matters and some of those involved in the topics dealt with in this collection.

A second category of fairness rules are those which deny contractual effect to certain terms or which limit the contractual effect of these terms.

---

1 For recent work on this area see Cohen 1995, Birks and Chin Nyuk Yin 1995, and Fabre-Magnan 1995, (all in Beatson & Friedman 1995), and also Carter and Furmston 1995

There are two sorts of rules here. First there are the rules on incorporation and construction of terms. Some of these are clearly fairness oriented and attempt to protect one of the parties from the other's terms. However the approach is not to say directly that terms are unfair but rather to hold that a term has no contractual effect because it has not been incorporated into the contract; or to hold that as a matter of construction the term does not have the effect which the party relying upon it intended.

Even if a term clears these hurdles there are a number of rules which may have the effect of invalidating the whole contract or a particular term. The contract may be voidable if there has been misrepresentation, duress or undue influence. A particular term may be unenforceable for unconscionability; it may fall foul of the rules on penalties, deposits or forfeiture; or it may be invalid under the Unfair Contract Terms Act (UCTA) 1977, or the Unfair Terms in Consumer Contracts Directive (implemented by the Unfair Terms in Consumer Contract Regulations 1994, SI 1994/3159).

What forms of unfairness do the above rules combat? The incorporation rules limit the extent to which party A can be surprised by partyB's terms, requiring that there at least be some form of chain of reference to the terms being relied upon and also requiring special disclosure of onerous and unusual terms.[2]

The contra proferentem construction rule construes any ambiguity against the party who is relying upon the term.[3] Often it will be this party who has drafted or at least chosen the terms, and it may be that the terms were offered to the other party on a take it or leave it basis. It may be thought to be unfair that one party can impose terms favouring his interests upon the other party. The contra proferentem rule may produce a meaning for the term which is more favourable to the interests of this other party.

UCTA and the Unfair Terms in Consumer Contracts Directive/UK Regulations offer a more direct control over terms which may have been imposed by one party and whose existence or import may not even have been known to the other party.

UCTA makes some terms void altogether and makes other subject to a test of reasonableness (see s.s. 2, 6, 7 and 11). The Directive/UK Regulations subject most terms in consumer contracts to a test of fairness (see Article 3 and Regulation 4). Both the UCTA reasonableness test and the Directive's test of fairness question the substantive fairness of the individual term in the context of the other terms. Both tests also question

---

2 Parker v. S.E. Ry Co. (1877) 2 CPD 416 and Interfoto v. Stilleto (1989) QB 433CA.

3 See Andrews Bros (Bournemouth) Ltd. v. Singer & Co. Ltd. (1934) IK.B. 17.

how fair the procedure was leading up to the conclusion of the contract. Of particular relevance here is whether the party prejudiced by the term know of and understood the terms, whether a choice of terms was available and what the relative bargaining strengths of the parties were (see further in Part 3 and see chapter 2 below).

Next, we have the equitable unconscionability rules. This is not the place for a detailed analysis (see Part 3 for further commentary). However we can say that there seems to be the facility to set aside a contract in equity if one party shows moral impropriety in taking advantage of a special bargaining weakness of the other party in order to secure terms which are very disadvantageous to the weaker party.[4]

The rules on misrepresentation, duress and undue influence concern themselves with even more blatant procedural unfairness and if it is shown that the misrepresentation, duress or undue influence has induced the contract the contract is voidable. There is no need to establish that the terms are in any way disadvantageous to the innocent party.

Finally in this second category of fairness rules are those rules which invalidate certain types of agreed remedies e.g. penalty clauses. Here the law's objection seems to be purely to the penalty itself, and the fact that is does not represent a reasonable pre-estimate of the loss suffered by the innocent party. Such a term cannot be saved by the fact that the bargaining procedure was fair; or by the fact that the overall package of terms was substantively fair (see chapter 5).

The third type of fairness rule is where the law imposes some type of obligation or duty on one of the parties with some kind of agenda to promote fairness. For example it might be thought that consumers reasonably expect, and as a matter of social policy are entitled to, a certain level of protection against poor quality goods. This might operate as a justification for imposing an obligation of quality upon sellers of goods (see chapter 6 below). It might also be argued that manufacturers should be liable to customers for the same reason, although it may also be possible to rationalise the placing of responsibility upon manufacturers in terms of efficiency (see chapter 7 below).

Another example of the law promoting a type of fairness through the imposition of obligations is where the law fills gaps in corporate contracts by reference to values of trust and co-operation (see chapter 8 below).

A fourth category of rules that might be said to be fairness oriented are those which set down ground rules for the remedies parties may have

4 Boustany v. Piggot (1993) 69 P & CR 298.

against each other for breach of contract.[5] So, for example, an innocent party in a breach of contract must mitigate his losses. While this rule can no doubt often be justified in terms of efficiency it also seems to be a matter of fairness that one party should mitigate his loss where practicable, rather than suffer the full loss and extract compensation from the other.

Another example of this type of fairness rule is a rule which places some kind of restriction on the right of an innocent party to reject goods or terminate a contract where the other party is in breach. A typical concern in this context is that the innocent party will reject or terminate in bad faith i.e. not because the breach significantly devalues what he gets from the contract, but because the contract has become a bad bargain (e.g. due to a change in market circumstances). This concern is clearly of relevance in the context of the rules on conditions, warranties and innominate terms (see Brownsword 1992 and 1995 for a discussion). The issue has also been addressed in the recently amended Sale of Goods Act 1979. Under s.15A of this Act if there is a breach of contract by a seller in a sale to a commercial buyer the buyer can only reject the goods if the breach is not so slight as to make rejection unreasonable. This rule is discussed below at chapter 6.

There is a fifth area in which fairness might be said to be a concern. This is where we find the law setting up such mechanisms as small claims courts, ombudsman and codes of practice because it is felt that although one contracting party may have rights against another, they may be hampered from pursuing these rights due to such factors as ignorance, inarticulacy, lack of resources etc. So any fairness which exists in the strict legal right may be rather meaningless in practice for the party possessing the right. Fairness may, therefore, have to be assured by the use of the sort of instruments mentioned. Consumer law provides a good example of this. The Motor Industry Code of Practice requires that terms and conditions of a sale should be clearly set out in an order form (section 1(4)) and that the retailer should draw the customer's attention to manufacturer's warranties (section 1(9)). If adhered to, these rules may ensure that customers are aware of their rights. This may make it easier for them to obtain redress in that they have something concrete to focus on in the dispute with the seller. An aggrieved customer who cannot obtain satisfaction from the seller is also more likely to take the matter further if he is aware of his rights.

There are also now a number of ombudsman schemes (e.g. in the banking, insurance, building society and personal investment sectors),

---

5 I would distinguish the setting of ground rules for remedies from the setting aside of agreed remedies (see the second category of rules, discussed above).

which provide cheaper and less formal access to justice for consumers (see Howells and Weatherill, 1995 and Rawlings and Willett, 1994). Again it can be argued that one purpose of such schemes is to make it more likely that consumers actually get the benefit of any fairness rules which exist.

The above are examples of how it can be made easier for individual contracting parties to obtain the benefits of fairness rules. The law may also seek to ensure that fairness rules work more effetively for the mass market of consumers. So Article 7 of the Unfair Terms Directive says that persons or bodies with a legitimate interest in protecting consumers should have access to the courts so that unfair terms can be controlled (see chapter 2, below and see Willett, 1996). The idea is that a court or administrative body have the power to declare terms unfair and instruct sellers and suppliers not to use them. This approach clearly assumes that sellers and suppliers will not be deterred from using unfair terms by the very remote risk of private law litigation.

PART 2

This part introduces the subsequent chapters. Chapters 2, 3 and 4 are all concerned with the issue of unfair terms in consumer contracts, more specifically with the Directive on Unfair Terms in Consumer Contracts (93/13 EEC) adopted in April 1993. This Directive has been implemented in the UK by the Unfair Terms in Consumer Contracts Regulations 1994 (SI 1994/3159), which applies to contracts made after lst July 1995.

At the core of the Directive/Regulations is a test of unfairness. A term which was not individually negotiated is unfair if 'contrary to the requirement of good faith it causes a significant imbalance in the rights and obligations arising under the contract to the detirment of the consumer' (Article 3, Regulation 4(2)). There is also an 'indicative annex of terms that may be regarded as unfair' (Article 3(3), Regulation 4(3)).

If a term fails this test it is not binding upon the consumer. As I have already pointed out in Part1, fairness regulation (which can result in the invalidation of a term or a contract) already exists in the UK. None of these existing rules are affected by the new Directive/Regulations. So, as far as rules which can invalidate a term or a contract are concerned the state of the law is now as follows.

All contracting parties can rely, where appropriate, on the protection of the rules on incorporation of terms and construction of terms; the rules on misrepresentation, duress and undue influence; the controls on agreed remedies and the equitable rules on unconscionability. All of these rules apply irrespective of the parties making the contract, and irrespective of the type of contract made.

However the range of parties and contracts covered by UCTA and the Directive/Regulations is narrower. Significantly the provisions in UCTA affecting negligence, breach of contract and indemnities (ss.2-4) do not apply to contracts of insurance or any contract in so far as it relates to the creation, transfer or termination of an interest in land (schedule 1).

In addition UCTA (with very minor exceptions) only applies to clauses excluding or limiting liability, and then only if this is being done by a party acting in the course of a business (section 1(3)). So both consumer and commercial contractors can challenge exemption clauses used by those acting in the course of a business; but they cannot generally challenge exemption clauses used by private contractors.

The Directive/Regulations apply to contracts of insurance and possibly to contracts involving land. However they do not apply to contracts of employment, contracts relating to succession rights or rights under family law and contracts relating to the organisation and incorporation of companies and partnerships (UK Regulations, Schedule 1). In addition the Regulations will only protect consumers and only when they are dealing with those dealing in the course of a business (see UK Regulations 1 and 2).

Within the contracts which are covered by the Directive all terms except those defining the price and the main subject matter are subject to the test of unfairness (Article 4(2), Reg. 3(2)).

The Unfair Terms Directive/Regulations in this Collection

The test of unfairness in the Directive/UK Regulations introduces concepts which the law in the UK is not used to dealing with e.g. 'good faith'. 'significant imbalance', 'detriment to the consumer' and an 'indicative annex' of unfair terms . We need commentary on these concepts, on their interrelationship, and on their relative roles in the overall test or tests of unfairness. Such commentary is provided by chapter 2. The authors of Chapter 2 also analyse the test of unfairness in the context of welfarism and the goals of European market integration. They consider how the test of unfairness should be understood in the light of the welfarist instinct to protect consumers which underlies the Directive; and in the light of the Directive's harmonisation and integrationist aims.

In Chapter 3 Honduis provides further analysis of the unfairness test in the Unfair Terms Directive, along with other aspects of the Directive, including the annex of unfair terms. However, Honduis looks beyond the

Directive and considers the concept of fairness as it is generally developing in European private law. He points out, that the test of unfairness used in the Unfair Terms Diretive is also used in the Principles of European Contract Law, which will serve as non mandatory guidelines in commercial contracts.

Finally, on the subject of the Unfair Terms Directive, if we are going to have such a major harmonising measure it makes sense to attempt to gain some insight into some of the sorts of terms which might be subject to this measure, and who is using these terms. This is one reason for including chapter 4 by Micklitz, which is based upon an empirical study carried out by the author for the European Commission. Micklitz discusses the various contractual forms in which terms may come (e.g. individualised terms and standard contracts) and the sorts of trade sectors and countries in which different terms are common. He also looks at ways of classifying different sorts of unfair terms.

Other Topics covered in the Collection

I will now turn to the other subjects covered in the collection. First of all there is the question of fairness in agreed remedies (see Collins at chapter 5 below). Commercial contracts make enormous use of terms which set down the implications of a breach of contract by either party. Yet, as I have already noted above, the common law exercises considerable control over such agreed remedies, especially over penalty clauses. Why is this? Is it possible to elaborate some notion of fairness which underlies the controls on agreed remedies? Collins argues that the courts are in the business of allowing the parties to engage in 'risk averaging' via their agreed remedies. The controls on agreed remedies seek to uphold this principle.

My own Chapter 6 considers the recent reforms to quality obligations and remedies in contracts for the sale of goods. The reformed quality obligation can be seen as more effectively representing the reasonable expectations of buyers; as well as slightly improving the prospects of making practical use of the right which it confers. With some qualification it may be possible to say the same of the reformed rules on 'acceptance' as they relate to the right to reject. Finally, the reform of the rules on the commercial buyer's right to reject can be argued to impose a certain restraint on bad faith rejection of defective goods.

Next there is the question as to whether a manufacturer should be liable to the ultimate customer for his statements and for quality defects in his products; and the parallel question as to whether a sub-contractor should be liable to the employer for the quality of his work (see Beale, below at chapter 7). What justifications might there be for such liabilities and might efficiency be just as important as fairness in this respect? If mass and network contracting make it too costly to properly reflect the parties' expectations via contractual protection, then by imposing these liabilities the law may be simply providing efficient gap filling mechanisms.

Chapter 8 by Bratton *et al* considers corporate contracts, within the context of repeated game theory. This essay is distinctive in that it operates within a highly specific theoretical context, with a huge literature of its own. The authors argue that there will often be an inability to fully specify parties' intentions *ex ante.* This is due to transaction costs and the technical difficulty of writing a complete contingent claims contract. In consequence *ex post* decision making becomes involved in gap filling. The gaps are often filled by norms of trust and co-operation, which co-exist with traditional choice based values.

The chapter by Bratton *et al* also shows that the contractarian approach in corporate legal theory is not secure. It suffered a minor set-back when its deregulatory implications were rejected in the 1980's US corporate law discussion of the relative merits of mandatory and enabling corporate law regimes. Since then, more fundamental questions have been diffused into legal theory. These describe multiple equilibria and contract failure instead of first best equilibria resulting from universal contracting. They make it harder to argue that the device of contract, taken alone, achieves the co-ordination that is necessary for production in firms. At the same time, the game theoretic models lend force to the argument (that was dismissed as naive ten years ago) that contractual descriptions of corporate relationships lack plausibility in the absence of bargaining over governance terms. Meanwhile, the Game Theoretic Models have prompted a new generation of social theorists to examine the organisation of economic institutions. Their inquiry focusses on trust. These investigations draw legal theory toward a new confrontation with the normative side of productive relationships. That confrontation portends a new endorsement of the traditional justificatory construct.

PART 3

I will use the remainder of this introductory Chapter to draw together and comment upon some fairness themes. Some of these are covered in the essays to follow, and others are not. I am, in no sense, attempting to summarise the other essays or provide a systematic analysis of what they contain. The main aim is to provide a setting for these other essays, and some of the ideas which they contain.

Fairness and Self-Interested Bargaining

If we focus on the party who is the beneficiary of many of the rules discussed here, we see that there is a relatively low level of insistence upon the exercise of self interested bargaining. By this I mean a lower level than might be required if we adhered to an approach which always faithfully enforced what was expressly agreed; and which also refused to add anything to this.

When the law disallows a term, one of the parties (at least in the immediate contractual context) is in a better position than he would have been in if the term had not been disallowed. He is in this position not because of anything which he has done to protect his own interests at the time when the contract was made, but because the law has taken the view that the term is in some way unacceptable. When the law implies a term into a contract, or gap-fills by the use of some legal norm, whoever benefits from the implied term or legal norm does so without having had to bargain the term into the contract in the first place.

The same argument might be made in relation to the imposition of liability on manufacturers for the quality of goods or on sub-contractors for the quality of work. There may be expectations held by customers as to the responsibility of the manufacturer or sub-contractor (some of them generated by the manufacturer or sub-contractor); indeed there may, in entering into the main contract with the retailer of the product or the main contractor, have been reliance upon the skill and expertise of the manufacturer or sub-contractor. However it will be unusual for the law to say that there is a contractual relationship between manufacturer and customer, or sub-contractor and customer, giving rise to contractually enforceable obligations in respect of the quality of the product or service. This is due to contract law's focus on an agreement between two parties which is 'intended' to create legal relations; and, in English law, it is also due to the importance of the existence of consideration. There will often not be a relationship or set of circumstances between the customer and the manufacturer or sub-contractor which could be said to involve an agreement. Whatever promise has been made by either a manufacturer or sub-contractor will often not be held to amount to an intention to be bound contractually. Finally, the customer will rarely be found to have provided consideration. If the law, nevertheless, provides a quality remedy to the customer as against the manufacturer or sub-contractor, then the customer is being excused from the burden of bargaining his way to the point which the law would traditionally require for a contractual remedy.

Another example of a tension between fairness and self-interested bargaining is provided by the situation discussed in Part 1 in which there has been some negotiation between two parties, with a view to the conclusion of a contract. However, the negotiations have not reached a stage that a given legal system counts as a binding contract. At the same time there is some reason to feel sympathetic to the position of one of the parties who may have invested time and resources in the negotiations and been given reasons by the other party to believe that the negotiations would lead to a binding contract. For example, there may have been a promise not to negotiate with anyone else, a promise which has now been broken, the promisor having negotiated with another party and, in fact, contracted with that other party rather than the first party to whom he made the promise. Another example would be where there has been some form of promise by A to B, that A would hold open an offer which he has made to B. However the promise has been broken. Legal systems (such as the English) which are more preoccupied with contract as a bargain, and which therefore require consideration, will generally say that neither of the above promises are enforceable as contractual obligations despite the fact that they may have raised expectations, or generated reliances. Arguments for enforcing such promises are often thought of as being arguments in favour of good faith and fairness. What they certainly represent are arguments that one party be given a certain level of protection. This is a protection which arises before this party has bargained his way to what the English legal system recognises traditionally as a contract.

Regulation of Bargaining Procedures and Substantive Rights and Remedies

I have said above that fairness rules will often provide a benefit for parties who have not bargained for this benefit. Inevitably, therefore, such rules will (at least in this immediate sense)[6] be of special help to those contractors who are in a weak bargaining position relative to the other contracting party. So if A is in a weaker bargaining position than B in some respect and there is a contract between them, A may be helped by rules on unfair terms, implied terms, penalties etc. These rules may result in B not

6 There may be an immediate benefit in the form of improved rights or a reduction in responsibilities under the contract. At the same time a cost-benefit analysis may reveal that this benefit is outweighed in the long run by increased prices or a reduction in availability of goods and services.

being able to rely upon one of the terms in their contract; or they may result in B having an obligation imposed upon him, which is in some way protective of A (e.g. some form of legally implied term). The fact that those who are in a weak bargaining position benefit from fairness rules is one reason that there is a common inclination to associate fairness type provisions with the redressal of inequality of bargaining power.

However it is one thing to say that fairness rules have the effect of benefiting those who are in a weaker bargaining position; but it is quite another thing to say that protection of those in a weak bargaining position is the aim of all of these rules. Penalties provide a good example.

Penalties are set aside on the basis that they do not represent a genuine pre-estimate of the loss suffered by the innocent party on a breach of contract. Deposits may be set aside if they are unreasonable, an important factor being what is typical in the market in question. Regulation of terms allowing for forfeiture places emphasis upon the prospects for repayment of the secured debt in question (see Collins, below at chapter 5). These controls generally apply irrespective of the relative bargaining strengths of the parties. Indeed as Collins has argued, agreed remedies are often under attack by the courts where 'they appear to represent carefully negotiated terms of the contract between equal commercial parties who are aware of most of the possible risks' (see below, chapter 5).

It would seem that control of agreed remedies is more readily tied to a principle which prevents a contracting party imposing burdens on the other party which go beyond what is necessary for the purposes of 'risk averaging'. So the courts 'permit an agreed remedy, to fix a measure of compensation which will correspond on average to the plaintiff's losses from different breaches of the same contact, though in any particular case the losses resulting from breach may be greater or smaller' (see Collins, at chapter 5 below). So the focus is not on fairness in the bargaining procedure but rather on the scope of the particular agreed remedy and its relationship to the risks of loss which the innocent party faced at the stage of making the contract. So ultimately the focus is on the term as opposed to the procedure surrounding its inclusion in the contract.

In corporate contracts we again see that protection of those in a weak bargaining position is not the main aim. Where contractual gaps are filled in these contracts the priority would seem to be to maintain the trust and co-operation which is necessary for the relationship (see Bratton et al below). This may, of course, result in providing an improved deal for a party who was in too weak a bargaining position to have bargained for such a deal. However it would seem that this is incidental.

So where regulation of agreed remedies and gap filling in corporate contracts is concerned the focus is on the substantive provisions of the contract. Certain values are applied to regulate these substantive provisions, and these values are not directly influenced by a desire to protect those in a weak bargaining position.

In the case of some rules, however, there *is* a quite explicit aim to protect those in a weaker bargaining position. The Preamble to the Unfair Terms in Consumer Contracts Directive talks of protecting consumers from 'abuse of power' (recital 9).

The discussion of abuse of power in the Preamble has been taken from the 1975 Consumer Protection and Information Programme. The idea of the abuse of power was also discussed the following year in resolution 76 (47), *Unfair Terms in Consumer Contracts and an Appropriate Method of Control* which was adopted by the Council of Ministers in November 1976.

> A supplier generally has superior bargaining strength when he is dealing with a consumer. He often has better economic resources and technical skill than the consumer. He can frequently rely upon a branch organisation, e.g. when drafting standard contract forms which will be used for contracting with consumers. Consumers collectively are usually not organised in such a way that they can offer effective counterweight to the advantages of the supplier. The individual consumer rarely gets the opportunity to negotiate the terms of a contract with a supplier and even if such an opportunity is offered to him, he seldom has enough bargaining strength to protect his interests. By making use of the principle of freedom of contract prevailing in Member States suppliers therefore can, and frequently do, impose on consumers terms and conditions which satisfy the suppliers interest but disregard the interests of the consumers. There can hardly be any doubt that there is a need for consumer protection in these contractual relationships (at p. 11).

The basic problem therefore, according to this view, is that if there has been no collective consumer input into the negotiation of the terms, then the only counterweight to the power of the supplier will be the individual consumer. The individual consumer has limited 'bargaining power' which can be put to use to protect his interests.

The test of unfairness contained in Article 3(1) of the Directive (Regulation 4(1) of the UK Regulations) is itself concerned with bargaining strength. Under the test, a term which has not been individually negotiated is unfair if 'contrary to the requirement of good faith it causes a significant imbalance in the parties rights and obligations to the detriment of the consumer'. Recital 16 of the Preamble to the Directive sets out a number of criteria which it says are relevant to whether or not there has been good faith, one of these being the relative bargaining strengths of the parties (Recital 16 was implemented by Regulation 4(3) and Schedule 2 of the UK Regulations).

In fact the bargaining strength criteria has been taken (along with other criteria) from Schedule 2 of the Unfair Contract Terms Act (UCTA) 1977. Under UCTA these criteria are to be given special attention where the court examines the reasonableness of including a term which excludes or limits liability for breach of the implied terms as to description, quality and fitness in commercial contracts for the sale and supply of goods. As it happens the courts do not feel constrained from considering relative bargaining strength in the case of other exemption clauses to which the UCTA reasonableness test applies. Relative bargaining strength has become a particularly important criteria where there is an exemption clause in a consumer contract.[7]

Both the UCTA reasonableness test and the test of unfairness in the Directive/UK regulations also look at the other criteria which are relevant to fairness in the bargaining procedure leading up to a contract. These are the clarity of the term; the extent to which it was drawn to the other party's attention; whether a choice of terms was offered or was available elsewhere and whether the other party received an inducement to agree to the term.[8] There are two important themes here. First of all there is transparency. The meaning and import of terms is made more transparent if these terms are expressed in clear language and their existence is clearly disclosed to the consumer. Transparency and the cultivation of informed consumers is a strongly emerging theme in European policy and law making (see Weatherill 1995); and is certainly important to the test of unfairness in the Directive/UK Regulations (see Brownsword et al chapter 2, below). Lack of transparency has also been a concern in the attitude of the UK judiciary to exemption clauses, both before and since the passing of UCTA. In Suisse Atlantique Societé d'Armement Maritime SAV Rotterdamsche Kolan Centrale NV.[9] Lord Reid said that:

> 'In the ordinary way the customer has no time to read (the standard terms) and if he did he would probably not understand them'

UK common law rules have been capable of developing basic agreement rules into reasonable notice and disclosure rules. The high water mark of this is the decision in Interfoto v. Stilleto[10] where it was held that particularly onerous or unusual terms may have to be specially brought to the attention of the other party (who in this case was not a consumer).

---

7 *Smith* v. *Bush* [1989] A.C. 831.

8 See UCTA, Schedule 2, (b) and (c); *The Zinnia* [1984] 2 Lloyds Rep. 211; *Smith* v. *Bush* [1989] A.C. 831;Directive, Recital 16 to the Preamble; UK Regulations, Schedule 2; Brownsword et al, below at chapter 2; Willett, 1994.

9 [1967] IAC 361 at 406.

10 [1989] QB 433.

Interestingly transparency is explicitly a criteria in commercial contracts under UCTA (Schedule 2 para. (c)) although not in consumer contracts. However it seems that the courts would be less likely to find a term to be reasonable in a consumer case under UCTA if the term was intransparent.

The second important theme is that of choice: the idea that there should be alternatives available to the party who is agreeing to the other party's terms; or at least that an attempt should be made to make the term in question more attractive by offering some inducement to agree to it. UK common law has never had the conceptual facility to use these as criteria of contractual enforceability.

In both UTCA and the Unfair Terms Directive the concern over fairness in the bargaining environment links up with a notion that certain sorts of terms are potentially unfair in a substantive sense. The extract cited above (from the 1976 Resolution on Unfair Terms) referred to terms which 'satisfy the supplier's interests, but disregard the interest of consumers'. In the case of the Unfair Terms Directive there is an indicative annex of unfair terms (see the Appendix) which reveals certain substantive unfairness themes. Micklitz (at chapter 4 below) identifies those terms on the indicative annex which allow the supplier to alter the price or characteristics of the product or service, or which allow the supplier to release himself from the contract. Elsewhere I have grouped these sorts of terms together as having in common the existence of a discretion which is unilaterally available to the supplier (Willett, 1993, 1994). We can turn this around and talk about the consumer's autonomy and security being compromised, by terms which give the supplier undue control over the relationship (Wilhelmsson, 1995). Micklitz also identifies those terms which interfere with the consumer's access to justice, by regulating the place of jurisdiction or the dispute settlement procedure (see chapter 4 below). Finally he identifies those terms which exclude or limit liabilities imposed voluntarily under the contract, or by virtue of a legal guarantee (see below and see also Willett 1993, 1994). Exclusion and limitation clauses, as well as those clauses which interfere with access to justice, may enable the supplier to escape responsibility for the reasonable expectations which they have raised. They also compromise the financial security of the consumer (see Wilhelmsson 1995). [11]

The Unfair Contract Terms Act also targets particular terms, although its focus is narrower. Rather than having a general test of unfairness applying to all terms which do not define the price or main subject matter (the

---

[11] Of course other sorts of terms can be unfair under the Directive. However the point I wish to make is that we can see from the annex that there is a targetting of certain sorts of terms. These terms have features which are disapproved of.

approach of the Directive/UK Regulations), UCTA carefully defines all of those terms which are subject to its controls. Basically these are clauses either excluding or limiting various types of liability (e.g. ss 2, 3, 5, 6 and 7); clauses requiring one party to indemnify another party from liability (s.4); and clauses offering a contractual performance substantially different from that reasonably expected, or no performance at all (s.3). So, as is the case with many of the terms on the Directive's indicative annex the broad theme is avoidance of responsibility by the use of various exemption devices; so leaving the financial security of the other party compromised. Some terms are void under UCTA i.e. those exempting liability for death or personal injury caused by negligence (s.2(1)); those exempting liability for breach of the Sale of Goods Act implied term as to title (s.6(1) UCTA) and those exempting liability for breach of The Sale of Goods Act implied terms as to description, quality and fitness for purpose in consumer contracts (s.6 (2), UCTA). However the dominant approach in consumer and commercial contracts under UCTA is the application of the reasonableness test.

A final point needs making in relation to the normative values which regulate the substantive rights and responsibilities under a contract. As I have shown, there is a tendency to focus on certain sorts of terms – penalties, deposits, exemption clauses etc. – and this must be a starting point in identifying underlying values. In some cases – most notably where agreed remedies are concerned – the term in question is analysed in isolation from the other terms of the contract. So there is no attempt to determine whether the unfairness of the agreed remedy is balanced out by other terms which in some way favour the party prejudiced by the remedy, (see Collins below at chapter 5). In other words the dominant principle is not overall contractual balance, but rather (where agreed remedies are concerned) to hold compensation to a particular level (see above at pp. 8 and 10–12 and see Collins at chapter 5 below).

However in the case of other controls of substantive contractual rights and responsibilities, even if certain sorts of terms come under special suspicion, the overall adjudication looks at the other terms of the contract and often the other circumstances obtaining at the time of the conclusion of the contract. So the UCTA reasonableness test is concerned, inter alia, with the 'circumstances which were in the contemplation of the parties when the contract was made' (s.11(1)). This must include the other terms of the contract. The unfairness test in the Unfair Terms Directive/UK Regulations talks explicitly of taking account of 'all the other terms of the contract or of another contract upon which it is dependent' (Article 4(1), UK Regulation 4(2)).

So where UCTA and the Directive/UK Regulations are concerned, although certain terms are under special suspicion there is a concern to achieve some notion of overall contractual balance (the test of unfairness in the Directive/UK Regulations refers explicitly to the term under consideration causing 'a significant imbalance in the rights and obligations arising under the contract').

The equitable unconscionability rules would probably also look at an allegedly unconscionable term in the context of the contact terms as a whole.[12]

Fairness and Freedom

When there are legitimate interests of some kind which may justify a protection which was not bargained for, the fairness instinct to protect these interests may come into conflict with a freedom instinct. There is *positive* and *negative* freedom (see Cohen, 1995).

The positive freedom which is often spoken of as being in conflict with fairness is the freedom of contract. This is the freedom from the law's interference with the terms which, on objective appearances, have been agreed to by the parties. So that while there may be a fairness instinct to set aside a term, or add a term to protect one of the parties, this is in conflict with the freedom of contract principle because it involves an interference with what was freely contracted for. So the rules on control of unfair terms, penalties etc., come into conflict with a traditional view of the freedom of contract principle. This is because they involve interfering with the terms which (at least formally) have been freely agreed to by the parties.

The negative freedom is a freedom *from* contract i.e. the freedom not to be bound until the contract has been concluded. Of course this statement in itself is somewhat circular in terms of trying to understand the precise nature and extent of the freedom, because the 'contract' could be defined by the law to be legally concluded at any number of points if the law so chose. If it chose an early stage, then freedom would start to have the same impact as fairness, as there would be a tendency to uphold a wider range of expectations. In fact the idea of freedom *from* contract tends to involve freedom until a fairly late stage, i.e. there existing a relatively high number of legal criteria to be satisfied before there will be a binding contract. This will tend to mean that there will be cases in which expectations and reliances will be generated (and so a fairness concern arises) and yet there

---

12 For different ways of defining the overall substantive fairness of a contract see Smith, 1996.

may be no liability. So a freedom from contract approach favours a doctrine of consideration. A doctrine of consideration helps to keep a promisor free from contractual liability by only enforcing a promise as a contract where there is some forbearance by the promisee, or some benefit (or avoidance of disbenefit) where the promisor is concerned. A freedom from contract approach does not favour a duty to negotiate in good faith. The lack of a duty to negotiate in good faith means that there is less chance of liability for any pre-contractual representations, or for withdrawing capriciously from negotiations (see Carter and Furmston 1995). The existence of such a duty might result in liability being placed on those who choose to withdraw from negotiations at a late stage when the other party has placed some reliance on the negotiations, or simply formed expectations as to the conclusion of the contract (Cohen 1995). A freedom from contract position is also unlikely to be keen on providing a remedy where there is either a specific gratuitous pre-contractual promise (e.g. a promise to keep an offer open, not to negotiate with anyone else etc.);[13] or even an actual contract to negotiate with the other party or not to negotiate with someone else (see Cohen 1995).[14]

Again we see a conflict with a fairness instinct. A makes a commitment to B of the sort just described; a desire for fairness for B and/or good faith on the part of A seem to be important underlying rationales in arguing that such commitments should be enforceable. But the freedom from contract principle pulls in the other direction.

An analogous conflict between fairness and freedom from contract is apparent in the area of manufacturers and sub-contractors liability to customers, for quality defects. Here the fairness instinct is that there should perhaps be some responsibility upon the manufacturers or sub-contractors where the customer's reasonable expectations of quality are not fulfilled. The freedom from contract instinct, however, wishes to preserve the manufacturer from a contractual type of responsibility which he has not expressly undertaken within the context of a bargained for exchange of promises.

[13] A system not requiring consideration (e.g. Scots law) is clearly not so committed to the freedom from contract principle; and is more likely to enforce such pre-contractual gratuitous promises. For a discussion of recent case law in England see Carter and Furmston, 1995, and for the position in Scotland see Willett and O'Donnell, 1996

[14] *Walford* v. *Miles* [1992] 2A.C 128.

Justifications for Compromising Freedom

What justifications might there be for preferring fairness to freedom in some contractual situations? Over recent years there has been a lot of work on economic rationales for interfering with freedom of contract (most recently see Trebilcock, 1993). Indeed the approaches of chapters 7 and 8 in this collection are strongly influenced by economic analysis. In both chapters the authors focus upon the transaction costs involved in certain sorts of relationship. If these transaction costs are too high then the parties may leave some important risks unallocated as between them. The law's role can therefore be seen in terms of finding the most efficient way to fill the gaps. So although the law is imposing obligations which have not been voluntarily agreed to, we might justify this compromise of party freedom on the utilitarian grounds that the greater good is served by the fact that a more efficient distribution of resources has been achieved.

It may also be possible to justify regulation of terms such as exemption clauses (via provisions such as UCTA) in terms of efficiency. It can be argued that there is often insufficient information about the meaning and implications of exemption clauses (Beale, 1989). As such the customer may not make a rational decision as to whether the exemption clause is in his or her best interests; and so the risks may not be allocated according to who is in the best position to bear them (i.e. who is the best cost avoider).

However some regulation of contracts cannot so readily be explained in terms of efficiency (see, for example, the discussion of agreed remedies by Collins at chapter 5 below). Even if all rules which depart from freedom of contract could be rationalised in efficiency terms it seems perfectly legitimate to consider other possible rationales. In this vein I would like to suggest a couple of themes which I believe should be borne in mind when thinking of rules which have some kind of fairness agenda, and appear to compromise freedom.

First of all we can focus on the agreement of the party who is benefitting from the fairness rule. It is clear that there are a wide range of factors which might be said to have compromised the quality of consent which was given. The more libertarian approaches will only wish to recognise a limited number of these, perhaps minority, insanity, misrepresenation, duress and undue influence. However a more liberal approach inspired by a conception of social justice may wish to give recognition to a wider range of factors which might be said to compromise the quality of the consent given by one of the parties. This approach might push for greater transparency of terms and might require that there are actually alternative terms available(the approach taken by UCTA and the Directive/UK

Regulations – see Part 2 above and chapter 2 below). Both of these factors enhance the quality of the consent given by the party agreeing to the term. In addition we could argue that if there is a great disparity of bargaining strength between two parties then the quality of the consent given by the weaker party is more limited than it might otherwise be.

So this approach sees the autonomy of one of the parties as being compromised by intransparent terms, lack of alternatives and weaker bargaining power (see Wilhelmsson, 1995). The mission is to re-instate this autonomy by giving greater recoginition to these factors. Great value is placed upon this reinstatement of autonomy and the resulting compromise of the other party's freedom can therefore be justified.

A second theme which is often important is one which focusses less upon the autonomy of the party benefitting from the fairness rule and more upon the blameworthiness of the other party. One extreme of blameworthiness or bad faith is to engage in misrepresentation duress or undue influence. However a contract law which is concerned with promoting a degree of co-operation may also take objection to a party who takes advantage of the very weak bargaining position of the other party (see the discussion of unconscionability above and see Cartwright, 1991).

UCTA and the Directive/UK Regulations might also be seen as combatting bad faith. These provisions target terms used by those who operate in the course of a business. By operating as a business one sends out certain signals. It can be argued that business status suggests a general sense of decency and responsibility towards customers: a professionalism of sorts (of course some businesses will actually be professionals). In addition businesses build upon these signals by advertising, presentation etc. and by the specific things which are said to customers in the course of enquiries, negotiations etc. Finally, businesses operate within a particular market, which has certain typical performance norms. Note, here, that I am not referring to the formal *terms* which might be normal in the sector, but rather the practice which is typical in the vast majority of cases (when of course the formal terms will never become an issue).

It seems to me that all of the above signals come together to raise a certain level of expectation as to the performance which will take place; and the general balance of the relationship (on this see also Brownsword et al below at chapter 2). Indeed, as I argue in my own contribution to this collection (see Willett, below), the quality standard in contracts for the sale and supply of goods, can be seen as being constructed from such signals. The norms of trust and co-operation in corporate contracts might also be argued to emanate partly from the signals which the parties send to each other (see Bratton et al below at chapter 8).

The expectations idea may help to explain the tests of unfairness contained in the Unfair Terms Directive and the Unfair Contract Terms Act and why it is available as against business contractors. As I have said those who offer goods and services send signals and generate expectations as to the performance that can be expected, and perhaps also that there will be a reasonably balanced relationship which does not overly compromise the autonomy of the other party. Perhaps we can say that terms are potentially unfair or unreasonable partly because they may offer something less than what is reasonably or legitimately expected.[15] It may not be acceptable for businesses to use such terms because they have been responsible for the creation of the expectations in the first place. There is possibly an element of blameworthiness in their behaviour.[16] They have generated expectations, while at the same time using contracting formats such as standard forms, which (for all their advantages) may enable avoidance of responsibility for the meeting of the expectations. The blameworthiness element helps to explain the language of good faith which is used in the Unfair Terms Directive. The test of unfairness clearly does not mean to require subjective dishonesty reaching fraudulent levels when it speaks of a term being contrary to the requirement of good faith, (see Brownsword et al at chapter 2 below). Perhaps, however, it intends to denote bad faith in the sense of a term which attempts to avoid responsibility for expectations which have been quite consciously raised.[17]

In conclusion then it can be argued that those who consciously raise expectations and then seek to avoid responsibility in respect of them are punished by the law refusing to grant them full freedom of contract.

---

[15] There is considerable evidence to the effect that reasonable or legitimate expectations are central to emerging European concepts of fairness and justice (see Micklitz, 1994). The EC Product Liability Directive 1985 (implemented by the Consumer Protection Act 1987) says that a product is defective if it is not as safe as people are generally entitled to expect (Article 6 of the Directive, section 3 of the Act). The proposed Directive to harmonise the laws on quality obligations owed by manufacturers and retailers, uses the concept of legitimate expectation as determinant of the standard of quality to be owed (EC, 1993).

[16] There is a tendency to be more ready to find a duty of care in negligence where professionals are concerned (see Thomson, 1995, and Willett and O'Donnell 1996). Is this also because the law is holding such parties responsible for the signals as to expertise being sent out, and the expectations raised by these signals? This, perhaps, is what is meant by 'assumption of responsibility' in this context (it certainly does not seem plausible to equate assumption of responsibility in this context with an actual intention to undertake an obligation). We may, then, have a useful contract-tort link to help in development of a theory of obligations.

[17] This approach may help to resolve some of the problems raised by Waddams (1995) as to the relationship between reasonable expectations and good faith.

A third theme focusses upon a package of terms which is substantively unfair in the sense that it represents a balance of obligations which is significantly out of step with the market norm. It might be argued that freedom of contract can be compromised here because the law's role is to promote valuable social activities; and it is simply not a valuable social activity to commit oneself to such a bad bargain (see Smith 1996).

Finally we can focus upon those compromises of freedom of contract which might be said to be based upon the assertion of essential rights. These rights are enshrined even where derogation from them is perfectly efficient or is balanced out by the benefits provided by other terms. For example it might sometimes be most efficient for a consumer to insure against consequential loss flowing from breach of the satisfactory quality obligation in contracts for the sale or supply of goods. (When a defective television damages household property this will normally be covered by home insurance). Nevertheless the seller must accept full liability (see ss. 6 and 7, UCTA).

Penalties and other agreed remedies provide another example. Contractors are clearly seen as having an enshrined right to be protected against these even where the other terms of the contract might be said to balance them out (see Collins, below at chapter 5).

CONCLUDING REMARKS

This introductory chapter has been intended to give specific introductions to the chapters which now follow.

I also hope that is has been able to provide a useful framework within which to read these chapters. Of course these chapters can equally be read in their own right, and in the context of literature which is highly specific to the subject matters in question.

REFERENCES

Adams, J. and Brownsword, R (1995) *Key Issues in Contract,* London: Butterworths.

Bamford, N. (1995) Unconscionability as a Vitiating Factor, Lloyds Maritime and Commercial Law Quarterly, 338-358.

Beale, H. (1989) 'Unfair Contracts in Britain and Europe', Current Legal Problems, 197?.

Beale, H. (1995) 'Legislative Control of Fairness' in Beaton, J. and Friedman, D. (eds), *Good Faith and Fault in Contract Law* Oxford: Clarendon.

Birks, P. and Nyuk, Yin C. (1995) 'On the Nature or Undue Influence' in Beatson, J. and Friedman, D. (eds), *Good Faith and Fault in Contract Law* Oxford: Clarendon.

Brownsword, R. (1992) 'Retrieving Reasons, Retrieving Rationality' 5 *Journal of Contract Law,* 83-107.

Brownsword, R. (1995) 'Bad Faith, Good Reasons and Termination of Contracts' in Bradgate, R., Birds, J., and Villiers, C., Termination of Contracts, Wiley, Chancery.

Brownsword, R., and Howells, G. (1995) 'The Implementation of the EC Directive on Unfair Terms in Consumer Contracts – Some Unresolved Questions', *Journal of Business Law,* 243.

Carter, J., and Furmston, M. (1994), 'Good Faith and Fairness in the Negotiation of Contracts', 8 *Journal of Contract Law,* 1-15.

Cartwright, J. (1991) 'Unequal Bargaining', Oxford: Clarendon.

Cohen, N. (1995) 'Pre-Contractual Duties: Two Freedoms and the Contract to Negotiate', in Beatson, J. and Friedman, D. (eds), *Good Faith and Fault in Contract Law* (1995) Oxford: Clarendon at p. 25.

Collins, H. (1993) *Law of Contract,* London: Butterworths.

Fabre-Magnan, V. (1995) 'Duties of Disclosure and French Contract Law' in Beatson, J. and Friedman, D. (eds), *Good Faith and Fault in Contract Law* (1995) Oxford: Clarendon.

Howells, G., and Weatherill, S. (1995) Consumer Protection Law, Aldershot: Dartmouth.

Micklitz, H. (1994), *Principles of Justice and The Law of The European Union,* in Passivirta, E. and Rissanen, K., Proceedings of the Cost A 7 Seminar, Helsinki.

Rawlings, P., and Willett, C. (1994), Ombudsman Schemes in the United Kingdom's Financial Sector, 17 Jurnal of Consumer Policy, 307-333.

Smith, (1996) In Defence of Substantive Fairness, 112 *Law Quarterly Review,* 138-158.

Thomson, J.M. (1995), *Scots Law Times.*

Trebilcock, M. (1993) 'The Limits of Freedom of Contract', Cambridge: Harvard.

Waddams, S. (1995), Good Faith Unconscionability and Reasonable Expectations 9 *Journal of Contract Law,* 55-67.

Weatherill, (1995), Prospects for the Development of European Private Law Through 'Europeanisation' in the Europe Court - The case of the Directive on Unfair Terms in Consumer Contracts, *European Review of Private Law 3:* 307-328.

Willett, C. (1991) 'The Unacceptable Face of the Consumer Guarantees Bill', 54 *Modern Law Review,* 552-562.

Willett, C. (1992), Uninduced Misapprehensions in Contract Law, 5 *Journal of Contract Law,* 157-162.

Willett, C. (1993) Unfair Terms in Consumer Contracts, *Scottish Business Law Bulletin,* March 1993, Issue 2, 10-11.

Willett, C. (1994) Directive on Unfair Terms in Consumer Contracts, *Consumer Law Journal,* 114-124.

Willett, C. (1994) Can Control of Unfair Terms be Regarded as a Redistribution of Power in Favour of Consumers, *Journal of Consumer Policy,* 482-492.

Willett, C., and O Donnell, A. (1996), *Scottish Business Law:* Text, Cases and Materials, (2nd ed.), London: Blackstone.

Willett, C. (1996) 'From Reindeers to Confident Consumers: UK Consumer Bodies and the Unfair Terms Directive', in Micklitz, H., and Reich, N., 'Public Interest Litigation' (forthcoming), Berlin: VIEW.

Wilhelmsson, T. (1995), 'Social Contract Law and European Integration', Aldershot: Dartmouth.

2. Between Market and Welfare: Some Reflections on Article 3 of the EC Directive on Unfair Terms in Consumer Contracts

By Roger Brownsword, Geraint Howells and Thomas Wilhelmsson

INTRODUCTION

It is something of a commonplace that modern European legal systems have been concerned to protect weaker contracting parties against abuses of power by stronger contracting parties (Beale, 1986, 1989). Such protective legal regimes can be stipulatively labelled as 'welfarist' in their intent (see Adams and Brownsword, 1987; Wilhelmsson, 1994) – although, of course, to what extent the protective interventions of the law of contract have been connected to the development of the modern Welfare State (and the concomitant broader concern for the condition of the relatively weak and disadvantaged) is a matter for debate (see Brownsword, Howells, and Wilhelmsson, 1994a). In the area of contract law, welfarist protection can focus on unfairness in contracting procedures, or on unfair terms or outcomes, or both; and welfarist strategies can take a variety of forms, involving both public and private law, general rules and judicial discretions, preventive and remedial measures, and so on (see Häyhä, 1994; Bradgate, Graham, and Howells, 1994).

The principal beneficiaries of the welfarist concern for weaker parties have been contractors who have dealt as consumers. Although there might be some occasions when those who deal as consumers happen to be better informed than business contractors, and although markets sometimes are weighted in favour of (consumer) buyers, in general consumers are seen as weaker parties and, thus, fit for protection. To this extent, the recent EC Directive on Unfair Terms in Consumer Contracts (93/13/EEC) implemented by the Unfair Terms in Consumer Contracts Regulations, 1994, SI 1994/3159) is of great interest. It fits very easily into the modern pattern of European contract law. For the Recitals declare that, in line with the Community programmes for consumer protection and information policy,

> acquirers of goods and services should be protected against the abuse of power by the seller or supplier, in particular against one-sided standard contracts and the unfair exclusion of essential rights in contracts.

In other words, the Directive is concerned to protect consumer contractors (presumptively weaker parties) against abuses of power. Moreover, in identifying 'one-sided standard contracts' and 'the unfair exclusion of essential rights' as particular forms of abuse, the Directive accords with widespread European concern that consumer contractors should be protected against unfairness arising from standard forms and from exclusion clauses.

However, the Recitals also declare that where consumers are unaware of the rules of law governing transactions in other Member States, such 'lack of awareness may deter them from direct transactions for the purchase of goods or services in another Member State.' And, the Recitals continue:

> Whereas, in order to facilitate the establishment of the internal market and to safeguard the citizen in his role as consumer when acquiring goods and services under contracts which are governed by the laws of Member States other than his own, it is essential to remove unfair terms from those contracts.

This sounds a caution should we be tempted to jump too quickly to the conclusion that the Directive is simply concerned, in a welfarist spirit, with protecting consumers' rights. As Norbert Reich (1993) has perceptively argued, Community consumer policy is as much concerned with establishing the conditions for an internal market as it is with protecting consumer rights (not that these twin objectives necessarily pull against one another).

Although there is room for considerable debate about the precise trajectory of the market side of EC consumer protection policy (see especially Collins, 1994),[1] it is tolerably clear that the future of European

---

1 Hugh Collins (1994, at p. 246) distinguishes *inter alia* between those legal interventions which strive for substantive fairness and those which seek to promote the ideal of a social market. In the present context, this invites a distinction between two conceptions of the internal market approach. An internal market approach wedded to substantive fairness will seek to eliminate the most egregious examples of contractual exploitation. As Collins puts it: 'The objective is to ensure fair prices and the fulfilment of legitimate expectations, and the evil is the rip-off of the consumer' (*ibid.*). However, an internal market approach wedded to the ideal of a social market is slightly more interventionist, setting its sights on the achievement of 'a market in which

consumer contract law is a standardised future, products and services being supplied on regulated standard terms – standard fairness for standard forms. Accordingly, it would be a serious misinterpretation of the Directive to suppose that it is concerned to do away with standard form dealing. The Directive's primary target is not standard forms as such, but *unfair* standard form dealing in the mass consumer market.[2] Indeed, far from wishing to restrict standard form dealing, the spirit of the Directive, we can infer, is to promote standard form fair dealing in the European marketplace. Just as consumers across Europe can be assured that they will get basically the same acceptable deal with McDonald's, Marks and Spencer, Mobil and the like, the Directive seeks to promote an acceptable standardisation of consumer contracts, the better to facilitate the operation of the single market.

Insofar as EC consumer protection policy, Janus - like, sometimes shows it consumer rights face but at other times its internal market face, we can expect the Directive to reflect, and to attract, two schools of thinking. One school, which we can term the 'market' school, will see the Directive as a vehicle for promoting fair standard forms in the European marketplace. The other school, which we can term the 'welfarist' school, will be more concerned that the Directive should protect weaker parties, in this case consumer contractors.[3] Although both schools will have a broad interest in the several provisions of the Directive, an initial focal point surely must be Article 3, where the key provisions on unfair terms are to be found. Article 3 is implemented by Regulation 4 of the UK Regulations, and it is to Regulation 4 which the UK courts would first turn. However the Directive is the ultimate authority and we are interested here in the way in which the Directive fits into the market and welfarist schools described briefly above.

In this paper, we consider the Directive's central provisions on unfair terms from two perspectives – first, from the perspective of the market

---

consumer goods and services are of good quality' (*ibid.*). Although, as Collins emphasises, the Directive betrays 'an unresolved tension...between considerations of substantive fairness and the pursuit of the goals of the social market' (p. 252), he concludes by suggesting that the Directive ultimately is concerned with the social market ideal (see pp. 253-254).

2 In fact, strictly speaking, the Directive is concerned with the fairness of terms that have not been individually negotiated. For a detailed examination of this point in the context of the Unfair Terms in Consumer Contracts Regulations 1994 (implementing the Directive in the United Kingdom), see Brownsword and Howells, 1995.

3 Caution needs to be exercised in interpreting such widely-used descriptive terms as 'market' and 'welfare'. In some usages, these terms might be identified with a neo-classical economic approach to contract law (see e.g Trebilcock, 1993). However, in this paper, the terms are to be understood in the specific sense outlined in the text.

ideal, the ideal of promoting fair standard forms for standardised consumption in the mass European market, and, secondly, from a welfarist perspective. Our discussion is in three parts. In Part One, we introduce a number of difficulties arising from the interpretation of Article 3. At one level, these difficulties relate to the general thrust of Article 3.1, which provides that a term is unfair if 'contrary to the requirement of good faith, it causes a significant imbalance...to the detriment of the consumer'. Is the thrust of this that a term is unfair if it causes a significant imbalance to the detriment of the consumer (and, thus, is contrary to the requirement of good faith)? Or, does the reference to the requirement of good faith set an independent condition for the fairness of a contractual term – and, if so, what kind of condition is set thereby? At another level, the difficulties arise from the structure of the Directive. Here, whilst one difficulty concerns the relationship between Article 3.1 and Article 3.3 (and the indicative list of unfair terms in the Annex), another difficulty arises from the failure in Article 3 to distinguish between specific *ex casu* challenges to the unfairness of a contractual term as against general (or typical) pre-emptive challenges of the kind contemplated by Article 7.2 of the Directive. Having reviewed these difficulties, we proceed, in Part Two, to explore another level of interpretive difficulties raised by Article 3.1 – namely, the interpretation of the key constituent concepts of 'good faith', 'significant imbalance', and 'detriment to the consumer' – conducting this exercise specifically from the perspective of the market school. In Part Three, we conduct a parallel exercise, this time considering how this same provision must be read if it is to promote a variety of welfarist objectives.

Our conclusions with regard to the interpretation of Article 3.1 are twofold. First, the logic of both the market approach and those versions of welfarism that emphasise the need for substantive fairness is such that a number of overlapping interpretive imperatives emerge. Broadly speaking, these are:

1. that the requirement of good faith should not be read as an independent condition of fairness – that is, that the test of unfairness should simply be whether the term in question causes a significant imbalance to the detriment of the consumer;
2. that, failing (1), good faith should be read as setting a direct substantive rather than a procedural condition; and

3. that, failing (1) or (2), then attempts should be made to read the concept of good faith indirectly[4] as a substantive requirement, thereby excluding any procedural requirement from the criteria of an unfair term.

Against this, however, some strands of welfarist thinking attach importance to procedural rights[5] for consumers and so do not support the moves in (1), (2), and (3) above to write a procedural version of good faith out of the Article 3.1 script. Up to a point, this first conclusion is fairly obvious. After all, it is hardly surprising that those approaches that seek direct control over the substance of consumer contracts should endeavour to fashion the Directive as an instrument of substantive regulation; and, equally, it is no surprise that the logic of procedural versions of welfarism dictates a procedural reading of Article 3.1. Our second conclusion, however, is rather less obvious. This is that, should the moves in (1), (2), or (3) fail, then virtually all shades of welfarist thinking unite with the market approach in arguing:

4. i) a simple 'clear conscience' interpretation of the concept of good faith should be avoided;
   (ii) the (procedural) requirement of good faith should be given a strong interpretation (so that standard form dealers cannot easily avoid the control of the Directive);
   (iii) the concept of significant imbalance should not be given a rigid literal interpretation (as significantly one-sided, or the like) but should be interpreted flexibly; and

---

4 i.e. by unpacking a substantive interpretation of good faith from a supposedly procedural element. Below, we suggest that the procedural requirement of 'reasonable choice' might be manipulated in this way.

5 Hugh Collins (1994) distinguishes 'consumer choice' from 'consumer rights' positions in relation to the drafting and interpretation of the Directive. In Collins' discussion, consumer choice is related to informed choice which is related to notions of free competition and to market failure justifications for intervention. Moreover, Collins suggests that, in many respects, the agreed text of the Directive represents a victory for the advocates of consumer choice rather than the advocates of consumer rights (see p. 238). In our discussion, we treat welfarism as being concerned with the rights of weaker parties (including consumers), and we assume that, in principle, such rights can relate to matters of both contractual procedure and substance. It follows that, whilst we recognise the distinction between procedural 'consumer choice' and substantive 'consumer rights', we do not characterise this within welfarism as an issue of non-rights-based choice versus rights-based consumer claims. To some extent, these differences are merely terminological. However, there is a morally relevant distinction between a consumer choice position based on goal-based considerations and a demand for informed choice made on the basis of rights.

(iv) the requirement of 'detriment to the consumer' should be given its face value meaning, as simply indicating that the Directive is for the protection of consumers.

In other words, our conclusion is that, if substantivists are unable to instate a direct substantive reading of Article 3.1, the logic of their position is to argue for a strong interpretation of the procedural requirements, effectively along similar lines to the proceduralists.

PART ONE: ARTICLE 3 OF THE DIRECTIVE AND THREE INTERPRETIVE QUESTIONS

Article 3 is the cornerstone of the Directive's concept of an unfair term. However, in specifying its concept of unfairness, the Directive suffers from a lack of clarity at a number of levels. In this part of our discussion, we consider three general questions relating to the interpretation of Article 3. First, there is the question of how Article 3.1 (which purports to specify the general criteria of unfair terms) is to be read – in particular, does the reference to the requirement of good faith signal an independent condition of unfairness (over and above the condition that the term must cause a significant imbalance to the detriment of the consumer) and, if so, is that independent good faith condition a procedural or a substantive requirement, or both?. Secondly, there is the question of how we are to understand the relationship between Article 3.1 and Article 3.3 (which incorporates and refers to the indicative list of unfair terms in the Annex).[6] Thirdly, there is the question of whether, and how, Article 3 regulates (a) specific *ex casu* challenges to contractual terms alleged to be unfair and (b) general pre-emptive challenges made under the auspices of Article 7.2 (which provides that 'persons or organisations, having a legitimate interest under national law in protecting consumers, may take action...before the courts or before competent administrative bodies for a decision as to whether contractual terms drawn up for general use are unfair, so that they can apply appropriate and effective means to prevent the continued use of such terms').[7]

---

6 Article 4.1 provides that the unfairness of a contractual term is to be assessed 'taking into account the nature of the goods or services for which the contract was concluded and by referring, at the time of conclusion of the contract, to all the circumstances attending the conclusion of the contract and to all the other terms of the contract or of another contract on which it is dependent.'

7 In the UK, the DTI (1993) caused a furore when, in its first Consultation Paper on the implementation of the Directive, it claimed that Article 7.2 could have no effect because

(1) The General Reading of Article 3.1

Article 3.1 defines a term as unfair if 'contrary to the requirement of good faith, it causes a significant imbalance in the parties' rights and obligations arising under the contract, to the detriment of the consumer.' Now, whilst it is pretty clear that a term will not be unfair under Article 3.1 unless it causes a significant imbalance to the detriment of the consumer, it is not at all clear whether a term which does cause such a significant imbalance necessarily violates the requirement of good faith. In other words, are all terms which cause a significant imbalance to the detriment of the consumer thereby necessarily contrary to good faith? If not, what is it that distinguishes such a term that is contrary to the requirement of good faith from a term that is not contrary to the requirement of good faith? In the light of these remarks, it will be apparent that there are at least four plausible general readings of this Article as follows:

(1) A term is unfair if it causes (i) a significant imbalance (ii) to the detriment of the consumer. There is no independent condition that the term must be contrary to the requirement of good faith – effectively, Article 3.1 functions as a definition of a violation of good faith for the purposes of the Directive. Thus, we should read Article 3.1 as saying that a term is unfair if it causes a significant imbalance to the detriment of the consumer and in this sense is contrary to the requirement of good faith. We can call this reading of Article 3.1 the "two-step" interpretation.

(2) A term is unfair if it causes (i) a significant imbalance (ii) to the detriment of the consumer and (iii) it is contrary to the requirement of good faith. The requirement of good faith is an independent condition. Condition (iii) (the requirement of good faith) is a procedural condition. We can call this reading of Article 3.1 the "three-step procedural" interpretation.

(3) A term is unfair if it causes (i) a significant imbalance (ii) to the detriment of the consumer and (iii) it is contrary to the requirement of good faith. The requirement of good faith is an independent condition. Condition (iii) (the requirement of good faith) is a substantive condition. We can call this reading of Article 3.1 the "three-step substantive" interpretation.

(a) the courts, rather than administrative agencies, decide on the fairness of terms and (b) UK law has no provision for representative actions. In its second Consultation Paper (1994), however, a different view was taken; and the implementing Regulations duly give the relevant powers to the Director-General of Fair Trading: see further Brownsword and Howells, 1995.

(4) A term is unfair if it causes (i) a significant imbalance (ii) to the detriment of the consumer and (iii) it is contrary to the requirement of good faith. The requirement of good faith is an independent condition. Condition (iii) (the requirement of good faith) involves both procedural and substantive elements. We can call this reading of Article 3.1 the 'three-step procedural and substantive' interpretation.[8]

No one of these general readings stands out as obviously correct.[9] Some English speakers may be tempted by the two-step reading simply because of the grammatical flow of Article 3.1.[10] Others, however, mindful of the English tendency to equate good faith with procedural matters (see e.g. Goode, 1992), may find the three-step procedural reading more plausible. Yet others, familiar with legal systems in which good faith is a token for substantive fairness, may find the three-step substantive reading more convincing. And, of course, some may prefer the three-step procedural and substantive interpretation on the ground that it has the scope to satisfy several constituencies. We offer no opinion on this interpretive choice in this paper, for our principal purpose is to identify the interpretive logic of the market and welfare approaches. However, because the three-step procedural reading presents a particularly serious challenge both to exponents of the market approach and to many interpreters within the welfarist school, we will focus for much of the time on this particular reading.

The nature of the challenge presented by the three-step procedural reading can be put quite shortly. On this interpretation of Article 3.1, there are three necessary and sufficient conditions of unfairness, namely:

---

8 This interpretation is open to at least two readings. On one reading, a term is unfair only if *both* procedural and substantive conditions are violated. On another reading, however, a term is unfair if the dealer has acted contrary to *either* a procedural or a substantive condition. The former reading effectively turns the three-step procedural and substantive interpretation into a four-step reading; the latter reading maintains a three-step reading and eases the consumer's burden in relation to the good faith condition. For present purposes, we will presuppose the former reading and, at the price of some over-simplification, we will tend to bracket it with the three-step procedural reading in our discussion.

9 The relevant part of Article 3(1) was implemented verbation by UK regulation 4(1). So the UK government have not done anything to suggest which of the above interpretations they prefer.

10 Stephen Smith (1994) puts this interpretation crisply:

The concept of 'good faith' is an unfamiliar one in the common law, but the wording of Article 3(1) suggests that its meaning is irrelevant in any event. The status of the term 'good faith' in Article 3(1) is definitional. All that matters in substance is whether or not the contract causes a 'significant imbalance' in the parties' rights and obligations. In other words, the test of validity, according to Article 3(1), is a test of substantive fairness. (p. 8)

(1) a violation of the requirement of good faith (interpreted as a procedural condition);
(2) a term causing a significant imbalance in the parties' rights and obligations under the contract; and
(3) such significant imbalance operating to the detriment of the consumer.

In the absence of a uniform jurisprudence of good faith (cf. Powell, 1956), the most plausible reading of a procedural requirement of good faith – at least, in the context of standard form dealing – is that the law is seeking to regulate unfair surprise and lack of choice (see e.g. Dugan, 1980; Smith 1994). If this is correct, the three-step procedural reading of Article 3.1 entails that a term will be treated as unfair only if there has been a double abuse of power by the dealer: namely, unfair surprise or bad faith lack of choice (procedural abuse) in conjunction with significant imbalance to the detriment of the consumer (substantive abuse).[11] Clearly, this will make no kind of appeal to those who seek to employ the Directive to gain route one control over the content of consumer contracts.

(2) The Relationship Between Article 3.1 and Article 3.3

Alongside Article 3.1, Article 3.3 also purports to have some bearing on the Directive's concept of unfair terms, incorporating the Annex, which declares that it contains 'an indicative and non-exhaustive list of the terms which may be regarded as unfair'. As the Directive has been finally drafted, neither Article 3.3, nor the Annex, has any explicit link with Article 3.1. There is no mention in Article 3.3, nor the Annex, of the requirement of good faith, of significant balance, nor of detriment to the consumer. Conversely, in Article 3.1, there is no explicit reference to either Article 3.3 or the Annex.[12] Now, whereas the good faith element in Article 3.1 can be given a procedural reading, Article 3.3 and the Annex (if considered on their own terms) apparently have a natural substantive bias. For, apart from indicative term (i), which refers to 'terms with which [the consumer] had no real opportunity of becoming acquainted before the conclusion of the contract' and thus apparently touches on non-disclosure, there is no trace in either Article 3.3 or the Annex of any concern with procedural unfairness – the indicative terms listed are all examples, roughly speaking, of one-sided provisions or unfair exclusions of essential rights.

---

[11] Cf. the distinction in Finnish contract theory between external and internal criteria of unfairness (see e.g. Pöyhönen, 1994)

[12] The same is true of the UK regulations. The Article 3(1) test is stated in regulation 4(1), and the incorporation of the Annex takes place via regulation 4(4). Regulations

Potentially, the Directive's failure to articulate the relationship between Articles 3.1 and 3.3 (and the Annex) invites a number of different approaches to the interpretation of Article 3 (and the concomitant question of what makes a term unfair). In the Nordic countries, for example, it would seem natural to read the two tests as complementary to one another – thus, in a particular case, where a term is arguably unfair under the Article 3.3 test, recourse might be made to Article 3.1, such that a violation of good faith by the dealer would tip the balance against the fairness of the term (possibly on the basis that the term has not been freely agreed to: cf. Brownsword and Howells, 1995; and Willett, 1994). However, we will focus on just two possible approaches to the matter.

The first approach, which is the approach that has generally been taken for granted in England, and which the DTI has taken, treats Article 3.1 as the master test for an unfair term. Thus, in its Consultation Document on the Directive, the DTI (1993) says that, where a term in the Annex does not fall within the scope of the (English) Unfair Contract Terms Act, 1977, 'it will be for the consumer to demonstrate that the term is unfair ***according to the test in Article 3(1)'*** (emphasis added). On this view, Article 3.3 does not offer an independent test for an unfair term; it merely supplements Article 3.1. Quite what supplementary function is to be played by Article 3.3 remains unclear.[13] According to the DTI, the terms in the Annex are neither 'automatically unfair, nor are they deemed unfair unless proved fair' – in other words, the burden of proving unfairness (unlike under UCTA) rests with the consumer. Such a weak interpretation strikes us as offering the consumer rather less protection than must have been intended. For the sake of argument, therefore, we will assume that the function of the Annex is to offer an indicative list of terms which at least raise a presumption that they involve a significant imbalance to the detriment of the consumer.[14]

The alternative approach is to treat Articles 3.1 and 3.3 as independent tests of an unfair term. On this view, for the purpose of showing that a term is unfair, it is sufficient to satisfy the test in Article 3.1 (however this test is interpreted), but equally it is sufficient to show that the term is unfair by analogy with the annexed terms brought in under Article 3.3. Neither

---

13 And the position remains unclear in the United Kingdom in the implementing Regulations: see Brownsword and Howells, 1995.

14 Cf. Dean, 1993, who says that 'the Annex can be taken as identifying those terms which would rarely satisfy the test of fairness and are therefore effectively void' (p. 587); and Hondius, (below at chapter 3), who emphasises that the status of the Annex is 'far from clear' (section ix), but who nevertheless refers to the Annex as a 'black-list'.

Article 3.1 nor Article 3.3, however, constitutes a *necessary* test of unfairness.

The general assumption in England, as we have said, is that the first approach accords with the intention underlying Article 3. Yet, can it be said that, in principle, the alternative approach is untenable? It might be argued, for example, that although the relationship between Article 3.1 and 3.3 is not explicitly dealt with, it is perfectly clear that Article 3.1 lays down the definition of an unfair term. However, this hardly disposes of the alternative approach. To be sure, Article 3.1 sets out a definition of an unfair term, but according to the alternative approach this is also the function of Article 3.3 (which it performs, not by setting out general criteria, but by offering an indicative list of unfair terms). Equally, it might be objected to the alternative approach that, in the final version of the Directive, Article 3.3 merely indicates terms which *may* be regarded as unfair, unlike an earlier draft of the Directive where the Annex clearly amounted to a black-list of proscribed terms. However, although this might be thought to weaken any argument in favour of the alternative approach, it hardly undercuts it completely. After all, the notion of an independent test for unfair terms that leaves judges with considerable discretion is hardly a novelty in the jurisprudence of European contract law. The English are familiar with the reasonableness discretion under UCTA,[15] but consider, too, the broad terms of the judicial discretion conferred by section 36 of the Nordic Contracts Act, which (in its Finnish version) provides:

> If a contract or a term thereof is unfair, or its application would be unfair, it may be adjusted or left unapplied. When considering the unfairness the whole content of the contract, the position of the parties, the circumstances when the contract was made and thereafter and other circumstances shall be taken into account....Price is to be considered one possible term for adjustment.

In the Nordic countries, this broad general clause has largely superseded the protective jurisdiction available under other narrower (mainly procedural) provisions, even though the latter technically remain available (see Pöyhönen, 1994).

For the moment, we will pend judgment on the correct resolution of the structural indeterminacy in Article 3, for we need to review the issue in the light of a second structural deficiency in the Directive – a problem already hinted at by the formulation of section 36 of the Finnish version of the Nordic Contracts Act, in which a distinction is implicit between challenges to terms unfair *per se* (hence, 'If a contract or a term thereof is unfair') and

[15] Generally, see Adams and Brownsword, 1988.

individual challenges in particular cases (hence, 'If...its application would be unfair').

(3) Ex Casu and Article 7.2 Challenges

In principle, a contractual term might be argued to be unfair by a consumer making a specific *ex casu* challenge, or by a person or organisation making a general pre-emptive challenge as envisaged by Article 7.2. Ideally, the relevant test of unfairness for each kind of challenge should be clearly articulated. Thus, for example, Nordic law uses separate general clauses on collective and individual levels for the regulation of the fairness of contracts. The Directive undoubtedly contemplates both *ex casu* and general pre-emptive challenges, but it does not explicitly identify the fairness regime applicable to each kind of challenge; and, certainly from a Nordic viewpoint, the Directive's use of just one general clause (Article 3) is a matter for criticism (see Wilhelmsson, 1992b, pp. 86-89).

One approach to the single general clause in the Directive would be to treat Article 3.3 and the Annex as applicable to general pre-emptive challenges, leaving Article 3.1 (in conjunction with Article 4) to regulate *ex casu* challenges. However, if we follow the English assumption that Article 3.1 sets the master test for an unfair term, then this is the relevant test whether the challenge is *ex casu* or pre-emptive. As we have seen, though, the specification of this'relevant test' is moot – the master test under Article 3.1 can be read in more than one way, two-step or three-step, procedural or substantive, and so on.

If we read the master test in Article 3.1 as a two-step test, the existence of both *ex casu* and pre-emptive challenges causes no great difficulty. In both types of challenge, the gist of the two-step question is whether the term is a reasonable one to have been included in the contract. On this interpretation, the function of Article 3.3 is basically to offer a sample check-list of potentially unreasonable terms. However, if we interpret Article 3.1 according to the three-step procedural reading, things are altogether less straightforward. There is no problem in relating the three-step procedural test to an *ex casu* challenge, but it strains the imagination to see how the test might be applicable to a pre-emptive challenge. The point is that a pre-emptive challenge does not relate to a specific case; it alleges that a term in general circulation is unfair *per se*, and thus unfair in all cases. In other words, where a pre-emptive challenge is made, the focus is on the reasonableness of the term under review, and (unlike in an *ex casu* challenge) the conduct of a particular dealer in a particular case is irrelevant. Accordingly, if, in a pre-emptive challenge, there is to be no inquiry as to a particular dealer's conduct, it is unclear how it might be established that the term was procured contrary to the requirement of good faith – and it is unclear how Article 3.1 might govern the issue.

Once we run the distinction between *ex casu* and pre-emptive challenges through Article 3, in conjunction with the several plausible general readings of the test in Article 3.1, interpretation of the Directive threatens to become exceedingly complex. One way of cutting through the complexity is to assume that, in Article 3.1, it is either the two-step or the three-step substantive test that applies. On this basis, the essential question under Article 3, whether one works with Article 3.1 or Article 3.3 or both, is whether the term at issue is a fair and reasonable provision to have included in the contract. With a little bit of fudging, this test can be employed in both *ex casu* and pre-emptive challenges. However, if we presuppose the three-step procedural reading of Article 3.1, matters are less easily resolved. Indeed, on this reading, it is not at all obvious that Article 3.1 sets the master test of unfairness. On the contrary, the alternative approach now looks quite appealing – in other words, where the challenge is *ex casu*, the relevant test is set by Article 3.1, but, for the purposes of pre-emptive challenges, the starting point is Article 3.3 and the specimen unfair terms in the Annex. Of course, one might try to avoid this complexity by closing off the possibility of pre-emptive challenges – as originally was the case with the DTI in the UK. If *ex casu* (UCTA-type) challenges are the only ones available, there is no problem with having a three-step procedural master test under Article 3.1. In principle, however, the difficulty remains and, in practice, this strategy of avoidance surely cannot be sustained in the long run.

Taking stock, we are left with two general approaches to Article 3. On one approach, we can give Article 3.1 a two-step (or a three-step substantive) reading, in which case it can function as the master test for unfair terms in both *ex casu* and pre-emptive challenges, and Article 3.3 then serves as a checklist of sample unfair terms. Alternatively, we can give Article 3.1 a three-step procedural (or a three-step procedural and substantive)[16] reading, in which case it can operate as the master test for unfair terms in *ex casu* challenges. However, on this alternative approach, Article 3.1 cannot serve as the master test for pre-emptive challenges and this role must be played instead by Article 3.3 and the Annex. For present purposes, we need not agonise about which approach is the better interpretation of the Directive; for, whichever approach is adopted, Article 3.1 will set the test that governs *ex casu* challenges.

---

[16] Cf. note viii *supra*.

(4) Efficiency and the Alternative Approach

Although the alternative approach to the interpretation of Article 3 offers a plausible explanation of how the Directive works in relation to both *ex casu* and pre-emptive challenges, it leaves the three-step procedural reading of Article 3.1 as the master test for *ex casu* challenges. Before we look more carefully at this test, it is as well to underline what would be given up if Article 3.3 were to govern pre-emptive challenges but play only a supplementary role in relation to *ex casu* challenges.

If we are looking for an efficient and a direct way of establishing a fair European standard form (as is the case with the market school of thinking), pre-emptive challenges – with Article 3.3 as the test of unfairness – have considerable appeal as a strategy. Not only are pre-emptive challenges likely to be more efficient than *ex casu* challenges (given the well-known limitations of occasional private law relief), Article 3.3 implies a broad discretion for dealing with substantively unfair terms – particularly if we assume that the terms listed in the Annex are presumptively unfair and bearing in mind that this list is not exhaustive. It follows that, from the market viewpoint, it would not be a disaster if Article 3.3 were to be relegated to a supplementary role in relation to *ex casu* challenges. Nevertheless, it would be inconvenient – and, if some Member States were to fail to make provision for pre-emptive challenges, or if pre-emptive mechanisms worked unsatisfactorily, it would become a significant cause for concern. To repeat, the point is that, on the three-step procedural reading of Article 3.1, a non-conforming standard form would be immune to challenge unless the dealer had also engaged in some procedural abuse. In other words, in *ex casu* cases, instead of having a consumers' charter based on Article 3.3, we would have to judge unfairness on the basis of the criteria in Article 3.1, which if not exactly a dealers' charter for evasion, nonetheless could prove something of a hostage to fortune.

PART TWO: ARTICLE 3.1 AND THE PROMOTION OF STANDARD FAIRNESS FOR STANDARD FORMS

Whichever approach we take to Article 3, our assumption is that, in *ex casu* challenges, the framework for legal argument that a term is unfair is set by Article 3.1 of the Directive. If the two-step reading of the test in Article 3.1 is adopted, there is relatively little further interpretive work to be done – the concept of good faith need not trouble the interpreter and the idea of a significant imbalance to the detriment of the consumer is to be taken as an invitation to decide whether the term is reasonable or unreasonable. Much the same is true if we adopt the three-step substantive reading. However, if the three-step procedural (or the three-step procedural and substantive) reading of the test in Article 3.1 is adopted, a further layer of interpretive problems has to be faced. These further interpretive problems associated with Article 3.1 arise from: (1) the vagueness of the concept of good faith; (2) the vagueness of the concept of significant imbalance; (3) an ambiguity in the concept of detriment; and (4) some exceedingly opaque remarks in the Recitals, particularly in Recital 16, on these matters. We now turn to these difficulties, focusing on the three-step procedural reading, and considering the issues in this part of our discussion specifically from the perspective of the market school of thinking.

(1) Good Faith

For promoters of the European standard (the market school), the good faith condition in Article 3.1 is a source of potential concern. Ideally, the good faith requirement should be rolled up into an objective substantive matter, making it possible to regulate unfair terms in standard forms directly without getting entangled in secondary questions concerning procedural abuse. In principle, this could be achieved in a variety of ways – by arguing for either the two-step or the three-step substantive reading of Article 3.1, or by arguing that Article 3.3 should regulate all questions of unfairness. However, we are presently considering the matter on the assumption that Article 3.1 sets the master test of unfairness for *ex casu* challenges and that the test takes the form of the three-step procedural reading.

Given these premise, the initial concern for the market school arises from the possibility that good faith might be taken as implying a simple 'clear conscience' test. In his seminal discussion of the good faith provision of the UCC, E. Allan Farnsworth (1962-63) pointed out that, on one interpretation, the concept of good faith can be taken to connote simply a particular (innocent) state of mind, namely one free from suspicion or notice – good faith in the sense of 'the pure heart and the empty head' as Lord Kenyon once put it.[17] For promoters of the European standard, the implications of such a simple 'clear conscience' interpretation of the good faith condition in Article 3.1 would be dire indeed. First, it would be an invitation to standard form dealers to argue that they did not believe that

---

[17] See *Lawson v. Weston* (1801) 4 Esp 56, 170 ER 806. See also Waddams (1995) JCL 55 who seems to connect good faith solely with a clear conscience or innocent state of mind.

they were taking unfair advantage of consumers, that they did not believe that they were abusing their position, and so on. Granted, such arguments would only be successful if they were plausible on the evidence but there is an obvious danger of such pleading wrecking the market ideal of a generalised regulation of standard forms. Secondly, the principal beneficiaries of the clear conscience defence would be just those benighted dealers who were honestly ignorant of consumer vulnerability or who were familiar only with shabby practice. Even if continuing procedural abuse would not concern the market school, the availability of the clear conscience defence to down-market traders and to small businesses without legal advisers could result in a worrying distortion of desired conditions of equal competition. Fairly clearly, therefore, the market approach must prefer a standard-setting reading of the good faith requirement that goes beyond mere honesty; it must prefer, so to speak, an 'objective' test of good faith.

Even if good faith is not read as a 'clear conscience' test, it still looks like a procedural test. But, what sort of procedural test would this be? Whilst good faith clauses tend to be drafted as requiring good faith in the performance and enforcement of contracts (see Summers, 1968; Brownsword, 1994a), they are often extended to good faith in negotiation and it is a reasonable assumption that the good faith requirement in the Directive refers to good faith in negotiation. However, we are not concerned with good faith negotiating at large, particularly with general obligations of disclosure as have been developed in French law in recent years (see Legrand, 1986). We are concerned specifically with good faith in the context of standard form dealing, and it is a reasonable assumption that, in this context, good faith implies:

(1) a requirement of disclosure of terms (in order to avoid unfair surprise); and/or

(2) a requirement that the standard form should not be offered on a take-it-or-leave-it basis (in order to preserve some element of choice for the consumer).

Although the language of Article 3.1 does not specify that there must be a causal link between the violation of good faith and the significant imbalance, it is perfectly clear how non-disclosure and lack of choice can be implicated in a chain of events leading to a significant imbalance. Quite simply, but for such violations of good faith, the consumer (or, at any rate, the rational consumer) would not have agreed to contract on such terms.

For promoters of the European standard, *if good faith sets a procedural condition*,[18] it is important that the condition is easily met by consumer challenges to unfair terms. In other words, the broader and the more stringent the good faith requirement the better. As we have already said, promoters of the European standard must argue against a simple 'clear conscience' interpretation of good faith; and, reading the requirement objectively, they must favour: (1) good faith requiring both disclosure and choice; (2) disclosure being a demanding requirement; and (3) choice likewise being a demanding requirement – thus making it difficult for standard form dealers to comply with the good faith requirement. We can speak briefly to these three points.

(1) The dual requirement: The claim that the good faith requirement should be read as embracing both disclosure and choice is plausible, being supported by the highly respectable argument that the underlying rationale of good faith is that the consumer's consent to the standard form should be genuine. If this implies that the consumer's consent should be both informed and voluntary, as it surely does, then it follows that both elements should be read into the Directive.

(2) Disclosure: To argue for a strong disclosure requirement, one might derive some assistance from English law, which now distinguishes between token disclosure and effective notice (*Thornton*[19] and *Interfoto*[20]). This idea has been developed through the classical requirement of reasonable notice, and it has relied on some vaguely articulated notions, such as the distinction between 'usual' and 'unusual' (or 'exceptional') terms. The upshot of this is that English law still has to clarify whether the mark of an exceptional term is the fact that the particular term is out of line with equivalent terms elsewhere in the market (as in *Interfoto*), or whether the term is exceptional because it impinges upon essential rights (as in *Thornton*). Nevertheless, there is a clear organising rationale for these developments in the idea of reasonable (or legitimate) expectation. Consumers contract on the basis of both background and specific expectations – they deal on the basis of background expectations generated by advertisement campaigns, product reputation etc. but also on the basis of specific expectations generated by sales talk, assurances, and the like. To the extent that standard form provisions derogate from these expectations, consumers must be put unmistakably on notice.

---

18 We will consider shortly the possibility that good faith is given a substantive interpretation.

19 See *Thornton v. Shoe Lane Parking Ltd.* [1972] 2 QB 163.

20 See *Interfoto Picture Library Ltd. v. Stiletto Visual Programmes Ltd.* [1989] QB 433.

For the disclosure requirement to have some real bite it must require effective notice not simply of terms which derogate from *contrary* consumer expectation but also of terms which touch and concern significant consumer interests (irrespective of whether consumers have any settled expectations in relation to these matters). The point is that, although consumers can be quite discriminating in their purchases, and although they can be quite well informed about particular markets for goods and services, it is not clear that they would have many expectations, background or specific, that would relate directly to the kinds of matters set out in the indicative list. To test this out, one need only ask how many of the terms set out in the Annex consumers might have expectations about. One suspects that the answer is relatively few. Accordingly, if there are terms which are substantively unfair (because one-sided or exclusions of essential rights), but which fall outside a standard reasonable expectations approach, they can still be caught under an effective disclosure principle.

If the market school were not yet satisfied with this interpretation of the disclosure requirement, it could be further strengthened by unpacking the effective notice principle in such a way that it called for active explanation of terms to consumers, with dealers having to be reasonably satisfied that the import of the terms had been understood. On this interpretation, disclosure of burdensome terms would require more than pointing red fingers, bold type, or the like, it would require the dealer to take steps to ensure that the consumer fully comprehended the contract. In this way, the disclosure requirement would move, first, from requiring token notice to effective or conspicuous notice, and then to real understanding on the part of the consumer; and, moreover, this movement would seem to be wholly compatible with the underlying rationale of ensuring free and informed consent by the consumer.

(3) Choice: If the element of choice is to be made difficult for the standard form dealer to satisfy, one might learn some lessons from the treatment of duress in English law (in criminal law, family law, and in contract law). In the context of economic duress in contract, English law refuses to recognise alleged improper pressure as duress unless the party against whom the pressure was applied had no real choice in submitting to the demand. Initially, contract law followed the criminal law (and family law) in interpreting this as requiring that the party's will should be overcome (that there should be a coercion of the will such as to vitiate consent)[21] but, before too long, this was abandoned in favour of the idea of there being no

21 See *Pao On v. Lau Yiu Long* [1980] AC 614.

practical, or reasonable, alternative.[22] If this thinking is applied to the good faith requirement of the Directive, the requirement of choice will impose a more stringent regime of procedural fairness if it is interpreted in terms of there having to be a reasonable alternative (i.e. if there is held to be a violation of good faith, not merely in those exceptional cases where the will is overcome, but far more commonly where the consumer has no reasonable alternative but to accept the standard form offered).

Where the dealer is a monopolist, this might seem unduly harsh (even though we are considering a test that would be difficult for dealers to comply with). For, in such a case, the consumer would always have no alternative, reasonable or otherwise, other than to contract with the monopolist. What this requires in the first instance, therefore, is that the dealer should offer the consumer a choice of standard forms, no doubt with a range of prices calibrated according to the extent of risk allocated by the standard form. It might be argued, however, that this is not quite enough. Choice, it will be recalled, entails a *reasonable* alternative. But, what does this mean? On one interpretation, a reasonable alternative is merely an alternative that is reasonably easily available (that is, a reasonably practical alternative) – a near monopolist in England, for example, cannot argue that the availability of a different standard form deal in Italy represents a reasonable alternative. Choice at such a distance is simply too remote. On another interpretation, however, the idea of a reasonable alternative is given a substantive import – good faith demands that the consumer be given a reasonable choice, not, so to speak, Hobson's choice. Minimally applied, this view entails that, to satisfy the good faith requirement of choice, the standard form monopolist dealer must offer the consumer *at least one* reasonable standard form. The more plausible interpretation, however, particularly from the perspective of the market school, is that this interpretation of choice entails that at least two standard forms must be offered to the consumer, each form being reasonable in its terms.[23]

Now, this is certainly a bold elaboration of the requirement of choice. However, if it were to hold up, and if we were to generalise this analysis to non-monopolists, we would say that the requirement of choice was not satisfied unless more than one reasonable standard form was realistically on offer. This is a potent argument, for it turns the ostensibly procedural

---

22 See *Universe Tankships Inc. of Monrovia v. ITWF* [1982] 2 All ER 67.

23 If, exceptionally, a consumer contracted on an unreasonable standard form, having been offered a choice by a dealer of one reasonable and one unreasonable standard form, the dealer would still be vulnerable; for it would be arguable that the dealer had failed properly to disclose (or to explain properly) the import of the standard form terms to the consumer.

requirement of choice into a substantive requirement. *Ex hypothesi*, if a contract is tainted by an unreasonable term, the consumer cannot have been given a proper choice (and there is a violation of the requirement of good faith). For a moment, however, let us assume that this indirect conversion of procedure into substance might not work and that good faith is to be read wholly procedurally.

Let us take stock. If the good faith requirement is to be read entirely procedurally, albeit broadly (as involving both disclosure and choice) and strongly, such that the particular requirements are difficult for dealers to comply with, the market school might still fear that the regulatory impact of the Directive – at least, in the case of *ex casu* challenges – will be inadequate. Accordingly, promoters of an easily regulated fair European standard may be expected to seek out substantive interpretations of the good faith requirement. One indirect way of doing this, which we have outlined above, is to make choice an element of the good faith requirement and then to unpack this ostensibly procedural element in such a way that a reasonable alternative requires a reasonable standard form – and procedure folds into substance. Such a strategy, however, might seem altogether too indirect. Why not meet the good faith problem head-on and argue that it is a substantive requirement, akin to the doctrine of unconscionability (or akin to the UCTA reasonableness test)?

As we have said, in principle at least, there are a number of ways of running such an argument. First, there is the two-step reading of Article 3.1 which removes any independent requirement of good faith. It could be objected that such a reading renders the reference to the requirement of good faith redundant, but this is not correct. According to the two-step reading, a violation of good faith ***is*** the test of an unfair term, but what good faith means in this context is that the term causes a significant imbalance to the detriment of consumers – Article 3.1 is to be understood as an extended definition of what would be contrary to the requirement of good faith. Secondly, there is the three-step substantive reading of Article 3.1. The obvious objection to this is that, if a violation of good faith is equivalent to substantive unfairness, then the requirement of significant imbalance is redundant. However, one response to this is that the emphasis of significant imbalance is on 'significant'. Terms will not be deemed unfair if they are merely a little unreasonable: the target for the Directive is grossly unreasonable provisions and this is signalled by the good faith requirement in conjunction with the significant imbalance condition. On this view, in the language of Article 3.1, a term which violates the (substantive) requirement of good faith, when placed in the context of the full set of particular contractual terms, might 'cause' a significant imbalance in the contract as a whole. Thirdly, proponents of the market approach could avoid all these problems if they could persuade interpreters of the Directive that Article 3.3 is the master test. In practice, this last option probably is not viable. However, there is no reason why the other two arguments should not be regarded as serious candidates – and at least as plausible as the three-step procedural reading which is the root of the concern.

Finally, to return to the main track of our analysis, if the three-step procedural reading prevails, the best bet for the market school is either to argue for an interpretation of good faith as reasonable choice (indirectly importing a substantive requirement), or to argue for a strong interpretation of the the good faith requirement (such that dealers cannot easily comply).

(2) Significant Imbalance

Whilst, as Hugh Collins (1994) has remarked, the test 'of a significant imbalance of the obligations obviously directs attention to the substantive unfairness of the contract' (p. 249), the precise import of this concept is unclear. In the first draft of the Directive, significant imbalance appeared as a test for an unfair term alongside other grounds: in particular, terms that would cause the performance to be unduly detrimental to the consumer or that would cause the performance to be significantly different from what the consumer could legitimately expect, were also to be treated as unfair. While these latter grounds have been dropped, the concept of significant imbalance has survived.

As against the concept of an unfair or an unreasonable term, the concept of significant imbalance seems rather narrow, being specifically about imbalance and requiring the imbalance to be significant. This is suggestive of a manifestly one-sided contract, a contract in which one side bears a disproportionate amount of risk, or in which there is a serious asymmetry in the balance of rights and obligations under the contract. Taking the concept fairly literally, in such terms, it is nevertheless capable of catching a fairly broad range of terms. However, the Annex offers an indicative list of terms which may be regarded as unfair and, to the extent that this elaborates the concept of significant imbalance, it invites a broader reading of significant imbalance.

The Annex offers a catholic range of terms which may be regarded as unfair. Elsewhere (Brownsword, Howells, and Wilhelmsson, 1994b), we have suggested that the indicated terms may be classified in four categories, namely: terms which give just one party control over the contract terms or the performance of the contract; terms which effectively give just one party control over the duration of the contract; terms which involve an asymmetry of rights; and terms which are in the family of exclusion, limitation, and penalty clauses. No doubt, the annexed terms could be catalogued in other ways,[24] but the important point for present purposes is that, while some of the terms in the list fairly straightforwardly fit the description of significant imbalance, this is by no means true of all the sample terms.

So far as promoters of the European standard are concerned, the broader and more flexible the reading of significant imbalance the better – and this applies whichever reading of the test in Article 3.1 is presupposed. Given, as we have said, that there was some narrowing down of the grounds for finding a term unfair, as the Directive went from first to final draft, the market school has cause for concern. In principle, Article 3.3 offers a foothold for the argument that unfair terms should be identified by reference to the examples in the Annex rather than by a mechanical or literal application of the idea of significant imbalance. Granted, it is possible to read Article 3.3 and the Annex as relevant only to pre-emptive challenges. However, if we make the not implausible assumption that, in *ex casu* challenges, Article 3.3 also supplements in some way the definition of an unfair term in Article 3.1, then if the indicative terms in the Annex are not specimens of terms involving significant imbalance, we might well ask what else they could possibly exemplify in relation to Article 3.1.[25]

(3) Detriment

The concept of 'detriment' to the consumer looks reasonably straightforward, but it conceals a possible ambiguity. One reading of Article 3.1 is that the reference to detriment to the consumer simply indicates that the Directive is concerned with significant imbalance against the consumer, rather than against the dealer. To this extent, this merely states the obvious; and, once there is shown to be significant imbalance against the consumer, detriment to the consumer follows like night follows day. However, it might be argued that the reference to detriment sets a fresh (third) hurdle for the consumer challenger. On this view, a term which involves significant imbalance against the consumer does not

24 For a helpful comparison between the terms listed in the Annex and equivalent lists in Austrian, Belgian, Dutch, French, and German, legislation, see Hondius, below at chapter 3, pp. 40-41.

25 Of course, if it is suggested that the Annex exemplifies terms which may violate the good faith requirement, then because the indicative terms have a predominantly substantive emphasis, the market school should seize upon this as an argument in support of a substantive reading of good faith.

necessarily operate to the detriment of the consumer. Detriment is something that has to be independently proved by the consumer and this can only be done by placing the contract in the broader context in which the transaction was concluded and showing overall disadvantage to the consumer. Accordingly, if the contract has actually had some beneficial effect for the consumer (for example, if a consumer has bought a car that has enabled him to gain employment), there is no detriment even though the standard form terms otherwise fail the conditions of fairness.[26]

Overall, we suggest that the latter interpretation is less plausible than the former. Certainly, from the perspective of the market school, control over standard forms cannot sensibly be subjected to vagaries of this kind; and the logic of the market position is to argue for an interpretation of detriment that makes it a condition easily satisfied by the consumer.

(4) The Recitals

Having declared that 'it is necessary to fix in a general way the criteria for assessing the unfair character of contract terms', Recital 16 states:

> Whereas the assessment, according to the general criteria chosen, of the unfair character of terms, in particular in sale or supply activities of a public nature providing collective services which take account of solidarity among users, must be supplemented by a means of making an overall evaluation of the different interests involved; whereas this constitutes the requirement of good faith...

At this point, we may pause. The first part of the Recital surely qualifies for a place in the pantheon of obscure draftsmanship: presumably, those who drafted it had some meaning in mind, but it is impossible to say what that meaning might have been (although cf Thomas, 1991). This would be no great loss were it not for the fact that this piece of pure gobbledygook is immediately followed by the important Recital 'whereas this constitutes the requirement of good faith'. Unfortunately, it is unclear what the relevant 'this' is that apparently constitutes the requirement of good faith. Is good faith the supplement to the (unstated) general criteria of unfair contract terms? If so, is it also 'a means of making an overall evaluation of the different interests involved' (whatever this might mean)? The Recital continues:

> whereas, in making an assessment of good faith, particular regard shall be had to the strength of the bargaining position of the parties, whether the consumer had an inducement to agree to the term and whether the goods or services were sold or supplied to the special order of the consumer...

---

[26] Cf. the reasoning in *National Westminster Bank plc v. Morgan* [1985] AC 686.

Again, we should pause. At this juncture, it rather looks as though the English tried to anglicise the concept of good faith by attaching some of the UCTA guidelines on reasonableness to the concept; and this is apparently confirmed by the DTI Consultation Document (1993), where we read that, although the concept of good faith is new to UK law, the guidelines for its application are not dissimilar to the guidelines for the application of the reasonableness test set out in Schedule 2 of UCTA. Finally, the paragraph concludes with one of the most elusive of the Recitals:

> whereas the requirement of good faith may be satisfied by the seller or supplier where he deals fairly and equitably with the other party whose legitimate interests he has to take into account.

The import of this particular provision, as we have discussed at some length elsewhere (Brownsword, Howells, and Wilhelmsson, 1994), is altogether unclear.

This important paragraph of Recitals is so unclear that one can make of it virtually what one will. In the United Kingdom, the implementing Regulations boldly incorporate most of the Recital in a Schedule listing guidelines for the application of the test of good faith,[27] leaving everything to be played for – including perhaps a simple 'clear conscience' interpretation of good faith,[28] different conceptions of good faith as a procedural requirement, and not least the argument that good faith is to be read substantively.

(5) Summary

To summarise: for promoters of the market ideal, both in the UK and elsewhere in Europe, the first priority is to make sure that the Directive facilitates effective and standardised control over unfair standard terms in consumer contracts. If the substantive thinking behind Article 3.3 is employed as the test for unfairness in general pre-emptive challenges, and if the machinery for such challenges is put in place, it should be possible, at least to some extent, to clean up the consumer market. In the larger regulatory picture, specific *ex casu* challenges are perhaps less important.

---

27 See Schedule 2 of the Unfair Terms in Consumer Contracts Regulations 1994, which provides that, in assessing good faith, regard shall be had in particular to: (a) the strength of the bargaining positions of the parties; (b) whether the consumer had an inducement to agree to the term; (c) whether the goods or services were sold or supplied to the special order of the consumer; and (d) the extent to which the seller or supplier has dealt fairly and equitably with the consumer. Generally, see Brownsword and Howells, 1995.

28 Do the closing words of Recital 16 encourage a simple 'clear conscience' reading?

However, assuming that such challenges are governed by Article 3.1, the logic of the market approach is to argue for an interpretation of the provisions that removes any obstructions to the development of fair standard form consumer contracts. In line with this logic, the two-step or three-step substantive readings of the test in Article 3.1 must be argued for. However, if the three-step procedural (or the three-step procedural and substantive)[29] reading prevails, then a second-best logic comes into play. First, an objective reading of good faith must be argued for as against a simple 'clear conscience' reading, and ideally good faith should be understood *indirectly* as a substantive requirement – if this is not possible, then the next best line is to argue for a procedural interpretation of good faith that is both broad and stringent, making it difficult for standard form dealers to comply. Secondly, a broad and flexible interpretation of the concept of significant imbalance should be argued for, facilitating the trimming of unacceptable provisions in standard forms. Finally, in case control over standard forms should be tripped up by the requirement of detriment to the consumer, this should be read as merely indicating for whose protection the Directive has been enacted – namely, consumers rather than dealers.

PART THREE: ARTICLE 3 AND THE PROMOTION OF WELFARISM

In general terms, welfarism is concerned with the protection of weaker contracting parties. Given the limitations of private law as a protective strategy, particularly where relatively disadvantaged persons have to take the legal initiative to secure redress, welfarists will be as keen as followers of the market approach to see the Directive put to good effect. It follows that, for welfarists too, pre-emptive challenges will look more significant than *ex casu* challenges tied to Article 3.1. However, as in the previous section, it is the interpretation of Article 3.1 that is our principal concern.

Although welfarist thinking is organised around the protection of weaker parties, different conceptions of welfarism employ different regulatory objectives. Following Brownsword (1994b), we can work with three conceptions of welfarism (minimal, maximal, and personal welfarism), identifying in each case the regulatory objectives implicated in the particular version of welfarism. In the first instance, we will present these regulatory objectives in a somewhat summary form.

---

29 Cf. note viii *supra*.

(1) Regulatory Objectives

The general idea of *minimal welfarism* is captured in a familiar Churchillian vision of the good society:

> We want to draw a line below which we will not allow persons to live and labour, yet above which they may compete with all the strength of their manhood. We want to have free competition upwards; we decline to allow free competition to run downwards. (Churchill, 1909, p. 82)

Contract being viewed as a competitive activity, it follows that the regulatory objectives of minimal welfarism are twofold: to protect contractors who deal from below a notional line of minimal well-being; and to adjust outcomes which are liable to push a contractor below the line. In other words, the most adverse effects of social inequality and of contractual exchanges are cushioned. Minimal welfarism, it should be noted, chimes in with the idea of need-rationality in the law (see Wilhelmsson, 1989, 1992a). Where transactions produce cases of severe individual hardship (need), the law should be willing to protect the party in need.

Maximal welfarism, like minimal welfarism, is concerned with cushioning the effects of competitive contracting. However, rather than looking at a contractor's position in the overall social order (or hierarchy), maximal welfarism focuses specifically on the power relationship between the particular contracting parties. If one side has greater bargaining strength than the other, then the weaker party will be protected against abuses of contractual power. Thus, the general regulatory objective of maximal welfarism is to act against inequality of bargaining strength and unfair contractual outcomes that can be generated by such inequality. If minimal welfarism seeks to shield contractors who are the least advantaged members of society, and who are needy in absolute terms, maximal welfarism seeks to shield contractors who, relative to fellow contractors, are disadvantaged (without necessarily operating from below the minimal welfarist line). For obvious reasons, the protection of consumers as a class falls naturally within the maximal welfarist programme.

Personal welfarism has a rather different regulatory objective. As against the qualified competitive model of both minimal and maximal welfarism, it seeks to institute a regime of co-operative contracting such that contractors assume responsibility for looking after one another's welfare. Ideal-typically, contracts are mutually beneficial exchanges in which parties deal fairly with one another. Co-operative dealing thus replaces a purely self-interested contractual ethic (an ethic in which each side acts with a view to maximising its own utility) and perforce entails that the interests of weaker parties are fully protected.

Insofar as welfarism is articulated in terms of consumer rights,[30] the particular rights implicated in each form of welfarism are those linked to the respective regulatory objectives. Having outlined the regulatory objectives associated with these three forms of welfarism, we can consider now how, in the event of a specific *ex casu* challenge, Article 3.1 needs to be read to promote each of these objectives.

(2) Promoting Minimal Welfarism

For the minimal welfarist, procedural controls are not very important. To the extent that good faith dealing makes standard term deals more transparent, puts consumers on special notice of onerous terms, and gives consumers a degree of choice, all well and good. However, there is little reason to be optimistic about such measures having much preventive effect in relation to the least advantaged members of society – and these members, it must be stressed, are the distinctive concern of minimal welfarism. The poor, the unemployed, the illiterate will continue to enter burdensome contracts (see Howells, 1993). For the minimal welfarist, the critical legal resource is one which enables relief to be given against hardship where a contract has adverse effects on disadvantaged consumers. This requires control over unfair terms and it needs to be backed up by effective remedies on the ground.

So far as the interpretation of Article 3.1 of the Directive is concerned, the minimal welfarist basically falls into line with the market school of thinking. Ideally, the Directive should offer a direct regulatory handle on terms which are unreasonable, in the sense that they threaten to push consumers below the safety line. The logic of minimal welfarism, therefore, is to argue for the two-step or three-step substantive reading of Article 3.1 – under which, the thrust of argument would be that no dealer could in good faith rely on a term which would place a consumer at risk in the relevant sense. Failing this, if the three-step procedural (or three-step procedural and substantive) reading of the test is espoused, minimal welfarism dictates that a simple 'clear conscience' test of good faith must be rejected and procedural conditions must not be allowed to impede substantive relief against hardship-threatening outcomes. Accordingly, the logic is to argue for a stringent procedural requirement of good faith (standard form dealers must not be allowed to go through the motions in relation to, say, disclosure and thereby satisfy the requirement of good faith) in conjunction with, first, a flexible interpretation of significant

30 Cf. note v *supra*.

imbalance and, secondly, the obvious interpretation of detriment to the consumer.

(3) Promoting Maximal Welfarism

As we have said, the regulatory objective of maximal welfarism is to control inequality of bargaining strength and concomitant unfair terms. However, this general statement conceals some fine divisions amongst maximal welfarists. In principle, maximal welfarists might be proceduralists or substantivists. Moreover, we can divide the proceduralists into pure proceduralists and impure proceduralists.

Pure proceduralists hold: (1) that the existence of conditions of equal bargaining strength is to be tested purely procedurally, without reference to the resulting terms of the contract; and (2) that if supposedly unfair terms materialise, equality of bargaining strength notwithstanding, there is no ground for intervening against those terms.

Impure proceduralists hold: (1) that the existence of conditions of equal bargaining strength is to be tested partly procedurally and partly by reference to the resulting terms of the contract; and (2) that if unfair terms materialise, it is legitimate to infer that apparently equal bargaining conditions were not in fact equal, and that there are grounds for intervening against the offending terms.

Substantivists, by contrast, do not draw any real distinction between unequal bargaining strength and unequal contracts – in practice, it is assumed that the two tend to go together, and indeed what makes a term unfair is precisely that it is incompatible with equal bargaining conditions. Accordingly, substantivists hold that unfair terms must always be acted against even if apparently equal bargaining conditions obtain. Thus, unlike the proceduralists, substantive maximal welfarists are unequivocally concerned with protecting parties against unfair terms.

For *pure procedural maximal welfarists*, a procedural reading of Article 3.1 is appropriate, for good faith procedures are relevant to the question of equality of bargaining position. However, it is important that good faith is taken as setting an objective rather than a simple 'clear conscience' test – whereas a clear conscience test may not be sufficient to procure equal bargaining conditions, an objective test (under which the standard form dealer must disclose terms and the consumer must be given the option of dealing elsewhere (or of dealing on different terms with the same seller or supplier)) promises to even up the bargaining odds somewhat. If substantively unfair terms nevertheless materialise, strictly speaking, this is no cause for concern. However, *where there has been a clear violation of good faith*, if consumers have difficulty in meeting the substantive conditions in Article 3.1, then this is very much a cause for concern to the pure proceduralist – indeed, it is worth recalling that, under the first draft version of the Directive, there were grounds for arguing that a violation of good faith alone rendered a term unfair. The upshot of this is that the reading that the pure proceduralist must argue for is one in which:

(1) the good faith requirement is used as a device to simulate conditions of equal bargaining strength (aided, no doubt, by the declaration in the Recitals that, in making an assessment of good faith, particular regard shall be had to the strength of the bargaining position of the parties); and

(2) the significant imbalance test (likewise the detriment clause) does not obstruct consumers who have been subjected to procedural abuse.

It follows that, albeit for different reasons, pure proceduralists will be with the market school and minimal welfarists in arguing for a broad and stringent interpretation of the good faith requirement (although, of course, it should be emphasised that the preferred interpretation from the perspective of both the market and the minimal welfarist approaches is one in which good faith is not treated as an independent condition or, at least, is not given a procedural reading). Additionally, the pure proceduralist will want the significant imbalance condition interpreted flexibly so that procedural abuses are not left unchecked, and the detriment condition must be given its obvious meaning.

Impure proceduralists follow pure proceduralists in favouring a procedural reading of the test in Article 3.1. However, the distinctive question for an impure proceduralist is whether significant imbalance can be relied on as evidence of a violation of good faith. If this point can be taken on board, the framework of Article 3.1 should present no special difficulties for impure proceduralists. In appropriate cases, where there is a suspicion of unequal bargaining conditions, impure proceduralists will reason: (1) there is a term involving significant imbalance to the detriment of the consumer; and (2) because there is such a term, there is a (rebuttable) presumption that there has been a violation of the good faith requirement (in the procedural sense that unequal bargaining conditions must have obtained and have been abused by the dealer).

For *substantive maximal welfarists*, the primary concern is to regulate unfair terms. Subjective tests and procedural conditions are a threat to this enterprise. Ideally, Article 3.1 should be read directly (via the two-step or three-step substantive reading) or indirectly (eg via a strong interpretation of the requirement of choice) as setting a wholly substantive objective test. Failing this, provided that the notion of significant imbalance is interpreted flexibly, the substantive aspects of Article 3 offer plenty of scope for substantive control and the only problem is to ensure that the procedural conditions raised by the good faith condition are not a hindrance. This again points to arguing (a) that the good faith requirement should be difficult for dealers to comply with, and (b) that the significant imbalance test should be interpreted broadly in order to facilitate the regulation of unfair terms – in short, that it should be hard for dealers to show that they have acted in good faith, yet easy for consumers to show that a term involves a significant imbalance to their detriment.

(4) Promoting Personal Welfarism

Personal welfarists attach considerable importance to the fairness of the contracting process. Parties must co-operate with one another in negotiating a contract, always acting in a way that maintains faith with the idea of a contract as a mutually beneficial exchange. Accordingly, other things being equal, if one side has information which it would regard as material if it were in the position of the other contracting party, the information must be disclosed. However, personal welfarists also take freedom seriously and, given good faith dealing, they allow the parties to set their own terms. This does not mean that personal welfarists are out and out proceduralists – in order to ensure that co-operative contracting has taken place a measure of substantive regulation may be required. Equally, the proceduralism of personal welfarism does not imply that the good faith obligations associated with co-operative contracting run out once the contract has been negotiated – good faith is required, too, in performance and enforcement. Essentially, then, personal welfarists hold: (1) that the existence of conditions of co-operative contracting (fair dealing) is to be tested partly procedurally and partly by reference to the resulting terms of the contract; and (2) that if manifestly unfair terms materialise, it might be legitimate to infer that co-operative contracting has not taken place, and that there are grounds for intervening against the offending terms – not because the terms are unfair but because a procedural violation is presumed to have taken place.

For personal welfarists, a procedural reading of the test in Article 3.1 is appropriate. For some personal welfarists (subjectivists), a clear conscience test of good faith is appropriate. For others (objectivists), this will not do – the framework for good faith dealing must be set not simply by standards of honesty but also by standards of reasonable care and competence. For present purposes, we need not arbitrate betwen the subjectivists and the objectivists, for both divisions of personal welfarism require a pattern of interpretation in relation to Article 3.1 that traces the pattern given by procedural maximal welfarists. Thus, personal welfarists will interpret the good faith requirement in such a way that conduces towards co-operative dealing; and they will argue that neither the significant imbalance nor the detriment conditions should be permitted to obstruct consumers who have been subjected to procedural abuse.

There are, however, at least two important differences between the attitude of maximal welfarists and personal welfarists in relation to the good faith requirement. First, for maximal welfarists, good faith is a vehicle for establishing an arena for equal bargaining, within which both sides compete for the best deal available to them. For personal welfarists, however, the requirement of good faith in negotiation is not about evening up the odds; it is about instating a co-operative ethic. Disclosure of terms and choice must be understood and applied in a co-operative context. To repeat our earlier example, in the case of disclosure, personal welfarists would prima facie require contractors to inform one another of material facts beyond the terms of the standard form (quite possibly including market-sensitive information). Secondly, for maximal welfarists, good faith has no relevance other than in relation to equality of bargaining strength. However, for personal welfarists, good faith symbolises the co-operative ideal which must run right through the contracting process, from beginning to end. In this light, since the concept of good faith can no longer be said to be unknown in English law, there is a doctrinal basis for arguing for a much more extended co-operative requirement in contract. Admittedly, the Directive may narrowly concern consumers and terms that have not been individually negotiated, but for personal welfarists there is no reason why the potential of good faith should be confined to this area.

Finally, some may query our emphasis on the procedural side of personal welfarism. If personal welfarists are so concerned that contracting parties should look after one another's interests, must they not seek to intervene against terms which manifestly act against one party's interests (for example, a clause excluding liability for negligence)? As we pointed out above, personal welfarists take freedom seriously – an agreement, freely negotiated by a mature agent under conditions of fair dealing is to be respected. Granted, it would be quite extraordinary that a contracting party should freely agree to a term which manifestly acted against its apparent interests; and, of course, in such circumstances the personal welfarist would need to take a hard look at the fairness of the contracting process. If the contracting process was found to violate co-operative ideals, the term would be treated as unfair. However, if the contracting process was unimpeachable, personal welfarists could not treat the term as unfair, however imprudent they thought the particular contracting party in agreeing to the term.[31]

CONCLUSION

The regulatory intentions of the Directive are unclear. Its priority could be to pave the way for standardised fair consumer contracting in the internal market (as the market school holds), or its priority could be to protect consumers' rights against various abuses of power by stronger contractors (as the welfarist school holds). For either set of regulatory objectives to be promoted, the Directive must be interpreted in a way that is conducive to the realisation of such objectives.

A critical question, at the heart of the Directive, is how one should read Article 3, interpretation of which is rendered difficult by a variety of drafting deficiencies – particularly, the ambivalent thrust of Article 3.1, the failure to spell out the relationship between Article 3.1 and Article 3.3, and the failure to address the distinction between specific *ex casu* and general pre-emptive challenges. With regard to general pre-emptive challenges, if Article 3.1 is given any kind of procedural reading, it is unclear how it can set the relevant test for whether a term is fair or unfair, and the generally substantive approach in the indicative list of unfair terms in the Annex (incorporated by Article 3.3) looks an altogether better candidate for this function. Given that pre-emptive challenges are likely to be a more effective means of control than *ex casu* challenges, and given that Article 3.3 offers a direct line to substantive regulation of unfair terms, both exponents of the market approach and substantivists within the welfarist school will see the pre-emptive challenge/Article 3.3 combination as advancing their regulatory objectives.

Turning to *ex casu* challenges, Article 3.1 is drafted so unclearly that there are any number of interpretive questions to be settled and we can be confident that these questions will become focal points for disputes that reflect deeper positions concerning the ultimate purposes of the Directive.

If the objectives espoused by the market school are to be fully realised, it is important that Article 3.1 facilitates reasonably direct control over the

31 In principle, of course, one might wish to graft a paternalistic veto onto personal welfarism but, to do this, would be to weaken the attachment to freedom which is one of the base premises defining this position. The logic of personal welfarism qualified by a paternalistic veto would be to argue for a three-step procedural and substantive reading of Article 3.1.

more objectionable provisions of standard form contracts (even in relation to *ex casu* challenges). As an opening gambit, the two-step reading of Article 3.1 must be preferred. However, if good faith is taken as importing an independent condition, the three-step substantive reading is the next best option. Failing this, a procedural version of good faith has to be confronted and, so far as possible, tamed. It follows that an objective test of good faith must be instated – apart from distorting competitive conditions, a simple 'clear conscience' test leaves too many loopholes for dealers; the concept of good faith must be given an interpretation which makes it difficult for dealers to comply with its requirements; the concept of significant imbalance must be interpreted flexibly to yield broad control over standard form terms; and the concept of detriment to the consumer must be read as following automatically from a finding of significant imbalance in the contract against the consumer.

Turning from the market to the welfarist school, there is no surprise in finding that the logic of *substantivist* welfarist thinking converges with market reasoning in relation to the desired interpretation of Article 3.1. In particular, both schools would prefer to see a violation of good faith equated with significant imbalance to the detriment of the consumer (i.e., in line with the two-step reading of Article 3.1). *Proceduralist* welfarist reasoning initially takes a different line. For proceduralist welfarists, a procedural reading of Article 3.1 is perfectly in order. However, if such a procedural reading prevails (e.g. in the form of the three-step procedural reading), we find that the thinking of both procedural and substantive welfarists now runs in parallel. Basically, assuming a procedural reading of Article 3.1, if the objectives espoused by the welfarist school are to be realised, there must be:

(1) a strong (and an objective) interpretation of the requirement of good faith – this being required by proceduralists in its own right and by substantivists as a means of closing a loophole against substantive control;

(2) a flexible interpretation of the concept of significant imbalance – this being required by proceduralists in order to ease the pathway to redress where procedural unfairness has been established, and by substantivists in order to facilitate control over terms and outcomes; and

(3) a face-value reading of detriment to the consumer, such that detriment must be read as flowing naturally from a finding of significant imbalance in the contract against the consumer.

Moreover, given a procedural reading of Article 3.1, it will be appreciated that, not only does the interpretive logic of procedural and substantive welfarism run in parallel, the interpretive logic of the market approach also runs along the same track.

In sum, if Article 3.1 cannot be transformed into a wholly substantive test for unfairness, we find most roads (market and welfare, proceduralist and substantivist) leading to a common interpretive approach: namely, to argue for a demanding interpretation of good faith (such that dealers cannot readily meet this requirement) and a relatively flexible interpretation of significant imbalance. However, in this convergence, there is an ironic twist. For substantivists, procedural fairness has no independent weight – control over the content of contracts is what matters. Yet, in order to secure such control through Article 3.1, the substantivists (albeit as a second-best strategy) might have to join the proceduralists in arguing for a strong interpretation of good faith dealing. If this substantivist ploy were to serve as a catalyst for the idea of good faith taking on an altogether larger significance in English, and possibly more generally in European, contract law, the irony would be compounded – particularly if, not for the first time, developments in consumer law spilled over into the commercial law of contract.

REFERENCES

Adams, J.N., and Brownsword, R. (1987), *Understanding Contract Law* (London, Fontana) (second edition, 1994).

Adams, J N., and Brownsword, R. (1988), 'The Unfair Contract Terms Act: A Decade of Discretion' 104 *Law Quarterly Review* 94-119.

Beale, H.G., (1986), 'Inequality of Bargaining Power' 6 *Oxford Journal of Legal Studies* 123-136.

Beale, H.G., (1989), 'Unfair Contracts in Britain and Europe' 42 *Current Legal Problems* 197-215.

Bradgate, R., Graham, C., and Howells, G. (1994), 'Regulatory Fairness and Promoting Welfarism in Contract: An Institutional Perspective' in Roger Brownsword, Geraint Howells and Thomas Wilhelmsson (eds.) *Welfarism in Contract Law* (Aldershot, Dartmouth) 158.

Brownsword, R., (1994a), 'Two Concepts of Good Faith' 7 *Journal of Contract Law* 197-244.

Brownsword, R., (1994b), 'The Philosophy of Welfarism and its Emergence in the Modern English Law of Contract' in Roger Brownsword, Geraint Howells and Thomas Wilhelmsson (eds.) *Welfarism in Contract Law* (Aldershot, Dartmouth) 21-62.

Brownsword, R., and Howells, G., (1995), 'The Implementation of the EC Directive on Unfair Terms in Consumer Contracts – Some Unresolved Questions *Journal of Business Law* 243-263.

Brownsword, R., Howells, G., and Wilhelmsson, T. (eds.) (1994a), *Welfarism in Contract Law* (Aldershot, Dartmouth).

Brownsword, R., Howells, G., and Wilhelmsson, T. (1994b), 'The EC Unfair Contract Terms Directive and Welfarism' in Roger Brownsword, Geraint Howells and Thomas Wilhelmsson (eds.) *Welfarism in Contract Law* (Aldershot, Dartmouth) 275-301.

Churchill, W.S. (1909), *Liberalism and the Social Problem* (London, Hodder and Stoughton).

Collins, H., (1994), 'Good Faith in European Contract Law' 14 *Oxford Journal of Legal Studies* 229-254.

Dean, M., (1993), 'Unfair Contract Terms: The European Approach' 56 *Modern Law Review* 581-590.

Department of Trade and Industry (1993), *Implementation of the EC Directive on Unfair Terms in Consumer Contracts (93/13/EEC): A Consultative Document.*

Department of Trade and Industry (1994), *Implementation of the EC Directive on Unfair Terms in Consumer Contracts (93/13/EEC): A Further Consultation Document.*

Dugan, Robert (1980), 'Good Faith and the Enforceability of Standardized Terms' 22 *William and Mary Law Review* 1

Farnsworth, E.A., (1962-63), 'Good Faith Performance and Commercial Reasonableness Under the Uniform Commercial Code' 30 *University of Chicago Law Review* 666

Goode, R., (1992) 'The Concept of 'Good Faith' in English Law', Centro di Studi e Richerche di Diritto Comparato e Straniero, Saggi, Conferenze e Seminari 2, Rome

Häyhä, J., (1994), 'Scandinavian Techniques for Controlling Fairness in Contracts' in Roger Brownsword, Geraint Howells and Thomas Wilhelmsson (eds.) *Welfarism in Contract Law* (Aldershot, Dartmouth) 127

Howells, G., (1993), 'Contract Law: The Challenge for the Critical Consumer Lawyer' in Thomas Wilhelmsson (ed.) *Perspectives of Critical Contract Law* (Aldershot, Dartmouth) 327-347.

Legrand, P (1986), 'Pre-Contractual Disclosure of Information: English and French Law Compared' 6 *Oxford Journal of Legal Studies* 322-351.

Powell, R., (1956), 'Good Faith in Contracts' 9 *Current Legal Problems* 16-38.

Pöyhönen, J., (1994), 'Procedural and Substantive Fairness in Finnish Contract Law' in Roger Brownsword, Geraint Howells and Thomas Wilhelmsson (eds.) *Welfarism in Contract Law* (Aldershot, Dartmouth) 188

Reich, N., (1993), 'From Contract to Trade Practices Law: Protection of Consumers' Economic Interests by the EC' in Thomas Wilhelmsson (ed.) *Perspectives of Critical Contract Law* (Aldershot, Dartmouth) 55-105.

Smith, S. A., (1994), 'Contract' in Ben Pettet (ed.) *Current Legal Problems 1994* (Vol. 47—Part One: Annual Review)

Summers, R.S., (1968), '"Good Faith" in General Contract Law and the Sales Provisions of the Uniform Commercial Code' 54 *Virginia Law Review* 195

Thomas, P. (1991), 'Legal Skills and the Use of Ambiguity' 42 *Northern Ireland Legal Quarterly* 14

Trebilcock, M.J,. (1993), *The Limits of Freedom of Contract* (Cambridge, Mass, Harvard University Press)

Wilhelmsson, T., (1989) 'Need-Rationality in Private Law?' *Scandinavian Studies in Law* 223

Wilhelmsson, T., (1992a), *Critical Studies in Private Law* (Kluwer, Dordrecht)

Wilhelmsson, T., (1992b), 'The Proposal for an Unfair Contracts Directive – a Nordic Perspective' *European Consumer Law Journal* 77

Wilhelmsson, T., (1994), 'Philosophy of Welfarism and its Emergence in the Modern Scandinavian Contract Law' in Roger Brownsword, Geraint Howells and Thomas Wilhelmsson (eds.) *Welfarism in Contract Law* (Aldershot, Dartmouth) 63

Willett, C., (1994), 'Directive on Unfair Terms in Consumer Contracts' *Consumer Law Journal* 114-124.

3. European Approaches to Fairness in Contract Law

Ewoud Hondius

I INTRODUCTION

This paper will deal with the concept of fairness as it is developing in European private law. I will consider both the European Directive on Unfair Terms in Consumer Contracts and various other fairness rules drawing in particular upon Dutch law.

II UNFAIR CONTRACT TERMS DIRECTIVE

In pursuance of Article 3 of the Directive on Unfair Contract Terms, (93/13 EC), a contract term 'shall be regarded as unfair if, contrary to the requirement of good faith, it causes a significant imbalance in the parties' rights and obligations arising under the contract, to the detriment of the consumer'.

According to the Explanatory Memorandum:

> in making an assessment of good faith, particular regard shall be had to the strength of the bargaining position of the parties, whether the consumer had an inducement to agree to the term and whether the goods or services were sold or supplied to the special order of the consumer.

Contract terms will probably have to be subjected to the test whether or not they are at variance with statutory law. The level of domestic legislation will certainly not be below the Directive's.

III JUSTUM PRETIUM CONTROL EXCLUDED

Excluded from the fairness test under Article 4 (2) is the main subject matter of the contract and the price: 'Assessment of the unfair nature of the terms shall relate neither to the definition of the main subject matter of the contract nor to the adequacy of the price and remuneration, on the one hand, as against the services or goods supplied in exchange, on the other, in so far as these terms are in plain intelligible language'.

This is a well known exclusion in several jurisdictions, such as Germany and the Netherlands. It was designed to keep free from judicial control the question whether or not the price agreed upon by the parties for the goods or services to be delivered is the 'correct price' (*justum pretium*). Although the Society of Public Teachers of Law Consumer and Contract Sections criticise this approach in the Department of Trade and Industry's 1993 Consultation Document, (see Bragg, 1994) it really does seem in accordance with the ideas of the draftspersons of the Directive.

IV COUNCIL OF EUROPE

In 1976, the Council of Europe adopted a 'Resolution on Unfair Terms in Consumer Contracts and an Appropriate Method of Control' (Council of Europe, 1976). The Resolution recommended governments of Member States: '2. to lay down, as a principle in relation to the contractual situations described in paragraph 1, that any term or combination of terms which causes a balance of rights and obligations under the contract as a whole contrary to the interests of consumers, is to be regarded as unfair and to draw the appropriate consequences therefrom'.

At the time this Resolution was adopted, English lawyers were not yet used to the notion of fairness in contract – as opposed to cricket[1] – and it needed some imaginative engineering to make them accept the idea.

The continental countries, however, had little difficulty in accepting a fairness test, which was in line with their tradition.

A common language – Latin – and a common heritage – Roman law – once of course, existed in Europe. Although the present situation bears little resemblance to pre-XIXth century Europe, and therefore a 'return' to that period is highly unlikely, yet the present interest in a new European civil law is a fascinating challenge to legal historians. As a German author, Schulze, (1991a) has observed:

> The present and the past are linked in the concepts of European legal culture and European legal history in two ways: the awakening of interest in research into European

1 As opposed to Americans: 'We in the United States (...) have had a generally accepted concept of good faith for decades' (Farnsworth, 1993, p. 1).

legal history is prompted by the experience of the present, namely the present-day efforts towards the development of a body of common European law. The resulting research can in turn influence present-day thinking in that, contrary to another tradition and present-day experience, namely the legal thinking moulded by the nation-state, it contributes from a historical standpoint to a consciousness of a shared European identity. The concept of European legal culture is thus directed at the definition of an identity for the present based on the past whilst research in European legal history is both defined by and directed towards the present [2].

What is the present day tradition of fairness tests in continental Europe?

V MEMBER STATES

Most Member States of the European Union have a legislative provision which in one form or another lays down the fairness principle. Most if not all of these provisions have a Roman law background. A close look into their use does reveal two things. First, they have been used in quite different ways, with France and Germany as the extremes, at least until recently. Second, in applying these provisions, the courts seem to be less than interested in the exact wording of the tests.

France has long held out against a liberal use of article 1134 of the Code Civil. Only as recently as 1992 has the Cour de cassation applied a full control of *clauses abusives*. The French Parliament has traditionally been reluctant to confer discretionary powers of too broad a nature upon the courts. Perhaps they still remembered Voltaire's 'Dieu nous protège des parlements' (Parliament here being used in a different sense, meaning the courts).[3]

Germany, on the contrary, has a lengthy experience of extending fairness control to contracts. This was not a post-war reaction to curb unfair practices, but was already developed by the Reichsgericht.

In the Netherlands, article 1374 paragraph 3 of the old Civil Code was long held to state little more than a moral principle. However, ever since the early twentieth century, this provision has gained importance and ever since *Saladin v. Hollandsche Bank-Unie* (1967) it has become a major element in Dutch contract law, serving both to supplement and to derogate from what the parties themselves have contracted. This even goes so far as to apply when the parties are still negotiating a contract. This is very much

---

2 See also Schulze (1991b).

3 See Tallon, 1994 for more on the French position.

different from English law, where according to *Walford v. Miles*[4] parties who are still negotiating are under no such obligation.

In the new Dutch Civil Code, the good faith rule reads:

Article 248 Book 6

1. A contract has not only the juridical effects agreed to by parties, but also those which, according to the nature of the contract, result from the law, usage or the requirement of reasonableness and equity.

2. A rule binding upon the parties as a result of the contract does not apply to the extent that, in the given circumstances, this would be unacceptable according to criteria of reasonableness and equity.

The good faith/reasonableness/fairness test has long received competition from other open norms, such as the good morals/ public order test and the causa test. Causa, of course, brings into mind the common law consideration principle. At present these other open norms seem to have lost out to goodfaith, however.

What about the common law? In Treitel's *Law of Contract,* (1995) and David M. Walker's *The Law of Contracts and related obligations in Scotland*, (1995) one looks in vain for lengthy analysis under such headings as 'fairness', 'good faith' or 'reasonableness'. However, common law jurisdictions do know specific statutory provisions which allow courts to review unconscionable bargains. E.g. Moneylenders Acts 1900 – 1927, Consumer Credit legislation and the Unfair Contract Terms Act.

VI OPEN NORMS IN A MODERN CIVIL CODE

Above I mentioned Article 248 Book 6 of the new Dutch Civil Code, which is a general fairness provision. This section will consider other open norms in the Dutch Code which help to secure fairness.[5]

With regard to unfair contract terms, one important set of provisions which may serve to deal with this problem are rules on defects of the will, abuse of rights and contract renegotiations. Most of these new provisions have already been applied by the courts in anticipation of the New Code's entering into force.

I shall leave out the protection of minors and mentally deranged persons who have been placed under guardianship; such parties are well protected by articles 234 and 381 Book 1. Indeed the protection of minors is so

4 (1992) 1 All ER 453.

5 On the new code see Wessels 1994.

efficient, that the courts have been more concerned with protecting the co-contracting parties against the whims of minors who invoke a contract's nullity. Ever since the age of majority was lowered from 21 to 18, this problem has lost much of its social significance, however.

Defects of the Will

With regard to the 'defects of the will' the New Code lays down the following:

> Article 44 Book 3
>
> 1. A juridical act may be annulled when it has been entered into as a result of threat, fraud or abuse of circumstances.
>
> (...)
>
> 4. A person who knows or should know that another is being induced to execute a juridical act as a result of special circumstances – such as state of necessity, dependency, wantonness, abnormal mental condition or inexperience – and who promotes the creation of that juridical act, although what he knows or ought to know should prevent him therefrom, commits an abuse of circumstances.

This provision provides protection to those who suffer from a variety of weaknesses. In particular this provision may provide protection to the elderly. The elderly may also profit from the Door-to-Door Sales Act, which allows any buyer a one-week cooling-off period during which s/he may annull the transaction. Experience suggests that Article 44 can provide limited protection against those contracting with cartels. Indeed Dutch law is generally fairly limited in providing such protection; although a major revision to bring Dutch anti-trust law into line with EC anti-trust law is now on its way.

Article 44 para 1 Book 3 the Dutch code omits to mention error. However error is dealt with by Article 228 Book 3.

Abuse of Rights

The Dutch Code also contains a provision on abuse of rights:

> Article 13 Book 3
>
> 1. The holder of a right may not exercise it to the extent that it is abused.
>
> 2. Instances of abuse of right are the exercise of a right with the sole intention of harming another or for a purpose other than that for which it was granted; or the exercise of a right where its holder could not reasonably have decided to exercise it, given the disproportion between the interest to exercise the right and the harm caused thereby.

3. The nature of the right can be such that it cannot be abused.

Dutch law has so far made little use of this provision in contract law – it has done so mainly in civil procedure, family law and real property law. This is no doubt a consequence of the use of the good faith rule mentioned above.[6]

Contract Renegotiation

Finally, mention should be made of the principle of contract renegotiation or imprévision as it is often called in the Netherlands with its French name.[7] Until recently, Dutch courts refused to apply the old theory of *clausula rebus sic stantibus*. Now the Code contains the following provision:

Article 258 Book 6

1. Upon the demand of one of the parties, the judge may modify the effects of a contract, or he may set it aside in whole or in part on the basis of unforeseen circumstances which are of such a nature that the co-contracting party, according to criteria of reasonableness and equity, may not expect that the contract be maintained in an unmodified form. The modification or the setting aside of the contract may be given retroactive force.

VII MODERN PROTECTION TECHNIQUES

Modern fairness techniques to protect the weaker party do not concentrate on individual circumstances, but rather on a party's status. In some cases the intention is to protect a weaker party. Thus, in the Netherlands employees have been protected ever since the 1907 enactment of the present employment contract; buyers on an instalment basis are protected against their creditors; tenants of housing are protected against their landlords. Finally, consumers are protected against their co-contracting parties and against producers. This in itself is nothing new; we find such regulation all over Europe. What is new, is that this type of regulation is now inserted in the Dutch Civil Code.

The most important example of this type of regulation are the rules on general conditions of contract in articles 231 ff Book 6. The new provisions on unfair contract terms are quite similar to those contained in the German Unfair Contract Terms Act (*AGB-Gesetz*). They declare

---

6 As to the relationship between good faith and abuse of rights see Gerbrandy, 1992.

7 Parties may have included a revision clause in their contract; in long-term contracts this is often the case.

voidable a term in general conditions if, taking into account the nature and the other contents of the contract, the way in which these terms have been drafted, the interests of both parties and the other circumstances of the case, it is unreasonably onerous for the other party. This general clause is supplemented by two lists of clauses which are presumed to be unreasonable in consumer contracts; in one case the presumption of unreasonableness is rebuttable; in the other it is not. Under article 6:240 consumers' organisations may request a court to issue a cease and desist order (injunction) against the further use of an unreasonable contract term. This latter possibility had previously been denied to consumers' organisations.[8]

In the Explanatory Memorandum, the government has accepted the use of 'reflexwerking', permitting the courts to invoke the test of unreasonableness in the case of purely commercial transactions. This makes it possible to extend control to business transactions where one of the parties is in a weak bargaining position.

This is an example of how consumer protection measures in the Netherlands often serve as a catalyst for law reform in other areas.

Another modern trend is to design rules for specific sorts of contract. This is seen in Book 7 of the new Dutch Code which introduces separate regiemes for commercial contracts, consumer contracts and wholly private transactions. Of course the status of the parties is often relevant also. We will often find that a higher level of fairness is insisted upon where a consumer transaction is concerned. One example of this is the fact that many of the rules protecting consumers are mandatory, while in the other contracts such provisions can be contractually excluded.

An example of a provision which has been introduced specifically for a consumer sale is:

Article 18 Book 7

In determining whether a thing delivered pursuant to a consumer sale conforms to the contract, information regarding the thing made public by or on behalf of a previous seller of that thing, acting in the course of a profession or business, is deemed to be information from the seller, except to the extent that the latter neither knew nor ought to know certain information, or that he has clearly contradicted it.

In other words the statements made by manufacturers are relevant to the retailer's contractual obligation to consumers.

A second specific contract for which specific rules have been designed is the medical treatment contract. This is still an Act, (i.e. not yet a part of the Civil Code) but parliamentary approval is expected. The Act aims at

8 See my report *Unfair Terms In Consumer Contracts,* Utrecht, 1987.

incorporating a number of patient's rights such as the right to self-determination, informed consent, privacy and the like in the Civil Code. An interesting example of the Act's aim at protecting the patient is the following provision:

Article 1 Book 7

1. If in the execution of a contract for medical treatment acts are taking place in a hospital which is not a party to that contract, the hospital is jointly liable for any shortcoming as if it were a party to the contract.

The Act has been supplemented by a number of model contracts agreed upon by professional and consumers' organisations, which are already in force.

Other specific contracts, such as suretyship, distinguish between consumer transactions and commercial transactions. An example may be taken from the regulation of suretyship:

Article 857 Book 7

The provisions of this section apply to suretyships entered into by a natural person not acting in the course of a profession or business, nor acting for the benefit of the normal exploitation of the business of a company limited by shares or a private company with limited liability of which he is an officer and in which, alone or with his co-officers, he holds the majority of the shares.

The regulation of specific contracts has not yet been completed. The protection of the buyer of real property has been the subject of heated debate. First it was considered to extend the requirement of a notarial deed from the transfer of the property to the contract, but this was opposed by the real estate brokers who considered themselves the consumer's best friends. The solution now will be that in all real estate transactions there will be a three-day cooling-off period for the buyer.

VIII APPLICATION OF THE UNFAIR CONTRACT TERMS DIRECTIVE

What changes will the EC Directive on Unfair Contract Terms bring about in domestic legislation? Most member states will have few problems in adapting their legislation to the directive, since in the seventies and eighties they have introduced legislation on unfair contract terms. In *Austria* this is the *Konsumentenschutzgesetz* of March 8, 1979 (see Bydlinski, 1982); in *Belgium* the *Loi sur les pratiques de commerce et l'information et protection du consommateur* of 1991 (see Balate and Stuyck 1988 and Stuyck and Wytinck 1992); in *Denmark* the *Markedsf/oringslov* of 14 June

1974 (see Gomard, 1982); in *Finland* Chapter 3 of the Act of 20 January 1978 (see Wilhelmsson, 1992); in *France* the Act 78–23 of 10 January 1978 and 5 January 1988 (see Calais-Auloy) in *Germany* the *Gesetz zur Regelung des Rechts der Allgemeinen Geschäftsbedingungen (AGB-Gesetz)*, (see Sandrock, 1978); in *Greece* the *Consumer Protection Act* 1991, (see Alexandridou, 1992) in *Ireland* the *Sale of Goods and Supply of Servces Act* of 1980, (see Honduis, 1987); in *Luxembourg* the *Loi relative à la protection juridique du consommateur* of 25 August 1983 (see Hoffmann, 1982); in the *Netherlands* articles 6:231–248 Civil Code, (see Haanappel and Mackaay, 1990); in *Norway* the Act 47/1972, as amended in 1981, (see Wilhelmsson) in *Portugal* Decree 446/85 of 25 October 1985 (see Mallmann, 1987); in *Spain* article 10 of 19 July *Ley general para la defensa de los consumidores y usuarios,* 1984 (see Coca Payeras, Diaz Alabart, Tornos Más, Claveria Gosálbez and Malaret I García, in Rodríguez-Cano and Salas Hernández, 1992); in *Sweden* the Act 1971:112, (see Wilhelmsson) in *Switzerland* article 8 *Loi fédérale contre la concurrence déloyale* of 19 December 1986 (see Stauder, 1991); and in the *United Kingdom*, finally, the *Unfair Contract Terms Act* of 1977 (see Howells, 1995); (I only mention the most important legislation). Only Italy, with its 1942 Civil Code articles 1341, 1342 and 1370 is running behind (see Alpa and Bessone, 1991) Another country, which already was considering changing its legislation before the directive was published, is Spain.[9] In the case of the United Kingdom, although a revision of the Unfair Contract Terms Act would seem the most logical thing to do, the government has instead opted for using regulations to supplement this Act, which to a foreign observer is not easy to grasp.[10]

IX MAKING THE CLAUSE MORE CONCRETE

As I have said above the Directive revolves around the general clause on unfairness in Article 3(1) (see Part II above). Although not everyone likes them,[11] many modern Unfair Contract Terms Acts do contain, apart from a general clause, a list of terms which aims at giving the general clause some clarification. The Directive also contains such a list, but its status is far

9 As to the Anteproyecto of the Spanish Ministry of Justice (see Bercovitz 1993).

10 See the Unfair Terms in Consumer Contracts Regulations 1994, and Willett, and Brownsword et al above at chapters 1 and 2.

11 Trade and industry often sees such lists as unwanted patronising – see UNICE, in: Alpa and Bessone 1991. The Scandinavian countries consider lists useless in their control system of Consumer Ombudsmen – see Wilhelmsson, 1992.

from clear. Article 3 sub-section 3 refers to it in the following words: 'The Annex shall contain an indicative and non-exhaustive list of terms which may be regarded as unfair' (see the Appendix to this book where the list is reproduced).

In an earlier proposal the list was presented as 'mandatory'. But according to the Commission, it appeared impossible to reach agreement between Member States as to the terms to be put on the list.[12] The Commission considers the Annex's list 'nonetheless a useful indication for judges, national authorities and economic agents, and will help to specify the general criteria set out in Article 3 of the Directive'.

Useful the list surely is. Two examples may clarify this. Subparagraph (a) of the European list deals with a category of exemption clauses: those concerning death and personal injury. Under article 6:237 (f) of the Dutch Civil Code the seller or supplier has a possibility to rebut the presumption that this sort of exemption clause is unfair. Subparagraph (a) now makes it virtually impossible for a seller or supplier to provide such rebuttal. Some French authors as well as courts have already argued exemption clauses as envisaged in subparagraph (a) to be null and void. (See Huet, 1994). The directive strengthens their case.

Another example may be taken from the last subparagraph (q) of the European list, which blacklists clauses requiring consumers to take disputes exclusively to arbitration not covered by legal provisions. Such clauses are allowed by the Dutch Civil Code's article 6:236 (n), which was the object of a heavy battle between pro- and contra-arbitration lobbies. The pro-arbitration lobby won, but the European blacklisting of those arbitration clauses which do not allow consumers a choice between arbitration and the court may well influence the tendency of the Dutch judiciary to find arbitration clauses unfair under the Code's general clause.[13]

Unlike several European laws (Austria, Germany, the Netherlands), the Directive does not encompass two lists, a black one and a 'grey' one. However, several of the clauses do give the judiciary some discretion by using terms such as 'inappropriately' (b), 'disproportionately high' (e), 'reasonable' (g), 'unreasonably early' (h), 'without a valid reason' (j and k), 'too high' (l) and 'unduly' (q). What also strikes one, is that a number of clauses are blacklisted if the right which they accord the seller or supplier is not accorded to the consumer. Examples of such mirror image rules are to be found in subparagraphs (c), (d), (f 1) and (o).

---

12 In 1976, the Council of Europe did arrive at a list in its Resolution on Unfair Terms in Consumer Contracts and an Appropriate Method of Control, Resolution (76) 47.

13 Botman v Van Haaster, *Hoge Raad* 23 March 1990, *Nederlandse Jurisprudentie* 1991, No. 214 (note by H.J. Snijders).

Finally, a piece of Brussels lobbying may be observed in the Annex's exemption from subparagraphs (g), (j) and (l) of certain terms in financial services contracts.

X THE LIST IN SOME DETAIL

This is not the place to give an exhaustive account of what the black list does and does not encompass. Instead I will try to give an indicative and non-exhaustive overview, thereby making some comparisons with the lists contained in the Austrian, Belgian, Dutch, French and German legislation: basically § 6 Austrian *Konsumentenschutzgesetz;* article 32 Belgian *Loi sur les pratiques du commerce;* articles 6:236 and 237 Dutch Civil Code; the recommendations of the French *Commission des clauses abusives;* §§ 9 and 10 German *AGB-Gesetz;* and article 1341 Italian *Codice civile.*

Subparagraph (a) of the black list has already been mentioned above. Subparagraph (b) covers a number of terms concerning non-performance or inadequate performance by the seller or supplier. The Belgian Act deals with this in article 32(19)(general) and (14)(set off), the Dutch Code in articles 6:236(b)(specific performance) and 6:237(g)(right of set off), the German Act in § 11.3(right of set off). Subparagraph (c) is the first example of a mirror image rule: making an agreement binding on the consumer whereas provision of services by the seller or supplier is subject to a condition whose realization depends on his own will alone. The same provision is to be found in § 6(1)(1) of the Austrian Act and in article 32(1) of the Belgian Act; a similar provision is contained in art. 6:237(a) of the Dutch Code and in § 10.1 of the German Act. Subparagraph (d) contains an even better example of the mirror image rule, comparable to article 6:237(i) of the Dutch Code. Subparagraph (e) on liquidated damages and penalty clauses is regulated in article 32(10) of the Belgian Act, in article 6:94 of the Dutch Code, in article 1152 French Civil Code, as amended in 1975, as well as a number of recommendations of the *Commission de clauses abusives*[14] and in § 11.6 of the German Act.

One of the elements of subparagraph (f) – the seller's right of rescission – is dealt with similarly in article 32(9) Belgian Act and article 237(d) of the Dutch Code. Subparagraph (f)'s retention right for consumers is dealt

---

[14] Recommendations 81–01 relative à l'équilibre des obligations entre les parties en cas d'inexécution, 85–02 relative à l'achat de véhicules automobiles de tourisme, 87–2 relative aux agences matrimoniales et 91–01 relative aux contrats proposés par les établissements d'enseignements – Huet, *o.c.*, p 3.

with in § 6 (1)(7) of the Austrian Act. Subparagraph (g) deals with the termination by the seller or supplier of contracts of indeterminate duration, as is done by the Dutch Code's article 6:237(d). Subparagraph (h); § 15 Austrian Act; article 32(16-17) of the Belgian Act, article 6:236(j) and 6:237(l) in the Netherlands and § 11.12 in Germany, all relate to the continuation of contracts of fixed duration. Subparagraphs (i) and (j) do not have a close parallel in the Member States' lists. Subparagraph (k) forbids unilateral alteration of any characteristics of the product or service to be provided, as does § 6(2)(3) in Austria, article 32(3) in Belgium and article 6:237(c) in the Netherlands. The price increases dealt with in subparagraph (l) are regulated in § 6(1)(5) and (2)(4) Austrian Act, article 32(2) of the Belgian Act, article 6:236(i) of the Dutch Civil Code and § 11.1 *AGB-Gesetz.* Like subparagraph (m), § 6(1)(10) Austrian Act, article 32(5) of the Belgian Act and article 6:236(d) Dutch Code do not allow sellers and suppliers to determine whether the goods or services supplied are in conformity with the contract. Subparagraph (n) on the seller's obligation to respect commitments of his agents and on form requirements is regulated in the Dutch Code's article 6:238 (agency) and 6:237 (m)(form requirement). Subparagraph (o) deals with a term which requires the Consumer to fulfill obligations even where the supplier does not fulfill his; as does article 32(6-8) of the Belgian Act and article 6:236(c) of the Dutch Civil Code. Subparagraph (p) on transferral of rights by the seller finds support in § 6(2)(2) Austrian Act, article 6:236(e) Dutch Code and § 11.13 *AGB-Gesetz.*

Subparagraph (q) deals with forum choice, arbitration, restriction of evidence and the burden of proof, as do § 6(1)(11) of the Austrian Act, articles 32(18, 20) of the Belgian Act, article 6:236 (n) Dutch Civil Code and article 1341 section 2 of the Italian Civil Code.

XI EXTENSION OF THE DIRECTIVE

The Principles of European Contract Law, which are at present being drafted by the Lando Commission, are to apply an unfairness test for commercial contracts. The draft is nearly the same as the Directive's test:

Unfair terms

1. A party may avoid a contractual term which has not been individually negotiated if, contrary to the requirements of good faith and fair dealing, it causes a significant imbalance in the parties' rights and obligations arising under the contract, to the detriment of that party. The nature of the performance to be made under the contract, all the other terms of the contract and the circumstances at the time the contract was concluded shall be taken into account.

2. A term defining the main subject matter of the contract or the price may not be avoided under this Article merely because of an imbalance between the price and the performance to be made in exchange.

These principles are not mandatory, but are intended to serve as guidelines. However they clearly constitute yet further Europeanisation of private law.

XII ACCESS TO JUSTICE

Redress of consumer complaints is widely considered to be one of the major problems of protection by regulation.[15] Reform of substantive law will have little effect, if there is no effective control machinery. The enforcement of employment and tenant rights seems to be adequate. The weak point is with consumer rights. Enforcement of these rights may be undertaken by several means. The consumer him – or herself may take the initiative; s/he may be aided by a consumers' association; or an administrative agency may intervene. These are but the principal means of consumer redress. Other enforcement methods, in which the consumer will play a more limited role, include the enforcement of voluntary codes of practice by professional organisations and the enforcement of criminal law by the public prosecutor. These methods are more of a – private or public – penal nature. They can result in a reprimand or a fine for the supplier, but do not necessarily provide a remedy to the consumer.

This paper will deal only briefly with consumer redress in which the consumer him- or herself is the complainant or plaintiff. When no other way such as mediation or conciliation is open, the consumer will finally have to address a court in order to obtain relief. However, traditional civil procedure more often than not will deter any but the most daring consumers from addressing a court. Courts are simply too expensive, time-consuming and awe-inspiring. For the private citizen, traditional court procedure has several drawbacks.

The massification of the production and supply of goods and services has been one of the major developments in our economy over the past centuries. The legal process has been slow to adapt to this development. Traditionally, civil procedure is geared to an individual conflict between two parties, not to one between a large corporation on the one hand and a

---

[15] 'The existence of adequate redress systems is generally considered crucial to the actual efficiency of the substantive consumer protection measures as laid down in legislation, codes of conduct, contract terms or other legal standards', Graver, 1987.

loosely organised group of consumers. Providing private organisations – or public representatives of the consumer interest, such as the Consumer Ombudsmen in the Nordic countries and the Director General of the Office of Fair Trading in the United Kingdom and his counterparts elsewhere in English speaking countries – may help to solve this point. In the Netherlands, a 1994 amendment has introduced into the Civil Code's Book 3 a general right of collective action. The two new articles read as follows:

Article 3:305a

1. An association or foundation with full legal personality may institute legal proceedings which aim at protecting similar interests of other persons, insofar as they promote such interests by virtue of their bye-laws.

2. A legal person as envisaged in para 1 is not received, when in the circumstances of the case it has insufficiently tried to attain its object by entering into negotiations with the defendant.

3. A claim as envisaged in para 1 may not bear on financial compensation.

4. A legal action envisaged in para 1 may not be based on an act insofar as such act concerns a person who objects against such action.

5. A judicial decision does not have any consequences as regards a person for the protection of whom the proceedings serve who opposes compliance with the court's decision vis-à-vis him, unless the nature of the decision entails that the consequences cannot be excluded for this person.

Article 3:305b

1. A legal person envisaged in article 1 of Book 2 may institute legal proceedings to protect the interests of others, insofar the law has entrusted such legal person with the promotion of these interests.

2. Paragraphs 2 to 5 of article 305a of this Book apply by way of analogy.

XIII CONCLUSION

This paper has dealt with the concept of fairness as it is developing in European private law. The main object of the paper has been the EC Directive on Unfair Terms in Consumer Contracts and more in particular its fairness test. A similar fairness test is to be found in the Principles of European Contract Law which are intended to serve as a guideline for commercial contractors.

I have also looked at other fairness norms and at the modern tendency to design regulations for particular sorts of relationships.

REFERENCES

Alexandridou, E. (1992), European Consumer Law Journal p. 20-31.

Alpa, G. and Bessone, M. (eds), (1991), I contratti standard nel diritto interno e comunitario, Torino.

Balate, E. and Stuyck, J. (eds), (1988), Pratiques du commerce & Information et Protection du consommateur, Brussels.

Bercovitz, R. and Cano, R. (1993), La Reforma del Derecho de la Contratacion en Espana, in: Congreso Internacional sobre la Reforma del Derecho Contractual y la Protección de los Consumidores, Zaragoza, p. 237.

Bragg, R. (1994), *Consumer Law Journal,* 29-38.

Bydlinski, F. (1982), in Festschrift Meier-Hayoz, p. 65 ff.

Calais-Auloy, J. (1992), Droit de la consommation, third ed., Paris.

Collins, H. (1993), Law of Contract, London: Butterworths.

Council of Europe, (1976), Resolution 76/47, Strasbourg, 1977.

Farnsworth, A.E. (1993), The Concept of Good Faith in American Law, Roma.

Gerbrandy, S. (1992), Redelijkheid en billijkheid op de drempel, Weekblad voor privaatrecht, notariaat en registratie Nr. 6061.

Gomard, B. (1982), Revue internationale de droit comparé p. 5910671.

Graver, K. (1987), Consumer Redress Systems in Seven European Countries, The Hague.

Heerma van Voss G.J.J. 1992, Ontslagrecht in Nederland en Japan/De spanning tussen zekerheid van de dienstbetrekking en flexibiliteit van de onderneming, thesis Utrecht.

Hoffmann C. (1982), in: Revue internationale de droit comparé p. 851-886.

Honduis, E. (1987), Unfair Terms in Consumer Contracts, Utrecht.

Howells, G. (1995), Consumer Contract Legislation/Understanding the New Law, London: Blackstone.

Huet, J. (1994), Propos amers sur la directive du 5 avril 1993 relative aux clauses abusives, La Semaine Juridique (JCP) 1.309.

Mallmann, D. (1987), *Recht der Internationalen Wirtschaft* p. 111-114.

Patti, G. and Patti, S. (1993), Responsabilità precontrattuale e contratti standard, Milano.

Payeras, M.C., Alabart, S.D., Más, J.T., Gosálbez, L.H.C., Malaret, E. and García, I. in: R. Bercovitz Rodríguez-Cano and Salas Hernández, J., (eds), (1992), Comentarios a la Ley general para la defensa de los consumidores y usuarios, Madrid p. 223-353.

Sandrock, O. (1978), The Standard Terms Act 1976 of West Germany, 26 American Journal of Comparative Law 551.

Schulze, R. (1991a) European Legal History – A New Field of Research in Germany, 13 Journal of Legal History 270-195.

Schulze, R. (1991b), Die europäische Rechts-und Verfassungsgeschichte – zu den gemeinsamen Grundlagen europäischer Rechtskultur, Saarbrücken.

Stauder, B. (1991,)European Consumer Law Journal p. 138-153.

Stuyck, J. and Wytinck P. (eds), (1992), De nieuwe wet handelspraktijken, Brussels.

Tallon, D. (1994), Le concept de bonne foi en droit françaid, Roma.

Treitel, G. (1995), Law of Contract, London: Sweet and Maxwell.

Walker, D.M. (1995), The Law of Contracts and Related Obligations in Scotland, Edinburgh: T and T. Clark.

Wessels, B. (1994), Civil Code Revision in the Netherlands: System, Contents and Future, 41 Netherlands International Law Review 163-199.

Wilhelmsson, T. (1992), European Consumer Law Journal p. 77-92.

4. Directive 93/13 In Action: A Report On A Research Project On Unfair Terms In Consumer Sales Contracts

Prof. Dr. Hans-W. Micklitz

I INTRODUCTION – DESIGN AND PURPOSE OF THE STUDY

The paper sums up the results of a study which was carried out on behalf of the European Commission in 1994 on the possible effects of Directive 93/13[1] in consumer sales in the then 12 Member States. The overall objective was to collect 100 consumer sales contracts per Member State and to submit the contract terms to the standards of the Directive, i.e. to the indicative and non-exhautive list of unfair terms contained in the Directive's Annex (reproduced below in the Appendix); and to the general test of unfairness in Article 3. Notwithstanding possible differences in the scope and reach of national laws and the Directive 93/13, the study aimed to evaluate the relationship between the use of unfair contract terms and different brands, as well as the relationship between the use of unfair contract terms and different types of sellers.

Four areas out of the whole range of products coming under consumer sales contracts have been chosen for analysis: motorcars, video-appliances washing machines and living room furniture. So the aim was to collect 25 contracts per sector, providing a total of 100 contracts for each country. The report begins with the quantitative selection of terms and contracts, turns to an analysis of the type of clauses and type of vendors and then places specific emphasis on substantive analysis under the Directive. There is then a comparison between evaluation under EC and the existing national law. This leads to a final conclusion focusing on the key position of the general clause as adopted and read by the national reporters. The project

[1] OJ No. L 95, 21.4.1993, 29 et seq.

has never been meant to allow for representative analysis of unfair terms in consumer sales. Therefore and in order to avoid misleading conclusions, the charts present the findings in absolute figures.

The paper presupposes knowledge on the different legal systems. The paper is meant to describe the unfair contract terms directive in action.

II QUANTITATIVE SELECTION OF CLAUSES/CONTRACTS IN CONSUMER SALES

The reporters were unable to obtain the full number of contracts aimed at. At 100 contracts per country the total should have been 1200. However no information was available from Lumembourg. *Chart I* (see next page) shows that 545 data sheets have been collected from 11 countries, France taking the lead with 97 contracts and Spain being the tail ender. Broken down into sectors, 155 contracts have been collected for cars, 119 for washing machines, 147 for video-appliances and 124 for non-fitted furniture.

With the exception of France, Italy and the Netherlands, the results are quite poor and do not come very close to the 100 contract per country ceiling. Under the pressure of collecting 25 contracts for each sector, the study revealed substantial difficulties in getting access to consumer contracts

1. Differences in the use of standard terms

There are countries where standard terms are commonly used in the sort of consumer contracts studied. This is the case in Germany, the Netherlands, France, Portugal and Italy. Countries in which the use of standard terms is not at all common in these contexts are Denmark, Ireland and the United Kingdom. Greece and Spain occupy a particular position. In Greece, standard terms appear mainly in the form of manufacturers guarantees, handed out by the local retailer to the consumer together with the product. Spain knows standard terms only in relation to hire purchase transactions this seems to be true for the United Kingdom too. Differences exist within the product categories. In the UK and in Ireland, there are no standard

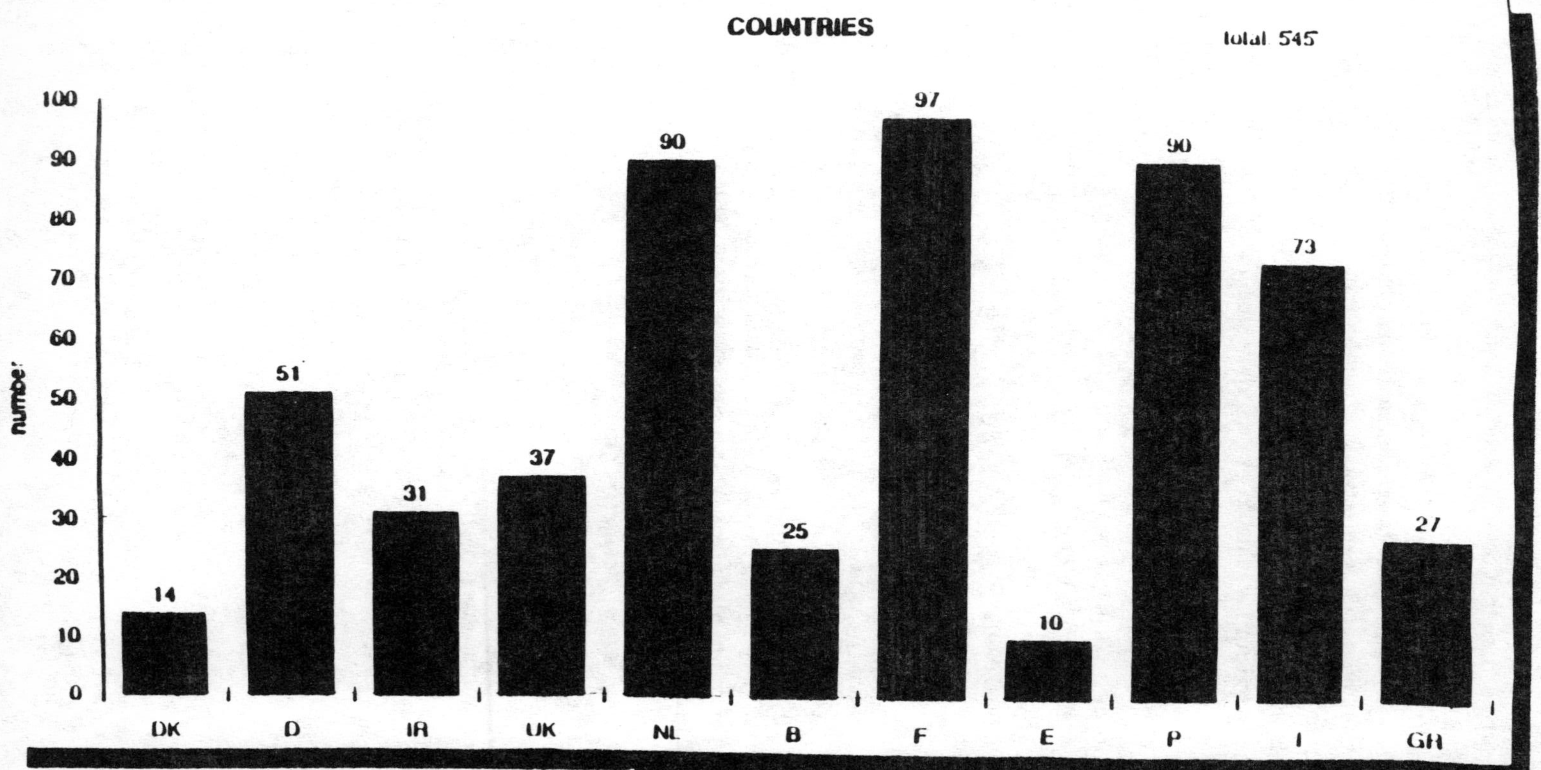
COUNTRIES
total 545
numbe
100
90
80
70
60
50
40
30
20
10
0
14
51
31
37
90
25
97
10
90
73
27
DK
D
IR
UK
NL
B
F
E
P
I
GR

CHART I

terms to be found at all in contracts for sale of furniture. In Denmark, there is only one type of standard contract which is used for video-appliances and furniture.

2. *The access problem – how to get contracts from business*

The access to standard terms differs considerably in the 12 Member States. These differences explain, to a large extent, why only 545 data sheets have been collected. Access is easy when standard terms belong to the categories of mandatory legal rules or sectorial agreements.[2] Outside these two categories, access depends on the legal system as well as on business practice. A duty to disclose information on the terms of the contract would be by far the most successful means. This is the case under French law where the reporters had grosso modo no difficulties to get the required number of contracts. Quite the contrary applies to Spain where it is documented that less than 10% of a hundred undertakings who were contacted replied and provided their standard terms. The situation was similar in Ireland where even a systematic and comprehensive inquiry did not lead to the desired results.

These restrictions had been overcome to a limited extent only by individual research strategies. It would be a story in itself to describe what the national reporters did to collect contracts for sale. One quite successful way was to persuade friends and colleagues to provide copies of their contracts. Another way was to contact the retailers personally and convince them of the feasibility of the project, sometimes by referring to competitors who had disclosed information.

3. *Filling the gap – manufacturers' guarantees*

When it became clear that it was difficult to collect the 25 contracts, it was decided to accept manufacturers' guarantees as legitimate substitutes. When there are no standard terms introduced by the retailer, it makes sense to switch to manufacturers' guarantees, especially when the retailer hands the guarantee as the only written document to the consumer. Guarantees provided by manufacturers will be covered by the Directive if we say that they form the basis of a contract between the manufacturer and the consumer. If they do form the basis of such a contract (and this will be most likely in systems which do not require consideration), then there is arguably a contract between a 'seller' or 'supplier' (the manufacturer) and a

---

2 The importance of the two categories and their role and function with relation to standard terms and pre-formulated individual contracts are set out in section III below.

'consumer'. This being the case the Directive will apply (see Articles 1, 2 and 3).

4. The type of brands focussed on

In the various sectors the following brands were studied:

(a) cars: Peugeot, Fiat, Volkswagen and Rover;
(b) washing machines: AEG, Phillips (Whirlpool), Miele and Bosch;
(c) video-recorder: Sony, Phillips, JVC, Panasonic;
(d) non-fitted furniture: Ikea.

The following contracts per brand could be collected, cars: Peugeot (24), Fiat (21), Volkswagen (12), Rover (16); washing-machines: AEG (18), Phillips (1), Whirlpool (15), Miele (17), Bosch (10); video-recorder: Sony (27), Philips Video (19), J.V.C. (15), Panasonic (17), non-fitted furniture: Ikea (1).

III TYPE OF CLAUSES

The following categories of terms were considered:

(1) **mandatory legal rules** or **voluntary legal rules** i.e. those made or approved by statute or by statutory supervisory boards or institutions.

(2) **sectorial agreements** i.e. those made by trade professional and consumer organisations, perhaps benefiting, in one form or the other, from statutory recognition;

(3) **pre-formulated standard terms** i.e. those drafted in advance by the supplier (including manufacturers' guarantees). Here we are talking about terms which are not based upon or approved by mandatory or voluntary legal rules or sectorial agreements, but which have simply been drafted by the supplier on his own initiative.

(4) **pre-formulated individual terms or pre-formulated individual contracts.** The difference between (3) and (4) is that pre-formulated individual terms or pre-formulated individual contracts are made for that specific contractual relationship rather than for a multitude of contracts;

(5) **individually negotiated contract terms** i.e. those negotiated with the particular consumer for the particular transaction.

Even although categories (1) and (5) are not covered by the Directive we must include them if we are to have an overview of practice and of the impact of the Directive.

1. Types of terms collected (see Chart II on next page)

As we can see from Chart II standard terms which are not guarantees are the most frequently used. The next most commonly used category are guarantees. Statutorily approved rules only exist for cars in Belgium and in France only for the order form.[3]. Pre-formulated individual terms and contracts amounted to 64, which is about 1/6 of the total. (It seems as if the Directive covers quite an important category here).

In some cases where different types of clause were analysed under one data sheet, reference has been made to all categories involved.[4] That is why the total number goes beyong the number of the data sheets.

2. Types of terms in use in different countries and sectors

It was found that in all countries except Portugal between 50% and 100% of terms used were pre-formulated standard terms. The next most typical terms in use were sectorial agreements and statutory rules. Manufacturer's guarantees were less common than expected although they played a reasonably significant role in France, Greece, the Netherlands and Italy. They were in greatest use in Portugal. The predominance of pre-formulated standard terms was fairly consistent across the trade sectors studied.

IV A PROBLEM-ORIENTED APPROACH - THE SUBSTANTIVE ANALYSIS UNDER DIRECTIVE 93/13

The five categories of terms, from mandatory rules to individually negotiated contracts, cover a broad range of consumer problems. The indicative and non-exhaustive list of unfair terms contained in Directive 93/13 is meant to be used in all type of contracts to which the unfairness test applies (the annex is reproduced below in the appendix to this book). This project was concerned with contracts for sales in selected areas only. Based on the experiences and expertise of the working group, the following six areas of consumer concern in contracts for sale could be identified. They may all be attributed to specific letters in the indicative and non-exhaustive list:

(1) alteration of price (l);

(2) alteration of characteristics of the product (k) and (m);

---

[3] Cf.Decret no 78-996 of 4th October 1978, amended on 5th March by decret no. 86-603.

[4] This was the case in Ireland where guarantees have been evaluated together with the order form, or in Netherlands where standard terms are even combined with pre-formulated individual contracts or terms.

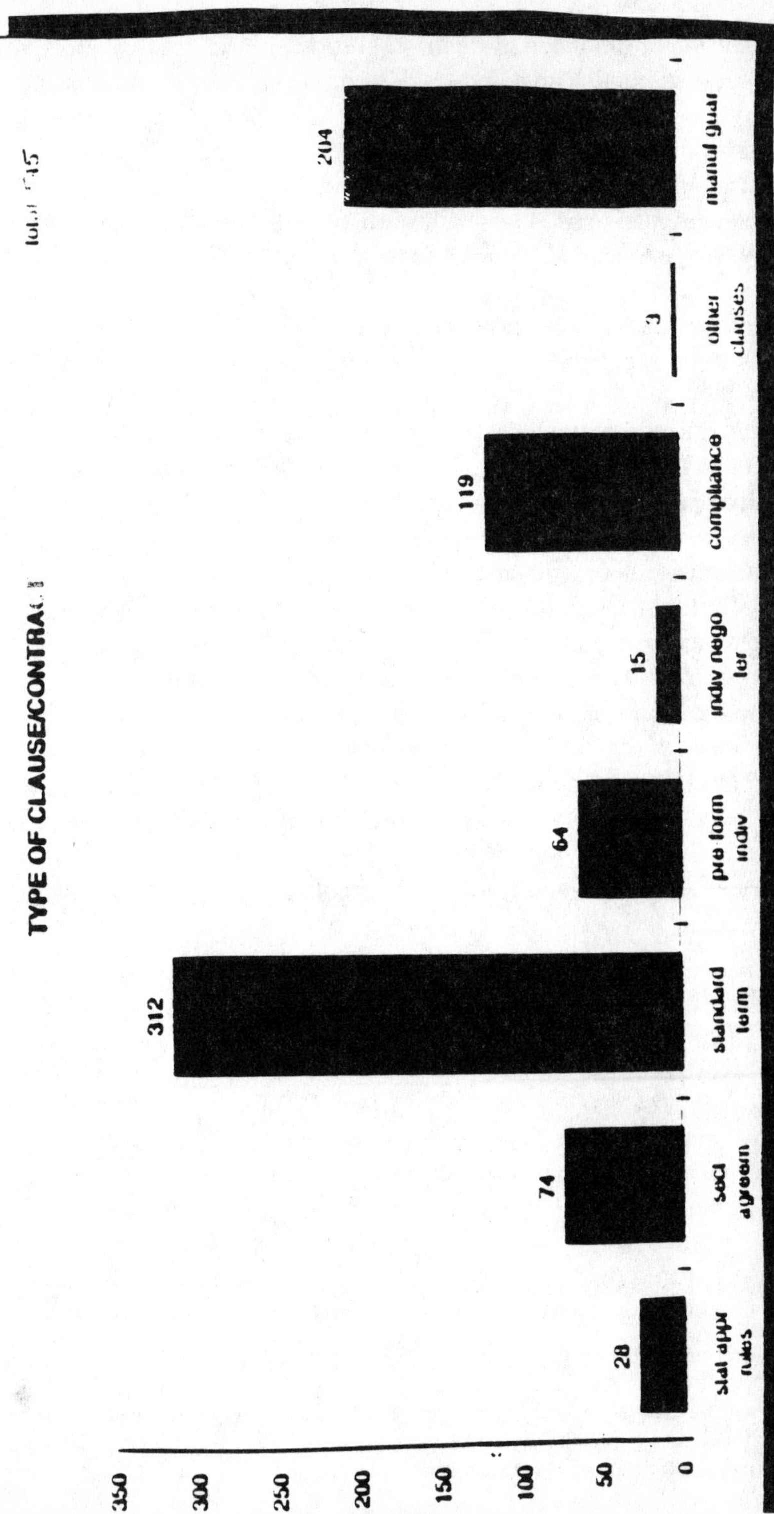
number
350
300
250
200
150
100
50
0
28
74
312
64
15
119
3
204
standard form
compliance
other clauses

CHART II

(3) exclusion or limitation of liability (a) and (b); (exclusion or limitation includes any restriction imposed on the consumer as to the time span in which he may claim for his rights);

(4) access to justice, (q);

(5) restricton of the legal guarantee, (b);

(6) unilateral release from contractual obligations, (c), (f) and (o). It may make sense to integrate (d) into this category.

1. Allocation under the six problem areas

Chart III (next page) gives an overview on how many violations have been found within the 545 data sheets. What have been counted as 'Violations' of the Directive fall into two categories. First are those terms which match one of the terms on the indicative annex. Second are those terms which national researchers felt would offend against the general Article 3(1) test of unfairness. Now it may well be the case that terms cannot be unfair on the first ground alone and that they (like any other term) must fail the Article 3(1) test, i.e. that this is **the** test and that the anex is only indicative of those terms having a good chance of failing it (see Brownsword et al at chapter 2 above). However it is possible that terms can be unfair simply by matching a term on the annex. The remainder of this section looks at the terms reported which would be unfair on this basis.

Chart III shows that by far the most common type of unfairness practised is exemption of liability. This is followed by exclusion of the legal guarantee, then alteration of price, alteration and characteristics, restriction of access to justice and finally the right to unilaterally release oneself from the contract.

2. A qualitative differentiation – what kind of clauses come under the six problem areas

The homogeneity of 'unfair clauses'in the 545 consumer sales contracts is striking. Language queries set aside the contracts terms are similar, if not identical. There were no real surprises to be found in the documents. We will now look at the six categories.

(1) Alteration of prices (l): **Three** types of clauses govern the consumer's position in this field. The **first** type concerns circumstances when the product is not sold over the counter but has been ordered. A delay occurs which postpones the payment to the time of delivery[5] or which combs down

[5] Cf. Greek report, Volkswagen order form.

ANALYSIS OF TERMS BY REFERENCE TO THE ANNEX

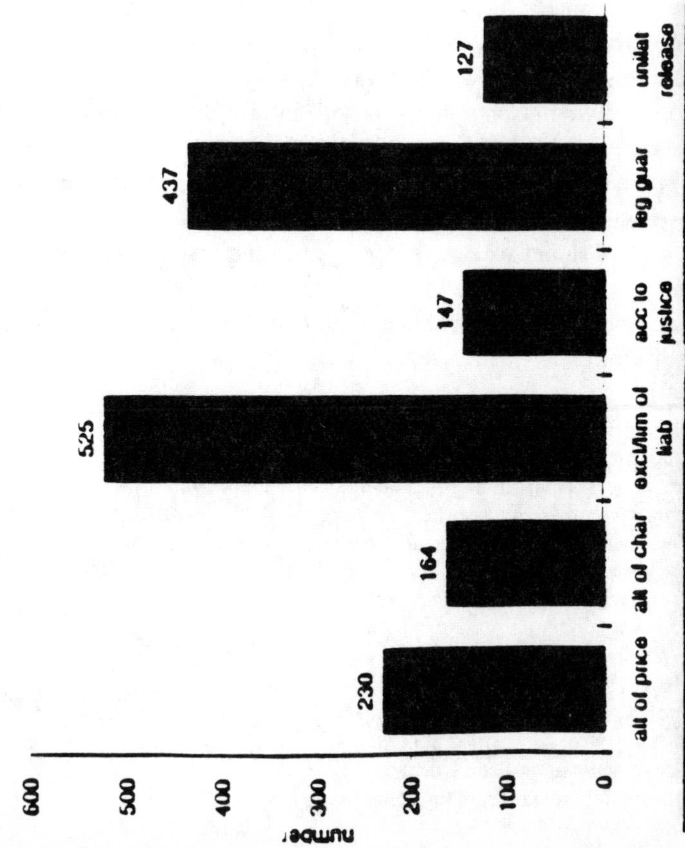

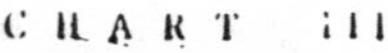

CHART III

the price to a down-payment.[6] In both cases however there is provision for a higher price to be charged at the time of delivery than was originally agreed. The **second** variant releases the supplier from indicating the full price. So, for example transport costs resulting from the delivery may be levied on the consumer without making clear the exact amount of costs which may result from the transport.[7] Quite a number of different occasions may arise : i.e. if the car is imported and the consumer has to pay the shipping costs, if the consumer has ordered furniture and has to pay extra costs if he lives in the third floor or higher. The **third** type of clause concerns increases in taxes which are to be paid by the consumer.

The opportunity to withdraw from the contract in case of price increases which go beyond a fixed percentage is not very well-known in consumer contracts in EC countries where such a right to withdraw exists,[8] it is sometimes bound to a period of notice which the consumer has to respect before he cancels the contract.[9]

(2) Alteration of characteristics (annex terms k + m): Three types of clauses may be distinguished: **Firstly**, clauses where the client must accept any type of alteration of the product. They appear in contracts for the sale of cars in i.e. France, Greece, the Netherlands and in Spain,[10] and here and there in contracts for the sale of furniture. Usually, the risk of a slight modification in the colour of the furniture lies with the consumer.[11] These clauses do not even provide for a duty to inform the consumer of a change of the characteristics.[12] **Secondly**, there are clauses which reserve the right of the supplier to decide whether the product is in conformity with the contract (whether it is manufactured imperfectly or not).[13] **Thirdly**, clauses obliging the consumer to give his consent to the alteration; or otherwise to pay a penalty.[14]

Clauses on alteration of characteristics most typically concern cars and non-fitted furniture.

---

6 Cf. France, report on furniture.

7 This pratice seems to be quite common in Spain and Portugal.

8 Cf. the example of Germany, where a consumers right to withdraw has been the result of extensive and long lasting litigations betwen the German automobile industry and the Verbraucherschutzverein.

9 Cf. German report and the Dutch report.

10 Cf. Spanish report.

11 Cf. German report on furniture.

12 Cf. Italian report, on cars.

13 Cf. Greek report. One might consider placing this clause under category b) (restriction of legal guarantee) as the decision left to the supplier is in substance one as to the existence or non-exitence of a guarantee.

14 Cf. Italian report on non-fitted furniture.

(3) Exclusion/limitation of liability (annex terms a + b):

Based on the findings of the twelve Member States and having in mind the difficulties in reaching a common terminology, the following clauses may be grouped together under this category: **first,** clauses aiming at the reduction of consumer rights when the delivery is delayed. One may further differentiate between clauses where no reason is given for the exclusion or limitation, and where the supplier refers to internal difficulties or external factors in order to legitimate and justify the denial of consumer rights. Whenever the supplier refers to internal reasons, such as strike or production difficulties, there might even be an overlap between exclusion and limitation of liability clauses on the one hand, and unilateral release clauses to the benefit of the supplier on the other, Annex (c+f+m). Such contract terms may touch upon the consumer's right to cancel the contract as well as the consumer's rights to claim for compensation. Classification depends on where the emphasis lies.[15] If the liability is excluded or limited, the clauses are put under category (a+b), if the right to cancel the contract is restricted, the clauses are put under the category of unilateral release (c+f+o). Also common are terms where the seller does not guarantee the delivery time (stating delivery time to be a mere estimate) in conjunction with exclusion of liability. The **second** group of exclusion/limitation terms are those which are meant to hinder the consumer from pursuing and enforcing his rights. Such terms presuppose that the liability of the supplier is not totally excluded but bound to the fulfilment of a specific complaint procedure. Just two examples: the consumer is required to write to the supplier asking for a definite answer within two or three weeks[16] or the consumer is obliged to write a motivated letter within a certain time period in order to justify why he is claiming compensation.[17] The **third** category of exclusion/limitation terms shifts the risk of delivery to the consumer. The terms require that there is a time span between the order and the delivery and that the product in question will be delivered to the consumer. In Greece, the costs of insuring the car during the transport is put onto the consumer. Such a clause might have to do with the Greek automobile market. All cars must be imported. But even outside Greek particularities, there is a strong tendency in the field of washing machines to shift the transport risk to the consumer. He often has to bear the consequences if the product is lost or is damaged during the transport.[18]

---

[15] Cf. German report, on furniture.

[16] Taken from the German report, on furniture.

[17] Cf. Netherlands report.

[18] Cf. The Greek the Italian and the German reports.

(4) Access to justice, annex term (q): This is an easy category as there are practically only two types of clauses which have been discovered in the Member States. The **first** regulates the place of jurisdiction to the benefit of the supplier, the **second** concerns the dispute settlement procedure. The former clause can be found in one way or the other in all Member States.

(5) Exclusion or limitation of the Legal guarantee, annex term (b): Before proceeding further it is necessary to point out three different approaches to the issue of exclusions or limitations of liability. There are the common law countries where the subject matter of legal guarantee is dealt with in the context of exclusion and limitation of liability, then there are countries which root their tradition in the German Civil Code and distinguish between exclusion and limitation of liability and exclusion and limitation of legal guarantees, last but not least, there are countries, which have adopted specific legislation on the inter-relationship between legal and commercial guarantees, such as Denmark and France.

Based on the information provided by the national reports, the following five categories of clauses can be identified: **first**, clauses which misinform the consumer on the relationship between legal guarantees and commercial guarantees. The French and the Danish had done much to clear the market from such terms. Only a few clauses still exist in these countries. The same cannot be said for the other countries where there are terms to be found which purport to limit the consumer to his rights under the commercial guarantee. The **second** category of clauses covers the exclusion of legal guarantees by the retailer. No clauses were found where the suppliers completely deny the existence of legal guarantees in their standard terms. However it is more typical for there to be terms which deprive the consumer of his rights indirectly. Greek and Italy may serve as examples where the consumer is obliged to accept the product as it is when he buys it, thereby depriving him of all his rights if he does not claim the defectiveness of the product at the time of the delivery.

Third: More widely spread are clauses which are meant to restrict, in one way or other, those consumer rights which come under the national legal guarantee scheme. Standard terms often tend to reduce the choice of rights, which the consumer has, when the product is found to be defective. It is also quite common to use clauses which only oblige the supplier to replace or repair. They sometimes appear in conjunction with the explicit exclusion of compensation rights. The **fourth** type of clauses aims at making it more difficult for the consumer to pursue his rights. [The working group agreed to exclude these clauses from the scope of Annex (q) access to justice and to put them under the category of (b).] Examples of this category are where consumers are obliged to return a guarantee card and to get the guarantee registered, and perhaps to prove the date. They may also be bound to a time period (varying between a couple of days to a couple of weeks) within which they can claim for the defectiveness of the product – otherwise they loose all their rights. The **fifth** category excludes legal guarantees, if the consumer tries to repair the product himself or if he does not bring the defective product to the supplier from whom he bought it.

(6) Unilateral release (annex terms c+f+o): The overwhelming objective of these sorts of terms is to allow the supplier to unilaterally release himself from the contract. Unilateral release seems to play quite a different role in the Member States. Italy (35), the United Kingdom (25) taking a lead position, Germany (13) and Belgium (12) ranking in the middle while the majority of the Member States do not seem to be concerned by the problem of unilateral release. For this majority there are very few – between zero and four nominations.

There are four categories of unilateral release clause: **first,** clauses stating that the contract is binding only after written confirmation by the supplier, although the consumer is bound to the contract without any written order; **second,** clauses obliging the consumer to pay despite partial or even total non-delivery or because of internal difficulties in the production,[19] **third**, restriction or limitation of the right of the consumer to cancel the contract although the delivery is delayed or incomplete. The **fourth** category concerns clauses on down-payments which have to be made by the consumer. It is worth mentioning that clauses focusing on down-payments have mainly been found in Italy and the United Kingdom. The Italian buyer of a motor car may be asked to pay a down-payment which remains with the seller in case the consumer fails to pay the full sum within two to three weeks. The English buyer of a motor car may also forfeit his down-payment when he breaches the contract or refuses to accept the delivery of the car.

3. Is there a relationship between unfairness and the country in question and between unfairness and the different sales sectors ? –

Looking at *chart IV* (below) it seems that most of the unfair terms are found in Netherlands, followed by France, Italy and Germany. It should not be forgotten, however, that only the Netherlands, France and Italy supplied the required 100 copies. So a 'hit-list' of countries is very difficult to establish.

---

[19] This is the case in Germany, where the supplier rejects any responsibility in case of strike etc.

The allocation of unfair clauses to the four investigated sectors shows substantial differences. 155 contract copies for motor cars show 623 violations of the Directive. This is a relation of 1:4. 119 nominations for washing machines with 316 unfair terms show a relation of 1:3; 147 for VCRs with 421 unfair terms shows a relation of 1:4; 124 for furniture with 501 unfair terms shows a relation of 1:4. The particular position of washing machines may be explained by the high frequency of manufacturers' guarantees being used here.

4. Is there a relationship between unfairness and the brand in question?
Chart V (see below) shows how the use of unfair terms varies across the different brands studied. Peugot seem to be the worst offenders.

5. Is there a relationship between unfairness and the type of clause?
Chart VI (see below) shows that unfair terms are most common by far in preformulated standard terms.

V RELATIONSHIP BETWEEN NATIONAL LAW AND DIRECTIVE 93/13

As the EC Directive is the yardstick against which the unfair terms should be measured, it is important to compare the national law with the EC Directive and to elaborate the main deviations. Quite different approaches have been chosen. Portugal and the Netherlands start from the idea that the national law is more protective of the consumer than Directive 93/13. Therefore unfairness under the national law means there is necessarily unfairness under the Directive. Quite the opposite approach is taken by Ireland and to some extent by the United Kingdom. Here each data sheet contained a careful weighing of when an annex term might be fair and if and how a violation under EC law would necessarily mean a violation under pre-existing national law.

Chart VII (see below) presents a comparison of unfairness in EC and national law in the six selected problem areas. The chart seems to point to the conclusion that the standards of the Directive are generally higher than the standards of the national law. What is meant by this is that the national law either does not control the type of clause in question, or that the test applied is not as rigorous. Alteration of price clauses are subject to a stronger control under EC law in Italy and the UK; alteration of characteristics are subject to a stonger control under EC law in Italy, the United Kingdom, Greece and Portugal; exclusion and limitation clauses are subject to a stonger control under EC law in Italy, United Kingdom, Greece and Ireland; access to justice clauses are subject to a stronger control under EC law in Italy, Greece, Belgium, Spain and Ireland; legal guarantee clauses are subject to stronger control in Italy, United Kingdom, Greece and Ireland and last but not least unilateral release clauses are subject to stronger control in Italy, the United Kingdom, Ireland and Greece.

Turning the question upside down and asking for circumstances in which the national law is stronger, the following cases can be reported: two cases from Ireland concerning alteration of prices, two cases from Italy and from Ireland concerning exclusion and limitation of liability, four from Ireland concerning legal guarantee clauses.

CONCLUDING COMMENT

It is hoped that the above analysis provides some useful insight into the sorts of 'unfair terms' in use in different countries and sales sectors.

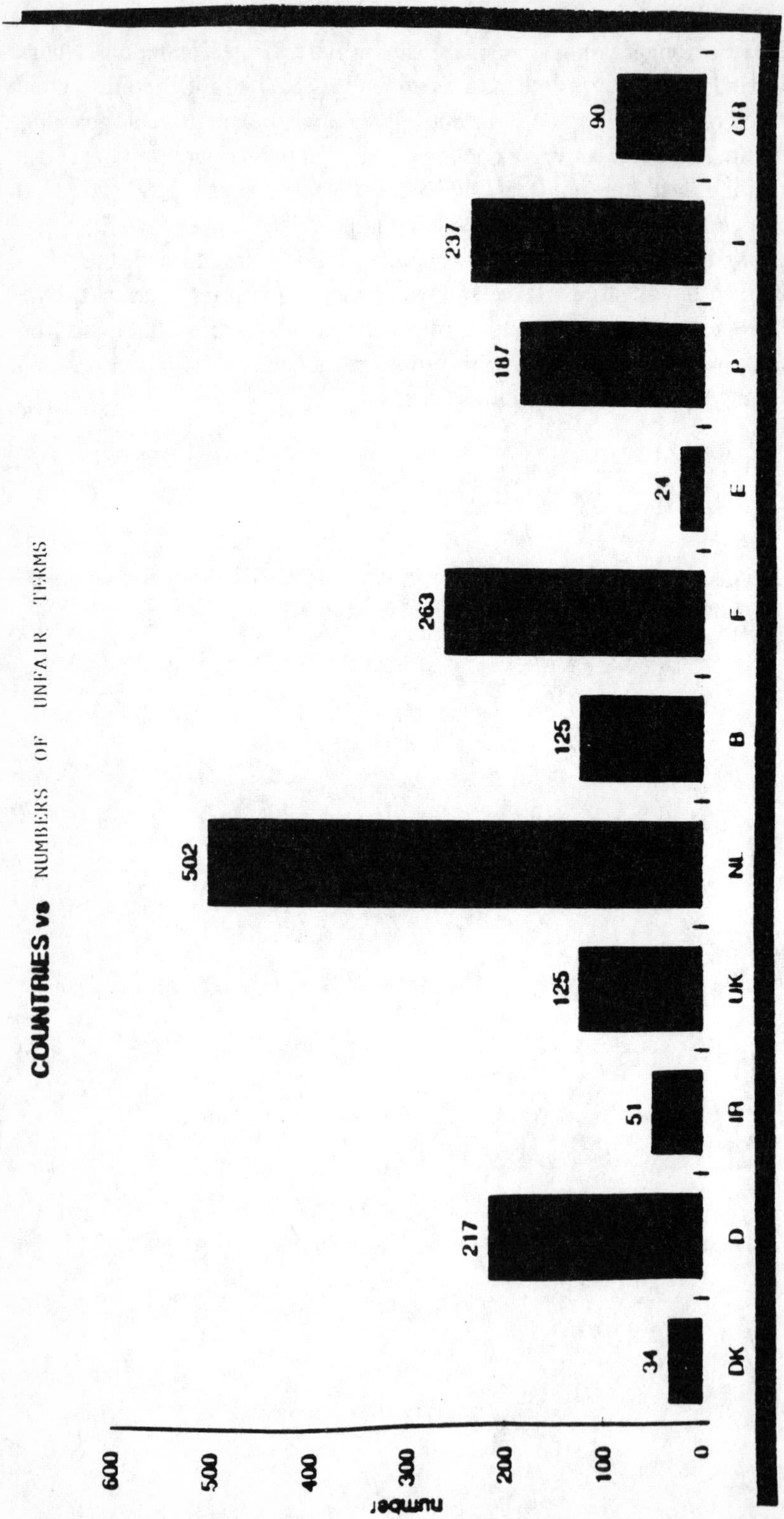

COUNTRIES vs NUMBERS OF UNFAIR TERMS
number
600
500
400
300
200
100
0
34
217
51
125
502
125
263
24
187
237
90
DK
D
IR
UK
NL
B
F
E
P
I
GR

CHART IV

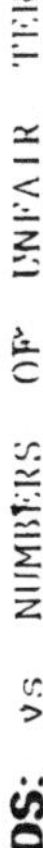

BRANDS: vs NUMBERS OF UNFAIR TERMS

number
0
10
20
30
40
50
60
70
Peugeot
Fiat
VW
Rover
AEG
Philips wash
Whirlpool
Miele
Bosch
Sony
Philips video
J V C
Panasonic
IKEA

CHART V

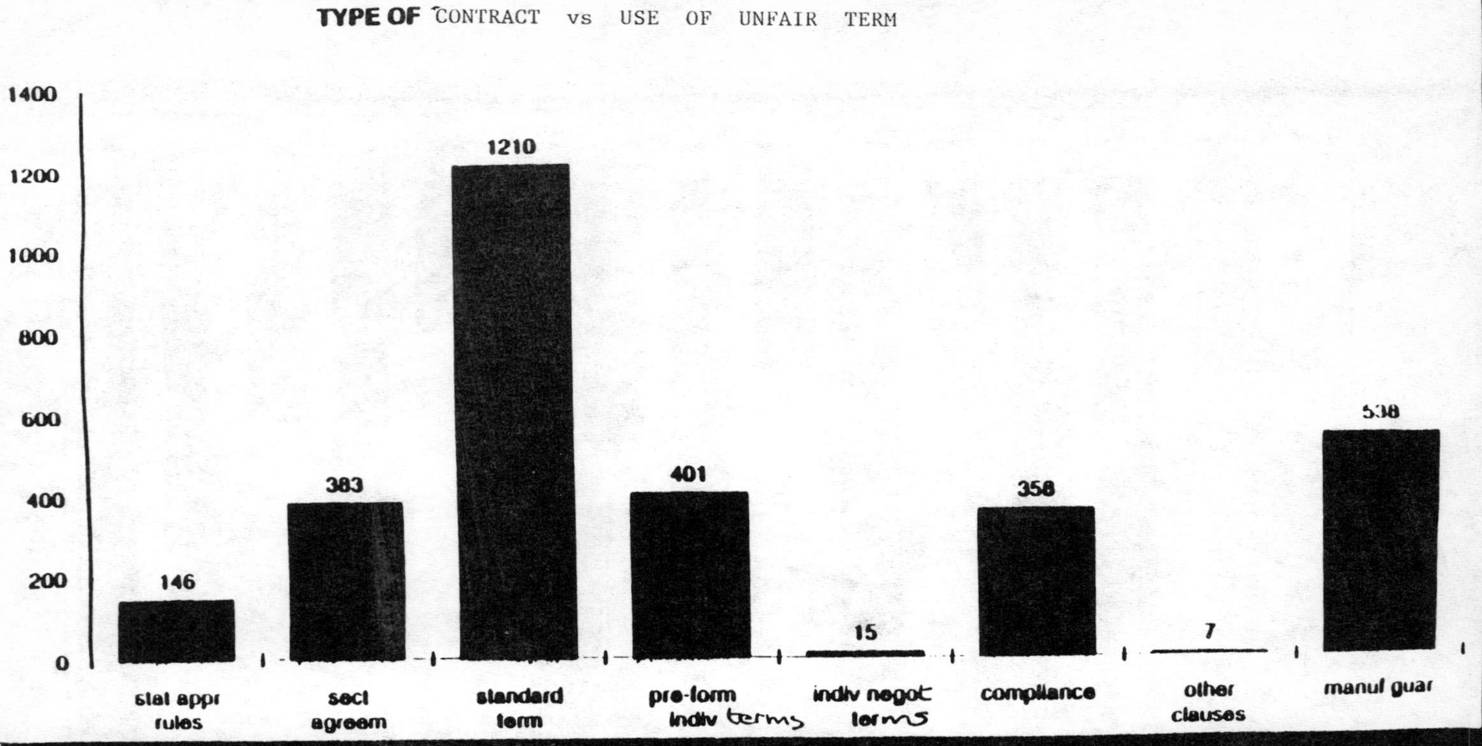
TYPE OF CONTRACT vs USE OF UNFAIR TERM
number
1400
1200
1000
800
600
400
200
0
146
383
1210
401
15
358
7
538
stat appr rules
sect agreem
standard form
pre-form indiv terms
indiv negot terms
compliance
other clauses
manuf guar

CHART VI

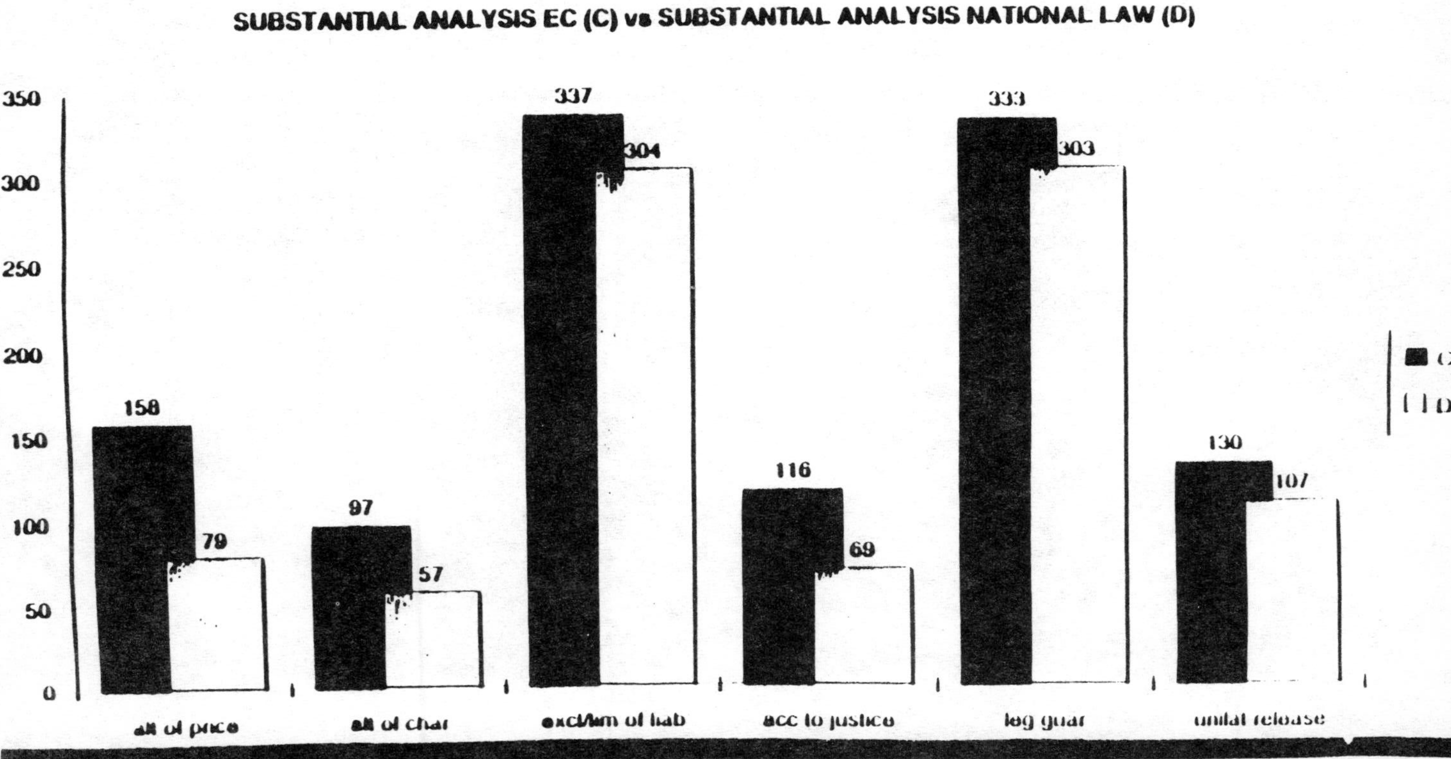
SUBSTANTIAL ANALYSIS EC (C) vs SUBSTANTIAL ANALYSIS NATIONAL LAW (D)
number
350
300
250
200
150
100
50
0
158
79
97
57
337
304
116
69
333
303
130
107
alt of price
alt of char
excl/lim of liab
acc to justice
leg guar
unilat release
C
D

CHART VII

5. Fairness in Agreed Remedies

Hugh Collins

Agreed remedies have been a neglected topic in the law of contract. In particular, the connection between judicial control over agreed remedies and issues of fairness in contract has not been explored rigorously. Here I examine the question of how judicial control over agreed remedies can be justified. I shall test in particular the hypothesis that judicial control is linked to a conception of fairness.

By agreed remedies, I refer to provisions in the terms of a contract which seek to replace or supplement the normal judicial remedy for breach of contract. Such provisions are illustrated by terms which fix an agreed level of compensation, which identify a security right over property which can be exercised in the event of breach, and which determine the forum in which any dispute should be resolved. The phrase agreed remedies should be understood by way of contrast with judicial remedies. As with other terms in a standard form contract, of course, agreed remedies present the risk of procedural unfairness in that the terms can be inserted without any negotiation or conscious agreement between the parties. It is possible that in this respect no sharp line distinguishes agreed remedies from other terms which shape and restrict contractual obligations. I focus here on the central case of terms which set out to replace the normal judicial remedies for breach of contract for the purpose of improving the position of the plaintiff against the party in breach of contract.

There is perhaps a loose assumption shared by judges and commentators that judicial controls over agreed remedies, such as the ban on penalty clauses and the jurisdiction to provide equitable relief from forfeiture, must be grounded in some conception of fairness. Yet there has been a marked reluctance to discover any coherent set of principles which justify these controls. In contrast, the subject of controls over the fairness of primary contractual obligations has been examined closely in the fields of procedural unfairness, such as undue influence, duress, misrepresentation and disclosure. Similarly, the role of fairness in guiding decisions has also been assessed in connection with the construction of contractual terms, the implication of terms, and controls over exclusion clauses.

My objective here is to turn the searchlight upon the justifications for judicial control over agreed remedies. I seek to test the hypothesis that such judicial controls are grounded in a particular conception of fairness in contracts.

I DIVERSITY OF GROUNDS FOR JUDICIAL CONTROL.

English law lacks any general rule for judicial control over agreed remedies. The legal rules are individuated by reference to the type of contractual term to be regulated. Special rules and standards apply to each type of term, such as liquidated damages, deposits, charges over property, and arbitration clauses. This approach then inaugurates both a diversity of standards of control and consequent problems of classification of terms.

Without going into much detail, we can present a snapshot of the standards employed by the courts by which to control agreed remedies which reveals their diversity. In relation to agreed fixed measures of compensation for breach of contract, a court will treat the term as an unenforceable penalty clause if it is unconscionable and extravagant, and one which no court ought to allow to be enforced,[1] but will permit enforcement of an agreed measure of compensation as a liquidated damages clause if it represents a genuine pre-estimate of loss.[2] If a fixed measure of compensation is identified as a deposit, that is a sum of money payable in advance by way of earnest of performance,[3] then the test of validity becomes one of the reasonableness of the amount of the deposit.[4] Where the contract term is identified as a forfeiture provision, which entitles the injured party to override possessory or proprietary rights of the party in breach of an obligation to pay money, then a court exercises a broad discretion to grant relief by way of extending the time available to pay the

---

1 *Clydebank Engineering and Shipbuilding Co. Ltd.* v. *Yzquierdo y Casteneda* [1905] AC 6, 10 per Lord Halsbury LC.

2 *Dunlop Pneumatic Tyre Co Ltd* v. *New Garage and Motor Co. Ltd* [1915] AC 79, 86 per Lord Dunedin. The terminology of penalty clause and liquidated damages reflects a long-forgotten contrast between forms of action between debt and assumpsit: Muir, 1983-85.

3 *Howe* v. *Smith* (1884) 27 Ch D 89 (CA).

4 *Linggi Plantations Ltd* v. *Jagatheesan* [1972] 1 MLJ 89 (PC); *Workers Trust and Merchant Bank Ltd* v. *Dojap Investments Ltd* [1993] 2 All ER 370 (PC); H. Beale, (1993).

debt before the property is forfeited.[5] Other types of terms might simply be invalidated at common law on the grounds of immorality or public policy, such as a term which grants a remedy to the injured party involving the physical chastisement of the defendant.

The diversity of tests of validity has been intensified by statutory interventions. Some agreed remedies may be judged under the test of fairness and reasonableness contained in the Unfair Contract Terms Act 1977, since the Act adopts an expansive view of what can count as an exclusion clause (McDonald 1994), and includes within its compass certain guarantees and indemnities. For consumer contracts, the EC Directive on Unfair Terms in Consumer Contracts generates a novel test applicable to agreed remedies which insists that a term will be unfair and invalid if contrary to the requirement of good faith, it causes a significant imbalance in the parties rights and obligations arising under the contract, to the detriment of the consumer.[6] Domestic legislation also introduces specific regulation of agreed remedies in such cases as consumer credit transactions and consumer arbitration agreements.[7]

Having adopted this approach of classification of particular types of terms in contracts, the courts must then confront the consequent problems of classification. These problems arise when the issue is whether or not a clause falls into a particular category. The controversy may concern which standard is applicable, or whether indeed any judicial control should be exercised at all, if the clause is arguably not within any of the categories of agreed remedies.

The task of classification of terms establishes a number of sharp contrasts which may be difficult to apply to particular terms. For example, the courts have to distinguish between deposits, pre-payment clauses, and instalments, because the applicable rules diverge. Whereas a deposit will be subject to a test of reasonableness, though exempt from criticism as a penalty clause, a pre-payment clause and an instalment will not be subject to either test, though they may be subject to control on the ground of unjust enrichment (Beatson, 1981). Similarly, the familiar contrast between penalty clauses and liquidated damages clauses must also deal with the more complex distinction between these types of clauses and conditions of the contract.[8]

---

5 *Shiloh Spinners Ltd* v. *Harding* [1973] AC 691 (HL); M. Pawlowski, The Scope of Equity's Jurisdiction to Relieve against Forfeiture of Interests in Property other than Land (1994) *Journal of Business Law* 372.

6 EC Directive 93/13, Art 3(1), Official Journal L 95/29 of April 21, 1993.

7 Consumer Credit Act 1974; Consumer Arbitration Agreements Act 1988.

8 *Lombard North Central Plc* v. *Butterworth* [1987] QB 527 (CA); *Gilbert-Ash (Northern) Ltd* v. *Modern Engineering (Bristol) Ltd* [1973] 3 WLR 421.

The courts also have to deal with a sometimes elusive distinction between price variation clauses and penalty clauses.[9] As the Law Commission has observed,

> what would be objectionable if expressed as a penalty for delay might be perfectly validly achieved if expressed, with appropriate adjustment of the main terms of the contract and of the date for completion, as a bonus for early execution of the obligation.[10]

Once these classifications have been made, or perhaps more realistically, once these classifications have been determined with a view to the appropriateness of the test of validity, then the court applies its diverse package of standards to each sort of term. These controls over agreed remedies obviously signal a measure of restriction upon freedom of contract. But can it be argued successfully that the restriction rests upon any particular theme, and if so, is this theme one concerned with the fairness of the terms of the contract?

There have been surprisingly few attempts to provide a considered justification for judicial controls over agreed remedies. Here I will construct out of various judicial dicta and academic commentaries a number of possible interpretations of the justification for judicial control. Although each justification may shed some light on the legal doctrines, no single justification appears to provide a unifying and coherent basis for judicial control over all types of agreed remedies.

II EXCEPTIONAL SUBSTANTIVE FAIRNESS

English contract law lacks a general principle of fairness. The courts have set their backs towards such general principles as inequality of bargaining power, a duty to bargain in good faith, and testing the adequacy of consideration. Such general principles are considered to conflict too directly with the basic disposition of the law to recognise freedom of contract. Instead, the courts rely upon particularistic, discrete doctrines, mostly drawn from equity, which can be utilised to counteract patent instances of unfairness. One strand of justification for judicial control over agreed remedies follows a similar route. Whilst it recognises that this

---

9 *Wallingford* v. *Mutual Society* (1880) 5 App Cas 685, 702; *Interfoto Picture Library Ltd* v. *Stiletto Visual Programmes Ltd* [1989] QB 433 (CA).

10 Law Commission, *Penalty Clauses and Forfeiture of Monies Paid* (Working paper No. 61) para. 14. A court that wishes to enforce a penalty clause can interpret it as a specification of an alternative performance: Sweet, (1972).

jurisdiction is based upon criteria of substantive fairness, it insists that the controls lack any basis in general principle.

The dominant conventional interpretation of judicial control over agreed remedies insists upon distinct tests for each type of term without any underlying principle. This view both reflects the practices of the courts in their classification of terms and their application of different formulae for regulation. Each type of control is presented as an anomalous exception to the general disposition to permit freedom of contract, which is justified, if any justification is offered at all, by the long tradition of judicial intervention with respect to a particular type of clause.

A typical discussion of this justification was offered recently by Dillon L.J. when considering the jurisdiction over penalty clauses. He observed that the courts do not claim a 'general power not to enforce any agreement which the courts regard as unconscionable and extravagant...but rules evolved as to the types of cases in which relief would be given, and one of those rules, now too entrenched to be challenged, is the equitable rule against penalties...'[11]. The justification offered for judicial control in this passage is primarily couched in terms of traditional authority. There is an implicit acknowledgement that considerations of fairness have informed the rule against penalties, yet there is no attempt to reconcile this intervention on grounds of fairness with the general rejection of such a jurisdiction at the level of principle.

This justification based upon tradition obviously leaves unanswered several crucial questions of principle. In the first place, it lacks an explanation of why control over the substantive fairness of terms is permissible in connection with agreed remedies whereas this type of control is rejected for the primary obligations under the contract. Secondly, it provides no explanation for the diversity of standards employed by the courts in the exercise of this jurisdiction. If the underlying principle is one concerned with substantive fairness, then we should expect the tests to be similar in their emphasis upon unfairness and unconscionability. But the most serious problem with this justification is that it lacks an explanation of why the courts do not apparently engage in a rational test for the substantive unfairness of agreed remedies.

A rational test of substantive fairness would examine all the terms in a contract. By looking at the terms as a whole, a court could perceive whether or not a substantial imbalance of advantage was created by the terms of the contract. A fierce penalty clause or a high deposit could be balanced out by a higher price or special insurance arrangements against

---

11 *Jobson* v. *Johnson* [1989] 1 WLR 1026 (CA), 1032.

risks. Yet the courts apparently examine the validity of agreed remedies in isolation. A fixed sum of compensation will be regarded as an invalid penalty clause if it fails the test of it being unconscionable and not a genuine pre-estimate of loss, and this will be the result regardless of the other terms of the contract. Similarly , the jurisdiction to give relief from forfeiture turns on whether the seeker of relief can offer reasonable prospects of repayment of the debt, not whether the allocation of risks under the contract represented a fair balance of advantage.

For these three reasons, the justification for control over agreed remedies couched in terms of an exceptional power to establish substantive fairness is extremely vulnerable to criticism. While the first and second points challenge the rationality of the scope of the exception to the rule against judicial control over fairness of terms in contracts, the third criticism reveals that this justification lacks a coherent idea of substantive fairness in contracts. Some combination of these reasons no doubt leads most commentators to reject substantive fairness as a plausible ground for justifying this jurisdiction to control agreed remedies. Indeed the weakness of this justification then provokes enquiries into the soundness of the argument based upon the ancient authority of the jurisdiction. The existence of the jurisdiction is attacked as an unfortunate result of a misinterpretation of earlier cases, which, because it lacks a coherent justification, should be abandoned (Muir, 1983-85).

III PROCEDURAL FAIRNESS

The normal way in which English law tackles unfairness in contracts seizes upon impropriety during the negotiations leading up to a contract. It joins together the substantive unfairness of the terms of the contract with evidence of coercion and taking advantage of another in the formation of the contract, so that the substantive unfairness confirms the abuse of power and position in the formation of the contract.[12] Under the province of such doctrines as duress, undue influence, and misrepresentation, the courts can then invalidate substantively unfair contracts, not on that ground, but on the ground that consent to the contract was impaired. Another potential justification for the judicial power to control agreed remedies could be to link it to this jurisdiction to supervise procedural fairness in the formation of contracts. This approach has the advantage of securing a much surer

---

12 *National Westminster Bank Plc* v. *Morgan* [1985] AC 686 (HL).

foundation for the jurisdiction over agreed remedies, but it also suffers from several damaging weaknesses.

Tests of procedural fairness can be justified either by reference to a theory which insists that free and informed consent should be the basis of contractual obligations, or by reference to a regulatory strategy which seeks to remove or alleviate market failures when there is an absence of a competitive market. On this procedural fairness interpretation of the judicial control over agreed remedies, the power will be exercised to invalidate the agreed remedy when the terms are the product of some defect in the bargaining process.

In some consumer transactions, no doubt, the small print of an agreed remedy clause can be described as an instance of market failure; that is a contract which would not have been agreed if the consumer had been properly informed of the contents of the contract. Other instances of agreed remedies may be the product of duress, pressured sales, or some informational asymmetry. Fuller and Eisenberg argue that there are often bargaining defects for liquidated damages, because the parties do not fully appreciate all the risks of breach and may not give the clause the attention it deserves, unlike the principal obligations under the contract. Some judicial explanations of the control over penalty clauses also give some credence to the importance of procedural fairness in assessing the unconscionability of the clause, but only as one relevant factor rather than the basis of the jurisdiction.[13]

Yet most of the cases before the courts where the validity of an agreed remedy is impugned do not appear to be the product of market failure or some defect in consent. On the contrary, they appear to represent carefully negotiated terms of the contract between equal commercial parties who are aware of most of the possible risks. In determining the validity of such clauses, the courts do not examine the process leading up to the formation of the contract, but simply examine the terms of the agreed remedy. One objection to the justification for judicial control over agreed remedies based on a concern for procedural fairness is therefore that it does not provide a satisfying description of the practice of the courts.

This justification also has considerable difficulty in explaining why the courts seize upon particular types of agreed remedies for the exercise of controls. If the problem being addressed is procedural unfairness, then the courts should be willing to perceive evidence of advantage-taking from any type of term in the contract. As Harris observes ,

---

13 *AMEV UDC Finance Ltd* v. *Austin* (1986) 162 CLR 170 (High Court of Australia) at p. 193 per Mason and Wilson JJ.

> What is the purpose of retaining the law on penalties? It seems that its only justification is to protect a weaker party against the unconscionable use of a superior bargaining strength. If this is its purpose, it is hard to justify limiting judicial scrutiny to this one type of clause. Any type of clause can be drafted unfairly, but the common law has never attempted overall control of the terms of a contract. If abuse of a stronger bargaining position is the real evil, it should be attacked directly by a principle which aims at any manifestation of the abuse, instead of one which aims selectively at agreed damages clauses and ignores other types of clause. (Harris, 1992; see also Muir, 1983-85).

It is for this reason, of course, that the topic of judicial control over agreed remedies becomes an independent subject for scrutiny. If the jurisdiction was merely confined to instances of market failure, then the normal doctrines designed to combat market failure such as duress, undue influence, fraud, and obligations to negotiate with care, would be applicable and there would be no need for further powers to invalidate agreed remedies. Furthermore, the remedies for such market failure might be expected to include rescission of the entire contract because consent to the contract was vitiated, but in practice there is no question in the control over agreed remedies of seeking to invalidate the entire contract. On the contrary, the contract normally remains valid and enforceable, with the exception of the objectionable clause.

The interpretation based upon market failure or procedural fairness therefore appears unpromising. It requires us to ignore traditional doctrinal distinctions which insist upon the discrete grounds for control over agreed remedies such as penalty clauses. It also requires us to ignore the criteria used to control agreed remedies, which examine the content of these terms rather than the process by which they came to be incorporated into the contract.

Given the weakness of both the proposed justification based upon substantive unfairness and procedural unfairness, it is natural at this point to turn to other possible justifications for the jurisdiction to control agreed remedies. We shall consider several of these proposed justifications, but they also turn out to share similar weaknesses.

IV PRIVATE PUNISHMENT AND THE COMPENSATORY PRINCIPLE

One recurrent theme in controls over some types of agreed remedies concerns the idea of private punishment. This interpretation suggests that an agreed remedy can amount to a form of private punishment for breach of contract, which is objectionable in relations of civil society in the market

(Burrows, 1987). We need to disentangle some of the elements of this argument before assessing it.

The requirement to pay an agreed remedy, such as forfeiting a property right or payment of liquidated damages, is not regarded as bringing with it the moral obloquy associated with punishment. Thus the analogy with punishment must be stripped of its retributive overtones. There can be no objection to private agreements which fix the sanction for breach of contract; otherwise, all agreed remedies would be invalid. It is therefore the content of the agreed sanction which must be objectionable.

If by punishment is meant those things which can only be done lawfully by the state, such as imprisonment, then certainly it makes sense to limit freedom of contract in order to prevent parties acquiring rights over others which would otherwise be unlawful exercises of force. Whilst private punishment of this kind would certainly be disallowed and any agreed remedy to that effect would be unenforceable as immoral or contrary to public policy, it is of course not this type of agreed remedy which is the normal stuff of commercial agreements.

In what sense can an agreed remedy which fixes a particular measure or form of compensation amount to a private punishment? The meaning of punishment here seems to imply a contrast with compensation. The objection to agreed remedies is that they may go beyond compensation for loss and in that sense be equivalent to punitive damages.[14] If this is the principal meaning of private punishment in this context, then the reason given for the intervention is not one of fairness, but is rather an objection to any punitive (i.e. greater than compensatory) measures of compensation. This interpretation meshes with the common law's general hostility to awards of punitive damages except in narrowly defined circumstances.[15] The hypothesis is that not only does the common law prohibit judges from making awards of damages in excess of the strict requirements of compensation, but also it prevents parties from contracting around this rule.

We can discover support for this interpretation of the justification for judicial control over agreed remedies in the courts. For example, Lord Diplock framed a description of the equitable rule against penalties in terms reflecting the compensatory principle. He said that an agreement:

---

14 Restatement of Contracts 2d (1981, St. Paul, Minn.) s. 356, Comment a: The central objective behind the system of contract remedies is compensatory, not punitive. Punishment of a promisor for having broken his promise has no justification on either economic or other grounds and a term providing such a penalty is unenforceable on grounds of public policy.

15 *Broome* v. *Cassell* [1972] AC 1027 (HL); Law Commission, (1993).

> must not impose upon the breaker of a primary obligation a general secondary obligation to pay to the other party a sum of money that is manifestly intended to be in excess of the amount which would fully compensate the other party for the loss sustained by him in consequence of the breach of the primary obligation.[16]

On the same subject, Lord Roskill has observed:

> one purpose, perhaps the main purpose, of the law relating to penalty clauses is to prevent a plaintiff recovering a sum of money in respect of a breach of contract committed by a defendant which bears little or no relationship to the loss actually suffered by the plaintiff as a result of the breach by the defendant. But it is not and never has been for the courts to relieve a party from the consequences of what may in the event prove to be an onerous or possibly even a commercially imprudent bargain.[17]

This description of the purpose of the jurisdiction over penalty clauses is doubly interesting, for not only does it endorse the compensatory principle as the main purpose of judicial control, but it also denies that the jurisdiction is connected to a general principle of substantive fairness in contracts.

Respect for the compensatory principle, however, does not rule out the possibility that the parties may agree a form of remedy which increases the likelihood of recovery. The normal form which improves chances of recovery consists of a security interest over property. This establishes the injured party as a secured creditor with much better prospects for recovery of compensation against the debtor. But where recovery can be achieved without exercising the security right, then the court can exercise its discretion to give relief from forfeiture, leaving the creditor to its claim in damages. This acceptance of alterations in the form of the remedy extends to the use of deposits as a security for money debts.

Nevertheless, this explanation of the jurisdiction over agreed remedies has to confront certain aspects of judicial practice which do not conform exactly to this mandatory compensatory principle. In the case of deposits, for instance, it is plainly accepted that the sum deposited may be forfeited even though it exceeds the actual loss. The control over deposits only catches those which are unreasonable, often judged by reference to the normal practice in the trade or business.[18] Yet the courts have revealed a disposition to find technical ways to avoid the outcome that a deposit which exceeds the compensatory measure of damages will be enforceable. Although an unpaid deposit can usually be recovered unless it falls foul of the reasonableness test, the courts have occasionally used devices to escape

---

16 *Photo Production Ltd* v. *Securicor Transport Ltd* [1980] AC 827, 850 (HL).

17 *Export Credits Guarantee Department* v. *Universal Oil Products Co* [1983] 2 All ER 205 (HL), at p. 224.

18 *Workers Trust and Merchant Bank Ltd* v. *Dojap Investments Ltd* [1993] 2 All ER 370 (PC).

such a conclusion. For example, in *Lowe* v. *Hope*,[19] the court argued that the contract had been rescinded *ab initio*, so that the contract including the provision of a deposit was no longer enforceable. This reasoning has since been disapproved,[20] because it is inconsistent with the rule that rescission for breach of contract only operates prospectively,[21] but it reveals a disposition to avoid enforcement of deposits when they exceed recoverable losses. Similarly, the exact terms of the contract will be scrutinised in order to check whether indeed the deposit had become payable prior to termination of the contract. If, for example, the deposit only becomes payable on the signing of a formal document, then in the absence of such a signature the condition precedent to payment of the deposit has not arisen, and the deposit may not be payable.[22] This use of technicalities in order to avoid the enforcement of otherwise valid deposits which conflict with the compensatory principle of damages perhaps signal that this principle provides the foundation of this jurisdiction even if it cannot always be fulfilled.

A similar problem confronts the reconciliation of the compensatory principle with the test for validity of liquidated damages clauses. In some circumstances a liquidated damages clause can be valid even though it exceeds the plaintiffs loss, provided that at the time of the formation of the contract the agreed sum represented a genuine estimate of the probable loss which would result from breach of contract. The jurisdiction to give relief against forfeiture also fits uneasily into this rationale, for the issue at stake is not the level of compensation at all, but rather whether the creditor can realise a security right over property at a particular time in order to extinguish the debt.

These objections to this justification for controls over agreed remedies are perhaps not insuperable. Further distinctions and refinements suggest themselves, and if these qualifications were added to the compensatory principle, it would not propose an intransigent test of validity. But once flexibility is introduced, we must ask about the basis on which this discretion is exercised. If, for example, a fixed measure of compensation can be valid in certain circumstances even though it exceeds actual loss, we require an explanation of how those circumstances should be identified. Why is the customary charge relevant in the case of deposits, and why does

---

19 [1969] 3 All ER 605, [1970] Ch 94.

20 *Damon Cia Naviera SA* v. *Hapag-Lloyd International SA, The Blankenstein* [1985] 1 All ER 475 (CA).

21 *Johnson* v. *Agnew* [1980] AC 367 (HL).

22 Per Goff L.J. dissenting, *Damon Cia Naviera SA* v. *Hapag-Lloyd International SA, The Blankenstein* [1985] 1 All ER 475 (CA).

a valid liquidated damages clause have to be a genuine estimate of loss? The compensatory principle on its own has no answer to such questions.

One remaining puzzle about the compensatory principle concerns the uneven treatment of limitation of damages clauses. We may ask why limitation of damages clauses which restrict the available compensation below the normal measure should be permitted when penalty clauses are invalidated. The logic of the court's support for a mandatory compensatory principle should also apply to clauses which restrict the measure of compensation. As a result of the Unfair Contract terms Act 1977, the courts now have jurisdiction to test many limitation of damages clauses on the basis of their fairness and reasonableness, but English law lacked any common law jurisdiction to control such clauses in the same way as penalty clauses. The difference in treatment can perhaps be explained on the ground that limitations of liability concern an allocation of risk of loss under the compensatory principle between the parties, whereas penalty clauses seek to supplant the compensatory principle altogether. It seems easier, however, to explain the contrast by reference to the coercive quality of penalty clauses considered below (Fritz, 1954).

This interpretation of the jurisdiction to control agreed remedies offers some important insights. It suggests that moral and public policy considerations will place limits on more extravagant agreed remedies, for these terms such as Shylock's pound of flesh, pose a challenge to the state's monopoly over the legitimate use of force. In addition, this interpretation suggests a link between the control over agreed remedies and the courts hostility to judicial remedies which go beyond mere compensation, as in the case of punitive or exemplary damages. Yet it lacks a complete explanation of how the control over agreed remedies will be exercised, for there are plainly factors at work other than a simple comparison with the compensatory principle. The question which remains is what is the missing additional criterion of validity?

V COERCED PERFORMANCE

It is possible that an entirely different justification explains the control over agreed remedies, or provides the necessary supplement to the compensatory principle. One such potential justification holds that objectionable terms attempt to coerce performance of the contract. It is certainly the case that many agreed remedies may deter breach and provide incentives for performance. This objection to agreed remedies makes sense, for instance, in a contract of employment where the weekly wage is £200 and the employee agrees to pay £1000 compensation for any day's absence. This agreed remedy would coerce performance through its threat of financial ruin for the employee.

There is judicial support for this interpretation of the rules controlling agreed remedies in the field of penalty clauses by the constant reference to the 'in terrorem' effect of penalty clauses.

> The essence of a penalty is a payment of money stipulated as in terrorem of the offending party; the essence of liquidated damages is a genuine covenanted pre-estimate of damage.[23]

This contrast suggests that what is wrong about penalty clauses is that they function as a threat against breach of contract. A similar criticism might be levelled against other agreed remedies.

There are two overlapping reasons why courts might object to agreed remedies which are designed to coerce performance. One reason is that such terms could amount to an unacceptable invasion of the freedom of the individual. This criticism would be powerful in connection with contracts to perform personal services, as in the employment example above, but seems much weaker when the contractual obligation merely involves the transfer of property or payment of money. Here the type of coercion adopts the same form as a judicial remedy for breach of contract, and though no doubt the threat of an award of damages functions in some respects to coerce performance of contracts, this degree of coercion must be regarded as acceptable for otherwise there would be little incentive provided by the law to perform contracts.

A second reason linked to criticisms of the coercive power of agreed remedies could be that the courts wish to reserve to themselves the power to order compulsory performance of contracts through their remedies of injunctions and specific performance, and that agreed remedies which surreptitiously seek to usurp that power should be disallowed. One reason why the courts may wish to keep exclusive possession of this power to order compulsory performance is that when they exercise it, they do so in the light of all the circumstances, and will refrain from making such orders when this would lead to oppression, unfairness, and interference with individual liberty. An agreed remedy which effectively demands specific performance would clearly pose a challenge to the exercise of this discretion.

This interaction between agreed remedies and judicial orders for compulsory performance assumes an interesting form in connection with

23 Lord Dunedin, *Dunlop Pneumatic Tyre Company Ltd* v. *New Garage and Motor Co Ltd* [1915] AC 79, 86 (HL).

claims for relief from forfeiture. When the facts concern the hire of a chattel, where, under the terms of the contract, any possessory interest in the chattel is lost in the event of late payment of hire charges, then relief from forfeiture would amount to an order to continue with performance of the contract of hire. The owner would not be able to recover possession under the forfeiture provision, and so would have no option but to perform the contract. It was this predicament for the owner which led the House of Lords in *Scandanavian Trading Tanker Co AB* v. *Flota Petrolera Ecuatoriana, The Scaptrade*,[24] to deny that the jurisdiction to give relief from forfeiture extended to contracts of hire and for services. In the normal case of relief from forfeiture involving security in the form of proprietary interests in land, the jurisdiction serves to limit the exercise of a self-help remedy which is equivalent to specific performance of a contract to transfer the property. By exercising the jurisdiction, the court prevents circumvention of its general power to determine when and whether specific performance of obligations will be ordered. In *The Scaptrade*, in contrast, the court viewed the exercise of the jurisdiction as having the potential to effect specific performance of contracts of hire, in this case a time charter, which would not usually be specifically enforceable at all.

Although these arguments linking judicial control over agreed remedies with a fear of coercion of performance have some weight and prove pertinent in particular cases, they do not appear to be sufficiently refined in order to account for legal practice. First, we must observe that agreed remedies providing for a fixed measure of compensation cannot achieve the same degree of coercive power as court orders for specific relief, since ultimately they result merely in seizure of property to the value of the judgment debt rather than the full rigour of remedies for contempt of court. The objection to agreed remedies providing for specific performance therefore does not apply to fixed measures of compensation.

Secondly, whilst it is true that the greater the amount of a fixed level of compensation, the greater the incentive to perform the contract, we must observe that the power of the incentive to perform the contract depends crucially on the variable cost of performance. If the courts had been concerned to prevent coerced performance, then they would have established a test of validity for agreed remedies which prohibited a fixed measure of compensation in excess of the costs of performance. But in general this does not appear to be the comparison which courts make. They compare the agreed remedy with the likely judicial remedy for breach, not the cost of performance. The two measures will only be the same in the

---

24 [1983] 2 All ER 763 (HL).

case of money obligations, where the cost of performance in the form of payment of money is likely to be the same as the measure of damages for debt. The measure of damages may reflect the cost of performance where the damages will be based upon a cost of cure principle, but this measure will not always be available. This justification therefore fits uneasily with the practice of the courts where the cost of performance is not usually regarded as a relevant consideration (Muir, 1983-85).

In addition, if the objection to agreed remedies centres on the coercion of performance, we might also expect the courts to have developed a test analogous to the doctrine of duress, under which it would be possible to determine whether or not the agreed remedy left the party in breach of contract with no reasonable choice but to perform the contract. Again, however, there is no sign in the judgments of the courts of such a test for coercion.

We should conclude that there may indeed by good reasons for objecting to agreed remedies which effectively compel performance of contracts. It seems likely that the jurisdiction over agreed remedies prevents such terms from achieving a coercive power equivalent to orders for specific performance. Yet the jurisdiction operates a much stricter control over agreed remedies than this justification would suggest.

VI UNJUST ENRICHMENT

A more subtle and selective justification for control over agreed remedies could be provided by the idea of unjust enrichment. Here the suggestion is that an agreed remedy may lead to the enrichment of the party not in breach of the contract if that party would be better off as a result of breach than if the contract had been performed or full compensatory damages had been paid. This justification overlaps with the argument based on punitive damages to the extent that it prohibits compensation for breach in excess of damages based on the compensatory principle, though it adds to that justification by requiring the excess compensation to be just. On this view, for instance, a liquidated damages clause would be enforceable even though it fixes a level of compensation in excess of actual loss, provided that this enrichment is not unjust.

How could a court assess the justice of any enrichment? At first sight, it might be urged that since the agreed remedy is part of a consensual agreement, then it could never be unjust to insist upon enforcement of the contract. Granting this point, however, it might be alleged that in a standard form consumer contract the degree of consent necessary to establish the justice of the enrichment was absent. In the alternative, where the reason for breach of contract indicates the absence of fault by the party in breach, then the court may be inclined to view such an agreed remedy as causing unjust enrichment if it leads to a measure of compensation in excess of the probable judicial remedy. In this vein, Sweet (1972) at p.89 observes in relation to Californian cases,

> Courts have therefore employed non-enforcement as an equitable compromise and corrective device in various situations, such as where the performing party had a good, but not legally sufficient, case for reformation, where a party's delay should have been excused, and where the legality of the contract was doubtful.[25]

English courts have not generally employed the language of unjust enrichment in this context, either in a loose generic sense or in a more technical examination of grounds for restitution. The major reason for this rejection of unjust enrichment as a relevant criterion is certainly a reluctance to permit restitutionary claims effectively to rewrite the terms of contracts. Instead, the agreed remedy will generally be regarded as displacing any potential restitutionary claim. For example, the use of a deposit will normally be interpreted as a contractual agreement to negative a potential claim for recovery of money paid in excess of the defendant's loss.[26] It is clear that if restitutionary claims were permitted to override agreed remedies, then these contractual terms would cease to have any practical importance.

Nevertheless, there are limited occasions when a restitutionary claim will be pertinent to an agreed remedy. The issue of the validity of an agreed remedy is usually raised as a defence to a claim, and if the defence is successful, then the agreed remedy will never be paid, so there will be no claim for restitution. But a restitutionary claim may arise where a contract creates obligations to pay money in advance, perhaps in the form of instalments. Here there is authority to support a restitutionary remedy for money paid in advance which exceeds the defendant's loss arising from breach of contract.[27] Such advance payments fall on a borderline between agreed remedies and ordinary primary contractual obligations. They share with agreed remedies the objective of reallocating risk, but they lack the intention to displace the ordinary judicial remedies. It is this intention to displace judicial remedies and set up a private remedial regime which

---

25 See citations to *Eva* v. *Mcmahon*, 77 Cal. 467, 19 P. 872 (1888); *Muldoon* v. *Lynch*, 66 Cal. 536, 6 P. 417 (1885); *Pacific Factor Co* v. *Adler*, 90 Cal. 110, 27 P. 36 (1891).

26 *Mayson* v. *Clouet*[1924] AC 980 (PC).

27 *Rover International Ltd* v. *Cannon Film Sales Ltd (No 3)* [1989] 1 WLR 912 (CA); *Stockloser* v. *Johnson* [1954] 1 QB 476 (CA).

signals the special character of agreed remedies and provokes the distinctive form of judicial control. It is also this intention which can be used to justify the rejection of any restitutionary claim.

This account of judicial practice reveals that unjust enrichment is not a satisfactory justification for control over agreed remedies. The normal principles governing restitutionary claims insist that they should always give way to express contractual provisions. The agreement signals that any ensuing distribution of benefits should not be regarded as unjust. For this reason, this justification based upon unjust enrichment seems distinctly unpromising as a basis for judicial control over agreed terms.

VII REDUCTION OF SOCIAL COST

An enforceable agreed remedy can have the effect of both reducing and increasing the costs arising from breach of contract. An agreed remedy such as a liquidated damages clause may reduce the costs of litigation and proof of loss by truncating disputes about the appropriate measure of compensation for breach of contract. On the other hand, a fixed level of compensation may have the effect of removing the incentive to mitigate loss by seeking alternative sources of supply. The law places a duty on the injured party to mitigate loss in the sense that claims for damages will be disallowed to the extent that the loss would have been avoidable by taking reasonable steps. A possible justification for judicial control over agreed remedies would comprise a principle that agreed remedies are valid in general, since they normally reduce the costs of breach of contract, but that where the agreed remedy substantially interferes with the duty to mitigate loss, then the agreed remedy must be invalid because the additional costs which it generates outweigh the savings on litigation costs.

The calculus initiated by this proposed justification for control over agreed remedies is both complex and uncertain. It commences with a comparison between the measure of compensation afforded by the agreed remedy with the likely measure of compensation to be awarded by a court taking into account the duty to mitigate loss. Since the ability to mitigate loss is normally assessed after breach of contract in the light of all the circumstances then prevailing, we encounter an uncertainty about whether the comparison should be made with the benefit of the knowledge about opportunities to mitigate loss available after breach, or whether knowledge should be confined to probabilities at the time of formation of the contract. Added to this uncertainty must be the complexity of making an assessment of the reduction of litigation costs achieved by an agreed remedy. Of course, these savings will only be achieved to a significant extent when the validity of the agreed remedy is not itself in doubt.

This justification based on reduction of the costs of breach of contract has an undoubted attraction as a policy for the law to adopt, but it must be questioned whether it presents a plausible interpretation of the practice of the courts. The calculus described above has certainly never been attempted. At most the courts will acknowledge that the potential savings in the costs of litigation afforded by agreed remedies should not be blocked by excessive controls over agreed remedies. It is also unclear whether or not a fixed measure of compensation will be invalid merely on the ground that it exceeded the likely loss because the possibilities for mitigation were not taken into account. There is something to be said for the view that the policy of reduction of the costs of breach should favour the routine enforcement of agreed remedies, since the benefits of savings on the costs of litigation are likely in practice to equal or exceed the additional costs generated by the removal of a duty to mitigate losses. If this is correct, then this justification fails in the end to warrant any judicial control over agreed remedies.

VIII WEALTH MAXIMIZATION

A similar criticism can be made against an economic justification framed in terms of wealth maximization for the jurisdiction to control agreed remedies. Given the usual commitment to the view that the parties are likely to maximise their own wealth if left to bargain freely, then this hypothesis is likely to reject judicial controls over agreed remedies. For example, Rea argues that a party to a contract will charge a higher price if it risks a penalty clause in the event of breach of contract; so the penalty clause is paid for by the higher price for the contract; and the contract is worth more to both parties than a contract without the penalty clause (Rea 1984). On this view, by invalidating a penalty clause, not only does a court prevent the maximisation of values through contracts, but also the court introduces unfairness by refusing to enforce a promise (the liability to a penalty clause) which has been paid for (by a higher contract price). The argument is more complex in fact, but it is clear that efficiency considerations cannot be offered as the underlying justification for the law, unless it is assumed that all objectionable agreed remedies are the product of market failures of some kind.

The precise implications of the criterion of efficiency for judicial control over agreed remedies have been hotly debated. The starting-point of the debate concerns an elaboration of the theory of efficient breach. If the competitive market is to allocate resources efficiently, then efficient breach (meaning a breach where the sum of the parties wealth is increased in comparison to performance of the contract) must be permitted. An agreed remedy which discourages an efficient breach must deter breach of inefficient contracts. So the agreed remedy should not be permitted to exceed a measure of compensation which permits efficient breach of contract. At first sight, this argument provides a basis for judicial control over agreed remedies in order to prevent them from exceeding the ordinary measure of contract damages (assuming that it is the expectation interest). But this conclusion has been challenged effectively by Clarkson, Miller & Muris (1978).

They point out that where the agreed remedy exceeds just compensation, (ie an expectation measure of compensation) two situations may arise. First, the parties may negotiate a settlement or compromise which divides the benefit accruing from breach of contract, thus permitting efficient breach still to take place, but allowing the injured party some share in the efficiency gains. Second, the agreed remedy, though greater than just compensation, may still permit efficient breach, because it was set at a level below which it is prohibitive of some efficient breaches. On this analysis, the agreed remedy will not prevent efficient breach, but will merely redistribute some of the efficiency gains between the parties. The defendant will not acquire all the benefits of efficient breach, which may be regarded as a fair outcome (Goetz and Scott, 1977). For these reasons Clarkson, Miller & Muris would enforce penalties and other types of agreed remedies which exceed an ordinary measure of damages.[28]

Goetz and Scott agree with these arguments and add that agreed remedies can improve the efficiency of contracts. The ordinary law of damages fails to compensate some interests of plaintiffs even when the expectation measure is employed. Examples are losses to idiosyncratic values, e.g. consumer surplus values, i.e. those subjective valuations which would not be compensated by market valuation of the law damages, and losses which are too remote. By means of an agreed remedy, the parties to a contract can protect themselves against such losses, thereby increasing the value of the contractual obligations. It is not clear that they approve wholly of this potential for agreed remedies. Recovery for remote losses might undermine the efficiency objectives of the rule which provides incentives for disclosure of risk. On the other hand, the presence of a term providing for a

[28] In addition, of course, there is the usual objection to judicial control of contract terms based upon vague standards that this increases transaction costs: Goetz and Scott, (1977).

specific remedy can function as a signal that certain risks are present, so that it implicitly discloses the risk. Similarly, attempts to undermine the mitigation rule by a fixed measure of compensation would inefficiently increase the losses arising from a breach of contract, though again we might argue that it would be wrong to invalidate such a term if the contract price had in effect purchased this freedom from the duty to mitigate loss. In these instances, therefore, it might be possible to justify judicial control over agreed remedies on efficiency grounds, but the argument is inconclusive. The main thrust of the analysis presented by Goetz and Scott is that agreed remedies can protect idiosyncratic valuations, which they regard as improving the efficiency of contracts (i.e. wealth maximization), and that therefore the courts should not at tempt to control agreed remedies on the ground that they exceed the ordinary measure of damages.

The general conclusion reached by the criterion of efficiency is that, in the absence of market failure considerations, agreed remedies should be enforced, even if they provide for greater compensation than an award of damages. This is not so much an interpretation of the law as a criticism of it.

IX RISK AVERAGING

We have examined a number of possible justifications for judicial control over agreed remedies. Most of these possible justifications look distinctly unpromising, since they fail to pass even a threshold test of fit over legal doctrine and practice.[29] Into this category we must place the justifications based on procedural fairness, reduction of social cost, and wealth maximization. Other justifications considered remain hazy in their details, but they should be rejected because they seem unlikely to fit judicial practice and fail to offer convincing criteria for control over agreed remedies. Into this category I would place the justification based upon unjust enrichment. Yet other justifications provide good reasons for control over agreed remedies, but they cannot account for the degree and type of control exercised by the courts. The objection to coercion of performance falls into this category. Similarly, the justification based upon the rejection of private punishment has force when the agreed remedy amounts to a criminal act, but this is not a common problem.

The justification which appeared most promising was the one which insisted that the courts should uphold the compensatory principle governing

[29] The terminology is drawn from R. Dworkin, (1986).

damages, and that attempts to circumvent that rule should be invalidated. The problem with that justification was that it failed to account for cases where a valid agreed remedy does apparently lead to a greater measure of compensation. Can the compensatory principle be supplemented in a way which explains why some agreed remedies can validly obtain for the injured party a higher level of compensation?

My hypothesis is that the compensatory principle is modified in order to tolerate a practice of risk averaging across different breaches of a contract. The courts permit an agreed remedy to fix a measure of compensation which will correspond on average to the plaintiff's losses from different breaches of the same contract, though in any particular case the losses resulting from breach may be greater or smaller. On this view, the significance of the requirement that a valid liquidated damages clause should be a genuine pre-estimate of loss is that it should represent an attempt either to quantify exactly the losses likely to result from every possible breach, which is an impractical requirement, or, and this is much more plausible, that it should represent a reasonable estimate of the average loss resulting from a number of different types of breach. Provided that the average measure of loss takes into account the likelihood of risks of loss occurring, it could be argued that such a clause represents a genuine pre-estimate of loss par excellence.

In the same vein, the requirement of reasonableness for deposits and the reference to customs of the trade or business could be interpreted as a requirement that the deposit should reflect the average losses resulting from breach of this type of contract, even though in any particular case of breach the losses may be greater or smaller. For this reason a ten per cent deposit may be an accurate assessment of average risk of loss, since although some breaches of contracts to sell land will cause no net loss, others may result in substantial waste of legal costs and rather speculative opportunity costs. The ten per cent deposit may represent a rough average of these losses which may occur.

Do the courts explicitly acknowledge this risk-averaging dimension to the jurisdiction over agreed remedies? In the case of penalty clauses, Lord Dunedin has insisted that there is a presumption against the validity of what he termed blunderbuss clauses which fix the measure of compensation regardless of the precise term broken in the contract, on the ground that they could lead to excessive compensation in particular instances. But it appears that this presumption can be rebutted provided that the liquidated damages clause does not represent an extravagant measure of compensation for any of the potential breaches of contract. This was the crux of the issue in *Dunlop Pneumatic Tyre Co Ltd* v. *New Garage and Motor Co Ltd.*[30]

In this leading case on penalty clauses, the manufacturer of tyres required under its contracts with distributors a payment of five pounds for every tyre sold to the public below list price, or sold after tampering with the manufacturer's markings, or supplied to prohibited persons, or exported. The defendant distributor sold to the public at below list price, which created the risk to the manufacturer that its other dealers would either demand reduced prices or go to other manufacturers. Here the loss which might arise from breach of contract was unpredictable and in many respects speculative. The plaintiff might lose market share, lose a deserved reputation for its product, lose its distribution system, or simply be forced into cutting its prices and profits, or some combination of these consequences. The House of Lords enforced the liquidated damages clause in this case. The court argued that the very uncertainty surrounding the measure of damages in such a case favoured the enforcement of the agreed measure of compensation . Yet the court was not prepared to enforce the clause if it led to an extravagant or unconscionable measure of compensation in the light of the actual losses caused. The five pound charge was not, however, an extravagant measure of compensation for any of the potential breaches of contract. Although the court made no attempt to assess actual loss in this case, it did say that the five pound charge did not look extravagant or unconscionable in the light of the sums of money at stake under the contract, so there may have been a broad brush judgment that the amount was not way out of line with any likely award of damages for any particular breach of contract. This approach conforms to a risk-averaging analysis.

Another recent decision of the Judicial Committee of the Privy Council, *Philips Hong Kong Ltd* v. *The Attorney General of Hong Kong*,[31] also supports the risk averaging approach. Here a large government construction contract contained clauses providing for liquidated damages for delay. The amount of compensation was calculated according to the stage at which the project fell behind schedule, and depended on variables including the cost of capital borrowing and probable staff costs in rescheduling the work. The plaintiffs sought to have the clause invalidated, even though on the facts the liquidated damages were equivalent to the actual loss caused by the plaintiff's delay. The plaintiffs argued that the liquidated damages clause could in some instances lead to greater compensation than the actual loss.

---

30 (1915) AC 79 (HL).

31 (1993) 61 BLR 41.

The Privy Council dismissed the claim, refusing to consider extreme hypothetical cases if the liquidated damages clause in general provided a reasonable estimate of the probable losses. The court conceded that the actual loss suffered in the case was relevant as a cross-check that the estimate of loss was reasonable, but insisted that it would not invalidate a clause simply because some disparity existed in some circumstances.

X CONCLUSION

My inspection of the possible justifications for judicial control over agreed remedies was designed to test the proposition that some conception of fairness lay at the root of the jurisdiction. This may be the correct conclusion, but it is clear that the relevant conception of fairness in connection with agreed remedies departs from any familiar standards of substantive and procedural fairness.

The key principle guiding judicial control over agreed remedies appears to be respect and protection for the principle that remedies for breach of contract should be merely compensatory. This principle may be an aspect of fairness in contract law, but it is not concerned with the fairness of the bargain, but instead insists that the remedial arrangements should not cause a redistribution of wealth which provides the injured party with greater compensation than his actual losses. This is the principle of corrective justice, which in a contractual context leads to the compensatory principle of damages.

Nevertheless, the courts admit a degree of flexibility in enforcing this principle of corrective justice for the sake of encouraging the parties to save costs by planning remedies. At its outer limit, the degree of tolerance extends to agreed remedies which fix a sum of compensation which represents an average of probable losses resulting from different breaches of the same contract. This is an acceptable deviation from the compensatory principle, since it admits the possibility that the agreed remedy may provide either higher or lower compensation than actual loss for any particular breach of contract. This qualification explains the approach to the validation of liquidated damages clauses and the degree of toleration exhibited towards deposits.

What English law has not done is to introduce a straightforward test of fairness which compares retrospectively the agreed measure of compensation with the actual loss resulting from breach of contract. Many other jurisdictions appear to operate this test of fairness, which led to its adoption in the Unidroit proposals for Principles of International

Commercial Contracts. Article 7.4.14 appears to regard all liquidated damages clauses as valid, but then gives a court an overriding power of control to reduce the agreed sum to a reasonable amount where it is grossly excessive in relation to the harm resulting from the non-performance and the other circumstances.[32] The main advantage of this test of fairness is that the parties can easily apply it themselves in order to test the validity of an agreed remedy. On the other hand, a retrospective test of fairness is likely to invalidate some clauses which would pass the English test based upon risk averaging, which suggests that the English approach has the potential to validate a broader range of clauses providing for a fixed measure of compensation.

The English Law Commission in its Working paper (No. 61) rejected any change to this approach because it would mean the introduction of an unacceptable amount of uncertainty even though the report recognised that the approach can lead to unfairness. Appeals to the danger of uncertainty are the standard rationale for any contract rules, but when examined closely the dangers often seem exaggerated. It is usually a cloak for a different rationale of protecting freedom of contract combined with an intolerance of any change in the law. In this particular case of agreed remedies, it seems to me that the English rule provokes greater uncertainty about the validity of agreed measures of compensation than a retrospective test of fairness. Its advantage rather lies in the greater freedom accorded to the parties to average risks of loss arising from breach of contract. This advantage appears to be remarkably slight in comparison to the uncertainty generated in determining the validity of agreed remedies under the current principles.

REFERENCES

Beale, H. (1993) 'Unreasonable Deposits' 109 *Law Quarterly Review* 524-532.

Beatson, (1981) 'Discharge for Breach: The Position of Instalments, Deposits and Other Payments Due Before Completion' 97 *Law Quarterly Review* 389-419.

Burrows, A. (1987) *Remedies for Torts and Breach of Contract*, London.

Clarkson, Miller & Muris (1978) 'Liquidated Damages v. Penalties: Sense or Nonsence?' *Wisconsin Law Review* 351-390.

Dworkin, R. (1986) *Law's Empire* Cambridge, Mass.

Fritz, (1954) 'Underliquidated Damages as Limitation of Liability' 33 *Texas Law Review* 196.

---

[32] The International Institute for the Unification of Private Law (Working Group for the Preparation of Principles for International Commercial Contracts) *Principles for International Commercial Contracts* (1992) 40:3 *American Journal of Comparative Law* 703.

Fuller & Eisenberg, (West, 1981) Basic Contract Law 4th ed.

Goetz and Scott (1977) 'Liquidated Damages, Penalties and the Just Compensation Principle' 77 *Columbia Law Review* 554-594.

Harris, D. (1992) 'Incentives to Perform, or Break Contracts' 45(2) *Current Legal Problems* 29-47.

Law Commission (1993) *Aggravated, Exemplary and Restitutionary Damages* Consultation paper No 132.

Law Commission *Penalty Clauses and Forfeiture of Monies Paid* (Working Paper No. 61).

McDonald, E. (1992) 'Exclusion Clauses: the Ambit of s. 13(1) of the Unfair Contract Terms Act 1977' 12 *Legal Studies* 277-301.

Muir, (1983-85) 'Stipulations for Payment of an Agreed Sum', *Sydney Law Review* 503.

Pawlowski, M. (1994) 'The Scope of Equity's Jurisdiction to Relieve against Forfeiture of Interests in Property other than Land' *Journal of Business Law* 372.

Rea, (1984) 'Efficiency Implication of Penalties and Liquidated Damages' 13 *Journal of Legal Studies* 147.

Sweet, (1972) 'Liquidated Damages in California' 60 *California Law Review* 84-145.

6. Fairness in Sale of Goods Act Quality Obligations and Remedies

Chris Willett

This essay considers the role of some new rules on quality obligations and remedies in sale of goods contracts, in promoting fairness between the parties. These rules are contained in the Sale and Supply of Goods Act 1994 which amends the Sale of Goods Act 1979. Basically the old 'merchantable quality' standard for goods has been replaced by a 'satisfactory quality' standard; the rules on when a buyer loses the right to reject by 'acceptance' have been reformed; and it has been made more difficult for commercial buyers to reject for minor breaches of contract.

HISTORY AND OVERVIEW

Since the last century there has been a statutorily recognised term imposing an obligation of quality upon those selling goods in the course of a business. This has existed as part of a package of implied terms, the others relating to title description, compliance with sample and fitness for purpose. Originally these terms only had a statutory basis in the case of contracts for the sale of goods (i.e. where there is a sale within the meaning of the Sale of Goods Act 1979 – see s.2).

However the implied terms were extended to contracts of hire-purchase by the Supply of Goods (Implied Terms) Act 1973. They were later extended to contracts of hire and contracts for the transfer of property in goods by the Supply of Goods and Services Act 1982. However this Act only applied to England and Wales. In Scotland, the common law remained the source of implied obligations on these matters. However the Sale and Supply of Goods Act 1994 has extended the provisions of the Supply of Goods and Services Act to Scotland (1994 Act, Schedule 1).

There are a number of issues in relation to the quality obligation and the remedies attached to it which have always been difficult. These have been subject to considerable judicial, academic and even political discussion over the years.

First of all there had always been difficulty with the quality standard itself. How many purposes did a product need to be fit for? Did it need to be durable and free from minor defects? To what extent (if at all) was quality to be determined by aesthetic criteria, such as the general appearance of the product (see Willett, 1991, 1993).

There are various fairness dimensions to these issues. One of these is whether the quality obligation properly reflects the reasonable expectations of consumer buyers. Perhaps such reasonable expectations were not reflected if the test was mainly concerned with the functionality of the product (i.e. whether a car could go from A to B); ignoring its freedom from niggling defects, durability, general comfort, appearance etc.

The Law Commissions' recognised that the merchantable quality standard might not meet consumer needs and they suggested a reformulation of the merchantable quality standard in their 1987 Report (No. 160, Sale and Supply of Goods, see Adams and Brownsword, 1988, Willett, 1991). The DTI published a consultation document in 1992 which, in the midst of various other proposals, favoured the Law Commissions' reformulated quality standard (Consumer Guarantees 1992; see Willett, 1993). The DTI consultation document actually came as part of a wider package of proposals on unfair terms, environmental claims and other matters (DTI, 1992).

Finally, in 1994 the Sale and Supply of Goods Act (SSGA) s.1 amended s.14 of the Sale of Goods Act (SGA) 1979, replacing the merchantable quality standard with one of satisfactory quality (s.14(2)). As with the merchantable quality standard the obligation is owed by those who sell in the course of a business (s.14(2)); and as before it does not apply in the context of defects which have been specifically drawn to the buyer's attention, or where there has been an examination, in respect of defects which the examination ought to have revealed (s.14(2)(c)).

Most importantly however, the reformed s.14 makes it clear that matters such as appearance, finish, minor defects and durability are relevant to the determination of whether goods are satisfactory quality (s.14(2)(b)).

The reforms to the acceptance rules and the commercial buyer's right to reject have the same history, having started as proposals made by the 1987 report of the Law Commissions. These proposals were then supported in the DTI's 1992 consultation document, and finally came to fruition in the 1994 SSGA. Section 2 reforms the rules on acceptance (by amending SGA, s.35); and ss. 4 and 5 reform the rules on the commercial buyer's right to reject for breach of contract (by creating new ss.15 A and B in the SGA).

These rules also raise fairness issues. The buyer has a legitimate interest in escaping in full from a transaction in which he has lost confidence, or at least in using the threat of withdrawal to secure an improved performance. The seller, on the other hand, requires some degree of protection against bad faith rejection and termination by the buyer. The seller also has an interest in commercial certainty which means being able to feel secure within a reasonable time after a sale that the buyer cannot reject and terminate. Striking a proper balance between these buyer and seller interests can be talked of as being a fairness issue. The problem arises in several ways. First, there is the question as to whether there should be *any* right of rejection and termination where the breach is small. The law on this issue has been reformed by ss. 4 and 5 of the 1994 Act, which add ss.15 A and B to the SGA. The balance which has now been struck is that consumers always have the right to reject and terminate; while commercial buyers cannot reject where the breach is so slight as to make rejection unreasonable, or in Scotland where the breach is not material (SGA, ss. 15A and B). One important question which will be discused below, is the extent to which the rules prevent bad faith rejection.

The second aspect of the fairness problem in the context of rejection and termination for breach, goes to the conditions to be attached to any right of rejection which does exist. Even those buyers who have a right to reject and terminate will lose these rights where there has been acceptance of the goods. These restrictions on the right to reject are intended to facilitate a degree of certainty for sellers by establishing an identifiable point at which the buyer can no longer reject. The circumstances in which there is aceptance are set out in s.35 of the SGA. Section 2 of the 1994 Act has reformed s.35 so as to tip the balance in the buyer's favour (SGA, s.35).

I will now consider the various reforms in more detail.

QUALITY AND REASONABLE EXPECTATIONS

The first issue which must be dealt with in relation to the satisfactory quality standard is why it, or the merchantable quality standard which preceded it, should be present in the contract in the first place. It appears in a contract of sale (and other contracts for the supply of goods) by sheer virtue of the fact that there is such a contract (see s. 14(2)). It is not there because the parties have agreed expressly that it should be there. This has two particular implications. First there is a compromise on the seller's freedom of contract, in that he is compelled to owe an obligation which he did not freely undertake. Secondly a protection is provided for the buyer which he has not explicitly bargained for. He is, from one perspective, being given something for nothing, rather than in exchange for exercise of personal responsibility and self interested bargaining. So what is the justification for compromising the seller's freedom and the buyer's responsibility to bargain in his own interest? It can be argued to be fair to attach responsibility to the seller for the reasonable expectations as to quality which he has played a part in generating. If one sells in a particular market sector at a certain price it would seem that a signal goes out to the buyer to the effect that a certain minimum level of quality can be expected. The seller knows perfectly well that this expectation exists, indeed he may have played a personal role in raising it via general reputation, advertising, pre-contractual negotiations, sales talk, etc. The buyer (who does not inhabit the artificial world of classical contract law) is hardly behaving unreasonably in focusing upon these various signals coming from the market generally and the seller specifically; and not believing it to be necessary to extract specific commitments in relation to basic quality issues. Indeed he probably imagines himself to be paying for a basic guarantee of quality via the price tendered.

We can now turn to the content of the quality obligation. If the quality obligation is based upon signals sent out by the seller, and the market in which he operates, then what implications does this have for the legal makeup of the obligation? First of all it seems clear that the signals which go along with selling a product at a particular price in a particular market extend beyond the functionality of the product. *Something* is signalled about more refined aspects of quality including appearance, finish reliability, durability etc. However this is not the same as saying that a quality obligation should offer set guarantees under all of these headings. I said that *something* is being signalled on these issues. It may be that, in the particular cirstumstances, what is signalled is that very little can be expected. However the point is that if the quality obligation is to reflect the reasonable expectations of the buyer then it must contain the *potential* to take account of all of the signals which are sent; whether these signals emanate from the market generally or from the reputation of sellers and their pre contractual descriptions, promises and statements.

The old merchantable quality definition in the now repealed s.14(6) ran as follows:

> 'Goods of any kind are of merchantable quality... if they are as fit for the purpose or purposes for which goods of that kind are commonly bought as it is reasonable to expect having regard to any description applied to them, the price (if relevant) and all the other relevant circumstances'.

One of the matters which was at issue in the case of this quality obligation was whether it did, in fact, contain the potential to look much beyond the functional aspects of products. However the judgement of Rougier, J. in the case of *Rogers* v. *Parish (Scarborough) Ltd.* seemed to indicate that the merchantable quality definition was capable to taking a suitably broad view of those factors which go to make up the reasonable expectations of a buyer. He said that a new car should be capable of being driven,

> 'with the appropriate degree of comfort, ease of handling and reliability and ... of pride in the vehicle's outward and interior appearance'

The new test explicitly refers to appearance, finish and freedom from minor defects.

Section 14 now reads:

14(2) Where the seller sells goods in the course of a business there is an implied term that the goods supplied under the contract are of satisfactory quality

(2a) For the purposes of this Act, goods are of satisfactory quality if they meet the standard that a reasonable person would regard as satisfactory, taking account of any description of the gods, the price (if relevant) and all the other relevant circumstances

(2b) For the purposes of this Act, the quality of goods included their state and condition and the following (among others) are in appropriate cases aspects of the quality of goods:-

(a) fitness for all the purposes for which goods of the kind in question are commonly supplied,
(b) appearance and finish,
(c) freedom from minor defects,
(d) safety, and
(e) durability

(2c) The term implied by sub section (2) above does not extend to any matter making the quality of goods unsatisfactory

(a) which is specifically drawn to the buyers' attention before the contract is made
(b) where the buyer examines goods before contract is made, which that examination ought to reveal, and
(c) in the case of a contract for sale by sample, which would have been apparent on a reasonable examination of the sample.

It is clear that we have a general test in sub section 2(a) and a list of criteria relevant to this test, set out in sub section 2(b).

The factors set out in 2(b) must be read in the context of the general test; we are not being told that simply because a product has, for example, a minor defect, (see 2(b)(c)) that is necessarily of unsatisfactory quality. All the factors must be set in the scales to determine if the goods meet the standard that a reasonable person would regard as satisfactory.

However, it is clear that this formulation contains the ability to take account of a wide range of factors on which signals may have been received and expectations raised. In this sense fairness is promoted. I will now consider how this will operate at a less abstract level.

There will be many other circumstances in which it is very clear that products fail the test e.g. by not being able to perform their function at all, or hardly at all, e.g. a car that will not start or will rarely start; a washing machine that does not clean clothes at all or hardly at all; an umbrella which is full of holes or one which collapses constantly, or with the slightest wind.

The real challenge for the test comes with the less clear cut cases e.g. where the car, washing machine or umbrella are erratic rather than nearly useless.

Here the criteria in the test are really put to use. A lower than average price might indicate a lower standard, although, as Ervine has pointed out, the reduction may have been to induce a quick sale rather than to indicate inferior quality (see Ervine, 1995). Of course price may have been reduced for *both* of these purposes e.g. where meat is 'reduced for quick sale' in a supermarket. This must lower the standard such that it need not, perhaps, be as tender as otherwise. Of course it must not give the purchaser food poisoning, or it is clearly not of satisfactory quality.

Description (in advertising material, on packaging, in verbal negotiation etc.) is also very important and can raise or lower the level that a reasonable person thinks is satisfactory. For example, a description which speaks in glowing terms of how a product has been manufactured to the highest standards of design is likely to help to make unsatisfactory a product which turns out not to be useless, but to be erratic.

It seems that the standard may be higher than before when it comes to the fitness for purpose criteria. There is no longer a reference to fitness for 'any of the purposes' for which such goods are commonly supplied but now the reference is to fitness for 'all purposes' for which such goods are commonly supplied. This means that there is less room for a seller to argue, for example, that, even although a four wheel drive vehicle does not perform well on rough terrain, at least it performs satisfactorily on the road.[1]

---

1 See Aswan Engineering Establishment v. Lupdine [1987] 1All ER 135.

If the buyer has a purpose in mind which is not 'common' at all (e.g. to inflate hot water bottles with his lungs as part of a strongman act) then failure to fulfil this purpose is unlikely to make the goods unsatisfactory.[2]

FAIRNESS IN DISPUTE NEGOTIATION

1. The Quality Obligation

If the quality obligation is to be meaningful then the reasonable expectation of quality which it represents must be able to be enforced in some way if it is broken. One difficulty facing consumer buyers in particular is that they are likely to have limited knowledge or understanding of the quality obligation and what standard of quality it entitles them to. In addition consumer buyers may not be able to match the supplier when it comes to the resources of time and money needed to pursue the dispute. It is, after all, the buyer who must do most of the work as it is he who has parted with money and who is in possession of defective goods.

The new obligation improves the position of buyers to the extent that it sets out, in an itemised way, the different aspects which are relevant to satisfactory quality. This restricts the seller's ability to misrepresent the buyer's rights. Under the old (and more opaque) merchantable quality obligation it would have been much easier for a seller to allege that minor defects were not covered or to generally confuse the buyer as to what the quality obligation represented. Now the buyer can point to the specific issues itemised in the new definition, thereby improving his negotiating position. In this way the theoretical fairness of the quality obligation becomes more of a reality in practice.

2. The Right to Reject and Terminate (A)

If a seller is in breach of the quality obligation the buyer may be entitled to reject the goods and terminate the contract (see SGA s.11). There is a distinction between rejection of the goods and termination of the contract. If there is only a right to reject then the buyer probably has to accept a re-tender of the goods. However if there is also a right to terminate the contract then the buyer need not accept a re-tender. If the seller has tendered unsatisfactory goods before the due date for performance then

---

2 However there will be a remedy under SGA s.14(3) if the special purpose has been expressly or impliedly made known.

there is normally no breach of contract; so that although the buyer has a right to reject for non conformity (see s.27 SGA), he has no right to reject *and* terminate under S.11 SGA. In such a case the buyer must allow the seller to re-tender. In a situation where the seller is actually in breach of contract because he has delivered unsatisfactory goods at the due time for performance a buyer's right of rejection will be accompanied by a right of termination. This section will concentrate on the situation where the seller is in breach of contract, so that if the buyer has a right of rejection this also brings with it a right of termination. However even if there is a breach of contract by the seller the right to reject and the concomitant right to terminate does not always arise. This and the following section consider the restrictions which exist, and the fairness issues surrounding these restrictions.

It would seem reasonable to suggest that a fair regime for rejection of goods in the case of supplier breach entails the balancing of the legitimate interests of the two parties. What are those legitimate interests? The buyer would seem to have a legitimate interest in a rejection regime which helps to secure satisfaction of his reasonable expectations of quality. This might suggest a rejection remedy for every breach of the quality obligation. This is because the buyer's expectation of quality is surely one of the most important expectations a buyer has; and it is the right to reject and terminate which comes closest to guaranteeing that the buyer's reasonable quality expectation will be fulfilled. I will elaborate on the reasoning underlying this assertion. A buyer of unsatisfactory goods will obtain goods of satisfactory quality in one of two ways. The first possibility is that the seller will repair or replace the goods. The buyer has no legal right to insist upon repair or replacement. In the absence of such a right, what will encourage the seller to repair or replace, and to do so within a reasonable time? Apart from market forces, or altruism on the seller's part, the seller is most likely to be encouraged to repair or replace by the legal sanctions which can be used against him. Damages will always be available for breach of the quality obligation and the threat of a damages claim may encourage the seller to repair or replace. However this will by no means always be the case. The seller will know that the average consumer buyer, for example, will be unlikely to invest time and resources in the pursuit of a damages claim. The same can probably be said where most commercial buyers are concerned, unless very significant losses are concerned. The threat that the buyer can legitimately reject the goods and terminate the contract seems more likely to encourage the seller to effect adequate repair or replacement.

The other way in which the buyer can secure goods of satisfactory quality is to have a rejection remedy which is actually exercised. The buyer then exercises his choice to terminate the contract, and, having obtained his refund he purchases elsewhere.

The conclusion, from the above analysis, is that buyers should always have the right to reject and terminate for breach of the quality obligation. Before the 1994 Act this was the position (SGA, s.11). However the seller clearly has legitimate interests which pull in the other direction. Rejection and termination are severe remedies resulting in the seller being required to refund the price and take back goods which may have been used. It might be argued, therefore, that the seller, is legitimately entitled to expect that a rejection remedy, and the option of termination which goes with it, should only be allowed where the buyer genuinely needs the remedy for the purposes of securing his reasonable expectations of quality, i.e. that the remedy is not available to the opportunistic buyer, dealing with a seller who is quite prepared to cure, but which buyer has collateral reasons for wishing to avoid the bargain. The most likely collateral reason is that market conditions have changed in a way which makes the purchase less attractive to the buyer.[3] It would, of course, be possible to use a general good faith test, which focused upon the motive of the seller. This could be used to determine whether, in the case of either consumer or commercial buyers, there should be any right to reject and terminate for breach.

This is not the approach that has been taken by the new regime; although it might be argued that this new regime does have the effect, in practice, of catching the worst cases of bad faith. Under the new rules consumer buyers still retain the right to reject for any breach of the quality obligation (SGA, s.15A). It is clear that this does enable some consumers to reject and terminate in bad faith. For example there might be a relatively small breach which the seller is perfectly happy to cure. There is, therefore, no reason for the buyer to use the rejection remedy to obtain goods of satisfactory quality. However it will be uncommon for buyers to insist on rejection and termination unless there is some ulterior motive. The most likely ulterior motive will be where the market has dropped so that the goods are not of the same value to the buyer as he expected them to be at the time of making the contract. However, this is uncommon where consumer purchases are concerned. It can be concluded, therefore, that in practice the basic right to reject and terminate will not normally result in bad faith rejection and termination where consumer buyers are concerned. It is probably better to

3 See Brownsword, 1995, for a discussion of a rational 'reason centred' approach to the whole question of withdrawal for breach of contract

stick to this approach in the case of consumer buyers. An explicit good faith test would require a possibly complex balancing of issues (degree of breach, attitude of both parties to resolution of the dispute, evidence as to broader market conditions etc.). In addition, even if the supplier bore the burden of establishing bad faith, there would be uncertainty. This uncertainty could be exploited by suppliers to persuade ignorant consumers that they had no right to reject (even where the consumer in question had perfectly good faith reasons for rejection and termination).[4]

Where commercial buyers are concerned, the rule now (for England and Wales) is that there can be no rejection and termination for breach, where the breach is so slight as to make rejection unreasonable (SGA s. 15 A). The seller must prove this to be the case. If he cannot do so, the buyer has the right to reject and terminate. We therefore have a departure from the traditional Sale of Goods Act approach, which has been to rest the right to reject and terminate on whether the term broken was classified as a condition (which the quality obligation was and remains). We must now look to the degree of breach. There is no definition of a slight breach. However, it is clear that for a breach to be slight it will have to be very small in proportion to the whole contract. There will be many breaches which are not very serious, but which are clearly more then slight. It must certainly be borne in mind that a slight breach is a long way from one which 'deprives the buyer of substantially the whole benefit of the contract'.[5] A slight breach is also something less than a 'material' breach.[6] So, for example, a computer sold to a business buyer might turn out to have a variety of electrical faults which make it of unsatisfactory quality. This may be fatal to the immediate use of the computer and therefore impossible to speak of as a slight breach. However, it may be that relative to the overall makeup of the computer the defects are not serious and can be put right fairly easily by the seller. However, as the seller cannot show the breach to be slight, the buyer will be able to reject and terminate the contract. There is, clearly, scope for bad faith rejection and termination. A buyer will be able to reject and terminate, even if the seller is being co-operative and is prepared to effect a quick repair or replacement; and in circumstances where the breach is clearly not so serious that it could

4 What would be even less fair on the consumer is the regime suggested by the EU Green Paper on Consumer Guarantees for a European Directive. This would give the seller the choice between offering repair, replacement, refund and reduction in price.

5 See the judgement of Lord Diplock in *Aforos Shipping Co.* v. *Pagnan* [1983] 1 All ER 449 at 455

6 Materiality of breach is the test in Scotland, both for sale of goods (SGA s. 15 B), and generally in contract.

legitimately be said that all confidence in the seller had been lost. Indeed it may, on the facts, be clear that the buyer's real concern is not with the ability or willingness of the seller to supply goods of satisfactory quality; but rather with avoiding a bargain which is less attractive due to a change in market circumstances. In contrast to consumer sales, such market fluctuations are quite likely to occur.

However, the law has chosen to eschew an outright good faith test, and to allow the possibility of bad faith rejections for breaches which are anything more than slight. At the same time we can at least be confident that the new test will catch the worst examples of bad faith rejection, i.e. those cases where the breach is slight.

The buyer can, however, contract out of the rule (see s.15A SGA), so that he can effectively give himself the right to reject (in good or bad faith) for a slight breach. There may be a fairness type control over the buyer's ability to do this. Such a term will be subject to s. 3(2)(b)(i) of the Unfair Contract Terms Act, which says that where using ones own standard terms against another, a term is subject to the test of reasonableness if the term claims to be entitled to 'render a contractual performance substantially different from that which was reasonably expected'.

It may be that a buyer's term which gives the right to reject even where the breach is so slight as to make rejection unreasonable can be said to offer the seller a contractual performance substantially different from that reasonably expected. The contractual performance to which I am referring is the buyer's duty to accept the goods under s. 27 of the SGA and not to reject where the breach is 'so slight, etc.', in terms of s. 15A. It would seem that the 'reasonable expectations' of the seller in this context would have to be constructed from the signals which are sent out by the commercial context, and what has happened in any previous relationships between the parties. If the term does compromise the reasonable expectations of the seller then the test of reasonableness will be applied. Here the court will consider, inter alia, the relative bargaining strengths of the parties; whether the term was in clear language and known of by the seller; whether the seller or buyer was best placed to insure, and whether the buyer offered the seller a choice of terms.[7]

---

7 See *Smith* v. *Bush* [1990], AC 831; *Mitchell* v. *Finney Lock Seeds* [1983] 2 All ER 737 HL; *Knight Machinery* v. *Rennie* 1995 SLT 166.

The Right to Reject and Terminate (B)

Even in circumstances where, having applied the above rules, there is a right to reject and terminate, it can be argued that the seller has further legitimate interests which must be taken into account. Sellers may suffer a considerable loss if they have to take back goods which have suffered a considerable depreciation in value. There must be circumstances in which, even where there has been a breach of the quality obligation, sellers are able to close their ledgers and feel secure that any risk of rejection and termination has passed.

In contracts of sale, this is facilitated by the rules on 'acceptance'. Once the buyer has 'accepted' the goods he loses the right to reject and terminate. The buyer is deemed to have accepted goods when he intimates to the seller that he has accepted them or when the goods have been delivered to him and he does any act in relation to them which is inconsistent with the ownership of the seller, or when, after the lapse of a reasonable time, he retains the goods without intimating to the seller that he has rejected them (Sale of Goods Act 1979, s. 35 as amended by Sale and Supply of Goods Act 1994 s. 2).

For the purposes of this essay I will focus solely on loss of the right to reject and terminate by lapse of a reasonable time.

Where this type of acceptance is concerned the issue is not connected to positive actions taken by the buyer; but rather the lack of action, the apparent acquiescence in the condition of the goods. The question is how long should it be before it can be said that the buyer has so acquiesced; and what are the various buyer and seller interests which should be taken into account in deciding upon what is a reasonable time. The type of product is obviously relevant. It must also be relevant to consider whether there are understandings between these two specific parties or in the commercial sector generally as to how long buyers have to check out goods and get back to the seller. In the absence of very clear guidance from these sources there will always be a difficult balance to strike between the seller's interest in commercial certainty and the buyer's opportunity to discover defects which may not have been patent at the time of sale, or for some time afterwards. The broad question here is whether the importance of certainty is such that a 'reasonable time' means a reasonable time to generally try out the goods; or whether it means a reasonable time to discover the particular defect. This latter approach is prepared to compromise on certainty if it can be said that the buyer could not reasonably have discovered the defect in question.

In the English case of *Bernstein* v. *Pamson Motors* [1987] 2 All ER 200 Rougier, J. took the former view, and held that it was too late to reject a car after three weeks, despite the fact that the defect had manifested itself on the car's first substantial outing and after 142 miles of driving. Rougier, J. placed considerable importance upon the need for commercial certainty. He said that from the seller's point of view it was important to foster 'the commercial certainty of being able to close his ledger reasonably soon after the transaction is completed' (at p. 230). So, on this approach, the need for certainty takes precedence.

The Scottish courts, on the other hand, place the emphasis upon the nature of the defect, and how long it should reasonably take to discover it.[8] Clearly this approach will favour the buyer in cases where there has been a latent defect which could not reasonably have been discovered for some time; and on this approach commercial certainty may be compromised.

Both the English and Scottish approaches described above were taken based on section 35 as it stood prior to amendment by s. 2 of the Sale and Supply of Goods Act 1994. The old provision gave no elaboration upon how to determine when a reasonable time had elapsed. However, there is now guidance in the new s. 35. Subsection 5 says that in considering whether a reasonable time has elapsed it is material to consider whether the buyer has had a reasonable opportunity of examining the goods to ascertain whether they conform to the contract. There are two points here. First of all it does seem that as this factor is now relevant to the overall test then the type of defect is clearly relevant. After all the reasonable opportunity for examination is for the purposes of determining whether goods conform to the contract. A latent defect which makes the goods of unsatisfactory quality means that they do not conform to the contract. Surely, then, this criteria demands a reasonable opportunity to discover latent defects. The second point, however, is that subsection 5 makes it clear that this criteria is only one which may be taken into account. The criteria are to 'include' the question as to whether there was an opportunity for examination. It might, therefore, be argued that, on the facts of a particular case, the needs of commercial certainty were most important; so that a latent defect could not reasonably have been discovered earlier. However I would submit that there is some significance in the statutory provision singling out the reasonable opportunity criteria. It must be Parliament's intention that some sort of priority be given to this criteria. The Scottish courts seem to treat this as a main and overriding criteria even on the old test which did not elaborate on the reasonable time concept at all. Even if it is not treated by

---

[8] *Hyslop* v. *Shirlaw* (1905) 7 F 875.

the English courts as an overriding factor then I would submit that it should be given priority. This can be done by only allowing the certainty criteria to cut into the equation after a reasonable period. In other words the fundamental question should be whether the buyer could reasonably have discovered the defect in question. There would however be a certain point (depending on the type of product) when the right to reject would be lost for certainty reasons even if the defect in question could not reasonably have been discovered.

CONCLUDING COMMENT

This essay has considered the role of several types of fairness rule in the creation of quality obligations and the resolution of disputes. It has associated the creation quality obligations with the enforcement of reasonable expectations. It has also discussed the balancing of interests at dispute stage, and the role of good faith in this context.

REFERENCES

Adams J. and Brownsword R.(1988) 'Law Jobs, Law Reform and Law Commission No. 160, 51 *Modern Law Review*

Brownsword R. (1995) in Bradgate R., Birds J., and Villiers C.,Termination of Contracts Wiley, Chancery.

Department of Trade and Industry (1992), Consumer Guarantees

Ervine, (1995) Sale and Supply of Goods Act 1994, Scots Law Times, 1.

Law Commission (1987), Report No. 160 on Sale and Supply of Goods

Willett C., (1991) 'The Unacceptable Face of the Consumer Guarantees Bill', 54 *Modern Law Review* 552-562

Willett C., (1993) 'The Quality of Goods and the Rights of Consumers', 42 *Northern Ireland Legal Quarterly* 218-232

7. Customers, Chains and Networks

Hugh Beale

INTRODUCTION

One of the difficulties of the notion of fairness is to distinguish it from rules which simply support the market. If, as economists have argued, one of the functions of contract law is to provide a set of 'default rules' to apply when nothing on the question at issue has been agreed expressly between the parties, and thereby to reduce the cost of transacting, many of the rules of contract law are simply to enable the parties to obtain what they wanted without the need for negotiation. But many of the rules of 'fairness' seem to me to have exactly the same function. Once we move away from cases where there has clearly been either obvious substantive unfairness (eg gross overcharging for goods or services) caused by conscious advantage-taking (fraud or unconscionable behaviour), several bodies of rules seem to me to be concerned merely to prevent the risk of parties accidentally agreeing to things that they didn't want. Thus the protection of the Unfair Contract Terms Act 1977 is, I have submitted elsewhere, primarily aimed at preventing unfair surprise and lack of choice (Beale 1986 and 1989). But both are caused by cost – the cost to the consumer of discovering what the small print contains and means; the cost to the supplier of using different terms for each customer. In each case the customer could in theory spend the necessary resources to get what he or she wants (Schwartz 1974). In other words, what is often thought of in terms of welfarism can equally be explained in terms of smoothing the operation of the market and the correction of inefficiencies caused by the presence of transactions costs. The rules on common mistake and frustration present the same kind of dilemma: they can be justified as basic fairness or in terms of the law mimicking what the parties would have agreed had the combination of the low probability of the event and the cost of negotiation not precluded this.

It is this broad notion of fairness which I am referring to in this paper. The rules and proposals which I wish to discuss are concerned not with unfair clauses but with a rather different problem which, if the argument just made is accepted, is just as much one of fairness.

Modern contracting is frequently not just a phenomenon of mass contracting, in which individual negotiation is uncommon. It is often also a phenomenon of 'dealing' with not only the individual with whom one happens to contract but with a group: a chain of distribution, for example, or a network of parties who are between them providing the goods or services being purchased. Thinking of my own experience of contracting I am conscious that my expectations are not just of performance by the party with whom I am immediately contracting, but also by others in the group; and that my expectations of what I am to get are created by others in the chain or network as much as by the party with whom I happen to contract. I do not have empirical evidence to back up my own anecdotes, but there is some caselaw which suggests that I am not alone. I think there might be rather more caselaw if English law provided any possibility of arguing for liability in some of the situations.

The paper looks at the two aspects just identified.

1. The first is the liability of the parties in the chain or network other than the immediate contracting party when the goods or services provided are in some way 'defective'. For example, the plaintiff has bought goods which were made not by the immediate contracting party (S) but by a manufacturer (M) (Case 1: this is simply a chain of distribution), or has contracted with a contractor (C) for services which are in fact performed by a Sub-contractor (SC) (Case 2: this will be a 'network' in the terms used by Adams and Brownsword 1990), and the goods or services are defective. Can the plaintiff recover from M or SC?
2. The second is the remedy the ultimate purchaser may have for things said by other parties in the chain or network and on which he relied in deciding to contract; for example the plaintiff has decided to purchase the goods or to contract for the services in reliance on information given not by S or C but by M or SC. Here the paper looks at both the liability of the other party to the immediate contract for what was said by M or SC and that of the party who makes the statement relied on.

To some extent English law already recognises the existence of the chain or network. First, where a defect in the goods or services causes personal injury or damage to property, there may well be liability in tort or under the Consumer Protection Act 1987. But if the goods or services are simply defective and have to be repaired, and if the defect causes the plaintiff consequential economic loss (eg the cost of hiring a replacement while repairs are carried out, or some other economic loss) recovery is much more problematic.

Second, the Consumer Credit Act 1974 recognises that there should be joint liability when the Creditor who supplies the finance and the Supplier who provides the goods are effectively engaged in a joint venture.[1] That may be described as 'horizontal' joint liability. This paper is concerned with 'vertical' liability.

The questions raised are to my mind not easy, if only because the traditional categories of contract and tort and the extent of responsibility associated with each do not provide appropriate answers, particularly on the measure of damages.[2] I think the questions are also quite important. There are a number of situations in which a plaintiff who is not very careful may find herself without an effective remedy against anyone. As mentioned earlier, I have no empirical evidence as to the extent of the problems caused by the lack of a remedy, but my guess is that they are not insignificant. And the matter is topical. A variety of moves to tackle these issues are being made by the Department of Trade & Industry and at EC level, most notably in the recent EC *Green Paper on Consumer Guarantees* (1993) and the discussion document circulated by DGIII on the 'inheritance principle' formulated by GAIPEC for construction. There are also interesting developments in other countries inside and outside the EU.

Obviously some of the proposals being discussed are primarily aimed at consumer protection (and, in the case of the EC, also at improving the internal market by levelling the playing field and increasing consumer confidence in cross-border shopping). This is the context in which I started to think of these issues. But I am not all sure that the reforms should stop with consumer cases. It is partly this which makes me wonder whether the underlying theme is fairness rather than support of the market. However, we are now accustomed to think of business being protected by Unfair Contract Terms Act 1977 against unreasonable exclusion clauses; that is really no more a question of fairness than my topic.

There is also the work being done by the Law Commission on reform of privity of contract (1991). For reasons which will become clear later, what I want to suggest as ways of dealing with the problems outlined go rather beyond what I personally would like to see as a general reform of privity.

---

1 Consumer Credit Act 1974, ss.12 and 75.

2 I do not have space to consider other questions such as the strictness of liability.

CASE 1: GOODS WHICH ARE DEFECTIVE BECAUSE OF A FAULT IN MANUFACTURE.

It is trite law that in this situation the plaintiff's remedy is against the seller, who is then expected to pass the loss back up the chain of contracts to the party whose breach, if not whose fault, was the origin of the problem. English law supports this process by holding each seller in the chain responsible for the defect, even if it was not its fault and it had no choice about which goods to supply or from whom it had to obtain the goods because the type had been specified by the seller and was only obtainable from one source.[3]

In practice there are a number of reasons why the chain of contracts may not give the plaintiff any effective protection. Most obviously the chain may be broken at the first link.

This can happen for purely legal reasons. In *Gloucestershire County Council* v. *Richardson*[4] a contractor was instructed to obtain pre-cast concrete beams from a supplier who would supply only on limited liability terms. The main contract did not give a right of objection to this nomination, although there was such a right of objection to the nomination of an unsuitable sub-contractor. The ratio of the case is not wholly clear but in that combination of circumstances the House of Lords held that the contractor was not subject to the usual implied obligations as to the quality of the beams. In practical terms the result is perverse; the party who has rights against the supplier (i.e. the contractor) suffers no loss, whereas the party who suffers the loss (the employer or customer) has no remedy.

More usually the chain will be broken for practical reasons. The most obvious one is that the retailer with whom the customer dealt has become insolvent or gone out of business. Should that leave the customer without a remedy? I would argue that it should not, for two reasons. First, although it might be argued that it is for the customer to assess the financial position or stability of the retailer with whom it deals, I doubt whether this is realistic under modern marketing conditions. It is of course common to run credit checks when 'monetary' credit is being extended; and it may sometimes be done when a product or process with an extended warranty, such as double-glazing or damp-proofing treatments, is being considered. I suspect that not even business buyers would run financial checks in simple sales cases except for very major purchases. The risk would not normally justify the cost. Of course, there is the obvious response that the customer

3 *Young & Marten Ltd.* v. *McManus Childs Ltd.* [1969] 1 AC 454.
4 [1969] 1 AC 480.

has chosen to take the risk and now should not complain. But that doesn't meet the second argument, which is that vis-a-vis the manufacturer, the retailer's insolvency or disappearance is entirely fortuitous. Why should the manufacturer escape just because the retailer has been wound up?

The other reason for a break in the chain is what I call the *Lambert* v. *Lewis*[5] problem; the customer bought the manufacturer's goods from a retailer but cannot prove which one. To have bought defective goods and to have forgotten from whom might look like carelessness; but I am less critical. To me it is simply a reflection of the modern reality of the purchase of branded goods. For example, I search around for some time to discover which computer printer I want to buy; but I then obtain it from whichever discount supplier is offering the best deal. If I am a consumer, I suppose I will be careful with the receipt, and the receipt will show me who I should sue; but if a business buyer is buying several of the items at different times it may be quite difficult to track which one came from which supplier. That was what happened in *Lambert* v. *Lewis*.

On the present law the customer who cannot recover from the retailer because the latter has gone out of business, or for one of the other reasons mentioned, will sometimes not be able to recover at all. Since *Murphy* v. *Brentwood District Council*[6], buying a defective product is treated as a form of economic loss. The customer cannot sue the manufacturer for the money wasted on the cost of the product, nor for any consequential economic loss such as the cost of hiring a replacement or loss of profit while the item is being repaired. Recovery is permitted only for physical injury or damage caused by the defect.[7]

There may be an exception to this if the *Junior Books* case[8] applies. But if this case is correctly to be seen as an application of *Hedley Byrne & Co. Ltd* v. *Heller & Partners Ltd.*[9], this exception appears to be limited to defects caused by the negligence of nominated sub-contractors and some nominated suppliers. It certainly will not cover liability to the normal purchaser, consumer or otherwise, of goods. Lord Roskill was quite definite about this in *Junior Books*:[10]

---

5 *Lexmead (Basingstoke) Ltd.* v. *Lewis* [1982] AC 225.

6 [1991] 1 AC 398.

7 If a component fails and damages the rest of the item, the customer may recover the cost of repairing that damage from the manufacturer of the component although he cannot recover anything from the manufacturer of the item as a whole. Pick your defendants for the next action carefully please...

8 *Junior Books Ltd.* v. *Veitchi Co Ltd.* [1983] 1 AC 520.

9 [1964] AC 465.

10 At pp.546-547.

> The concept of proximity must always involve, at least in most cases, some degree of reliance... and as between an ultimate purchaser and a manufacturer [proximity] would not easily be found to exist in the everyday transaction of purchasing chattels when it is obvious that in truth the real reliance was upon the immediate vendor and not upon the manufacturer.

If Lord Roskill intended this description to apply to most consumer purchases, with respect I cannot accept his reasoning. I think that consumers do not usually buy, as he seems to suggest they do, in reliance on the retailer. Very frequently they buy in reliance on the brand. But I think his conclusion was correct. The problem, I would submit, is parallel to *Caparo Industries plc v. Dickman.*[11] There it was held that there will be no liability in tort for negligent misrepresentation unless the maker of the statement knew that the statement would be communicated to the person relying on it, either as an individual or as a member of a specified class, specifically in connection with a particular transaction or a transaction of a particular kind. In relation to our situation, the second requirement appears to mean that the misrepresentation must have been made in connection with the contract in respect of which relief is sought, or at least that reliance on the representation in connection with the contract was likely. But the manufacturer will usually know nothing of the individual buyer unless there have been direct discussions between them. This will occur with nominated sub-contractors but not with all nominated suppliers, let alone other manufacturers.

Of course in many situations manufacturers of branded goods give a guarantee to the consumer or other customer. As Chris Willett (1993) has pointed out, there may be doctrinal difficulties over the enforceability of these, though I suspect the problems are more apparent than real: in practice it seems to me that if the customer has bought goods which had the normal 'repair or replace' guarantee the manufacturer will have difficulty displacing the common sense presumption that the customer did so in reliance on the guarantee, and this should overcome any problem of consideration. The DTI (1992) has proposed that in any event such guarantees should be legally enforceable, I cannot imagine that many would dissent from this. But manufacturer's guarantees are not always very generous, and they do not have to be, and are not always given even for branded goods. So should a guarantee with some minimum content in effect be made compulsory for goods sold under a manufacturer's brand name? And should this extend also to unbranded goods?

One possible way of approaching this would be via reform of the doctrine of privity of contract. The Law Commission (1991, para. 6.3)

---

[11] [1990] 2 AC 605.

provisionally proposed that a third person should be able to enforce a contract which the parties intended to benefit him and under which they intended him to have an enforceable right. If this were to be adopted, it would be possible to treat the ultimate buyer[12] as an intended beneficiary of the contract between the manufacturer and the distributor, wholesaler or retailer to whom the manufacturer sells. I am not sure, however, that this would be the best approach to reform of privity. My own view is that there is danger in presuming an intention to confer an enforceable benefit too easily, because it will be hard to predict one's contractual liability: it might lead to the indeterminate liability which the House of Lords in recent tort cases has done so much to try to avoid. Therefore my view is that if the doctrine of privity is to be modified along the general lines suggested, it may be better to treat parties as being intended beneficiaries only when that was stated expressly or by necessary implication. A strict test would exclude the customer who is not mentioned and of whom the manufacturer will know nothing (Beale 1995). Rather I am in favour of specific rules to enable the disappointed buyer to reach the manufacturer.

Several Western systems of law already have such rules. In Belgian and French law the *garantie des vices cachées* is treated as running with the goods and giving the owner a remedy against any seller in the chain, provided the defects are of a certain seriousness. Under Article 1646 of the Code Civil,

> Si le vendeur ignorait les vices de la chose, il ne sera tenu qu'à la restitution du prix, et à rembourser à l'acquéreur les frais occasionés par la vente.

Thus the manufacturer would have to repay the price plus the costs of returning the goods to him. Under Article 1645, a knowing seller is liable in damages:

> Si le vendeur connaisait les vices de la chose, il est tenu, outre la restitution du prix qu'il a reçude tous les dommages et intérêts envers l'acheteur.

It is well known that *la jurisprudence* in each country has established a presumption that a professional seller knew of the defect. In Belgian law this presumption is rebuttable, but in France it is irrebuttable.[13]

In this country the DTI has canvassed making the manufacturer liable along with the seller (1992, p.9). It proposes safeguards to ensure that the

---

[12] Or end-user. I have not considered the position of donees and the like here, though the problem needs to be tackled.

[13] The position in German Law is that the manufacturer is not liable. One might have thought that the contract between the manufacturer and the next party in the chain could have been treated as having protective effects vis-a-vis the end-user, or that the theory of transferred loss might have been used to assist the latter party (see Markesinis (1987).

manufacturer would not be liable when the goods are defective only because of some unexpected description applied to them by the retailer or because of the price at which the latter sells them. A similar rule with equivalent safeguards has already been enacted in New Zealand. The Consumer Guarantees Act 1993 provides:

25. Circumstances where consumers have right of redress against manufacturers -

This Part of this Act gives a consumer a right of redress against a manufacturer of goods where –

(a) The goods fail to comply with the guarantee as to acceptable quality set out in s.6 of this Act:

(b) The goods fail to comply with the guarantee as to correspondence with description set out in s.9 of this Act due to the failure of the goods to correspond with any description applied to the goods by or on behalf of the manufacturer or with the express or implied consent of the manufacturer:

...

(d) The goods fail, during the currency of the guarantee, to comply with any express guarantee given by the manufacturer in accordance with s.14 of this Act.

26. Exceptions to right of redress against manufacturers –

Notwithstanding s. 25 of this Act, there shall be no right of redress against the manufacturer under this Act in respect of goods which –

(a) Fail to comply with the guarantee of acceptable quality only because of –

(i) An act or default or omission of, or any representation made by, any person other than the manufacturer or a servant or agent of the manufacturer; or

(ii) A cause independent of human control, occurring after the goods have left the control of the manufacturer; or

(iii) The price charged by the supplier being higher than the manufacturer's recommended retail price or the average retail price:

...

The recent EC Green Paper on *Guarantees for Consumer Goods* (1993) also suggests that so far as the so-called 'legal guarantee' is concerned, the manufacturer and the seller should be jointly liable, with similar exclusions for expectations created only by the retailer (at p.87). The Green Paper also raises another reason for making the manufacturer liable: the goods may be bought in a country in which the consumer is not normally resident. There would be a tremendous practical advantage to the consumer if she could proceed directly against the manufacturer, particularly if legislation were to provide that the action might be brought against any subsidiary or authorized dealer of the manufacturer in the consumer's own country.

A proposal with very similar effects is currently under consideration in the U.S. by the committee working on a new draft of Article 2 of the Uniform Commercial Code. The draft of 29 July 1994 would make the manufacturer's warranty to its buyer extend to future buyers, and the proposal is not limited to consumer buyers.[14]

We may anticipate that manufacturers will not welcome additional liability; but if there is hostility, would it be justified? In so far as the cost of repairing or replacing the goods is concerned, I suggest that it would not. Manufacturers effectively bear the risk of this already, either via the 'commercial guarantee' given direct to customers or down the chain of contracts. Manufacturers frequently use limitation of liability clauses in their contracts, but in my experience they do usually accept at least this degree of liability.

What I suspect manufacturers might be much less ready to take on would be liability beyond the cost of repair or replacement. I believe[15] that guarantees are usually limited to this or perhaps allow for a refund of the price; and so, I believe, is the responsibility of the manufacturer down the chain of contracts.

Given that this type of limitation of liability clause is found even in commercial situations, one has to ask why. Even in commercial situations it may be an example of manufacturers passing risks onto unwitting contracting parties in order to reduce their costs;[16] but it seems more plausible to suggest that it is an efficient arrangement knowingly agreed to by the parties because of the cost of requiring the manufacturer to bear liability which is uncertain in extent.

Posner and Rosenfield, (1977) in the context of frustration, suggested that in the absence of transactions costs, the parties would normally allocate risks of losses to the superior risk bearer. This would primarily be the lower cost avoider, i.e. the party best positioned to prevent the loss occurring. For risks which neither can avoid, the risk should be allocated to the superior insurer. But these two indicators may point in different directions. Even if, as I assume is the case, the manufacturer is the lower

---

14 The text of the draft article 2-318 is appended. I am most grateful to Professor Don Clifford of the University of North Carolina for keeping me up to date on these developments.

15 As yet I have no empirical evidence.

16 Cf. what seems to happen with exemption clauses; particularly in consumer contracts: see Beale (1989).

cost avoider, if the extent of its liability is uncertain because it does not have adequate information about the buyer's or end-user's losses, it may be cheaper for the latter to insure (or self-insure). Provided that the manufacturer is left with sufficient liability to give it an adequate incentive to produce its goods carefully, it may be cheaper for the buyer or end-user to bear the uncertain losses itself, since it will have better information and can therefore insure more cheaply. In other words, it may be efficient for the manufacturer to limit its liability to repair or replacement.

Of course this analysis runs into the perennial difficulty of economic analysis; it all depends on the relative costs and these will vary from situation to situation. But the practice on guarantees, even (I believe) in relatively well-informed markets, and on contracts in the chain, make me suspect that what I have suggested may not be far from the truth in most cases. Thus I think the manufacturer should definitely be liable for the cost of repairing or replacing the goods, or possibly refunding the price; but I am much less sure that it should bear the same full liability for consequential loss as the retailer does.

It is noticeable that several of the proposed systems would limit the manufacturer's liability in this way. The DTI's proposal is not wholly clear,[17] but the EC Green Paper proposals seem to limit the manufacturer's responsibility.

> The purchaser would only be entitled to require the manufacturer to either to replace or to repair the product; however, the latter would also be liable for direct losses suffered by the consumer (price paid or reduction in value of the good) in the event that such a replacement or repair was not or could not be realised (at p.8).

The draft proposals for reform of the UCC seem to be the same. Draft Section 2-318 would make the manufacturer liable to the consumer, but under para. d(2) the manufacturer who has replaced the goods or refunded the price would then escape liability for damages except for 'cidental damages' – the cost of returning the goods in, etc.

It is this possible need to limit the manufacturer's liability which makes me think that the existing categories of tort and contract are not very helpful; it is a measure of liability not known to either.

I do wonder however whether the EC and the UCC reformers have the measure of liability quite right. The most obvious form of consequential economic loss is the cost of hiring a replacement while the defective article is being repaired or replaced. The extent of that liability does not seem hard to calculate and I would have thought there was a strong case for

---

17 As Chris Willett (1993) points out, on p.10 the DTI refer to repair or replacement; but I am not sure they meant to limit liability to this.

including this liability – if only to give the manufacturer an adequate incentive to get on and repair or replace.

CASE 2: THE DEFECTIVE SERVICE PROVIDED BY A SUBCONTRACTOR.

Although in many ways the subcontractor who has been accepted by the customer[18] seems to be in an analogous position to the manufacturer, and even though a construction subcontractor is *par excellence* an example of a network contractor,[19] I find this case rather more difficult. There are a number of reasons for this.

One complication is that it is far more likely that the chain will be broken because of what appears to have happened in the *Junior Books* case: the customer may have entered a final settlement with the contractor before realising the extent of the problem. As Atiyah (1989 at p.397) has pointed out, the settlement may have included an element for the risk that the sub-contractor's work would prove defective and, if it did, it would seem wrong to allow the customer to recover again from the sub.[20] How likely it actually is that the settlement would have included such an element I do not know.

A second difference is that, at least in major construction projects, parties are very much aware of the risks of insolvency, and there is not the same justification for allowing a party who has misjudged. his contracting party to by-pass the insolvency and sue the party at fault directly

The third complication may only be the product of my imagination; but I wonder whether the parties in such a case would not prefer the liabilities of the subcontractors to be 'channelled' through the main contractor. Perhaps I can best illustrate what I mean by a slightly different example. On a project involving several subcontractors a delay by one of them may well impede another. At present the subcontractor who is impeded will have a claim against the contractor; the contractor will in turn have to make a claim against the subcontractor in breach. I am not at all sure that the parties would want the subcontractors to be directly liable to each other because of the complications which might arise from multiple claims over

---

18 This would include both the nominated subcontractor and one to whom the customer has given assent (standard forms often require the Employer's or Architect's/ Engineer's consent to subcontracting). The case of the subcontractor of whom the customer knows nothing I mention below.

19 See Adams and Brownsword, 1990.

20 Discussed by Beyleveld and Brownsword (1991).

the same incidents. It may be – and I put it no higher than this – that the same concern might be felt in relation to defective work: it might be better for claims to be channelled through the Contractor to simplify procedures. I am not sure that this would really apply, however, in respect of claims arising after the end of the maintenance period; and in any event it may be a case for the kind of 'breakdown' principle – liability which applies only when the normal chain is broken – canvassed some time ago by Beyleveld and Brownsword (1991).

A last complication is that in a complex undertaking such as construction there is a greater chance that a defect will be caused by the fault of more than one party.[21] At present this will involve the parties each being liable but the one who is sued being able to claim contribution from the other.[22]

To some extent English law already makes the person doing the work liable. Defective Premises Act 1972, section 1 imposes responsibility on anyone taking on work in respect of a dwelling house to see that the work is done in a workmanlike manner. As Spencer (1974) pointed out, it is far from clear what the measure of damages under this section will be but I assume it will at least include the cost of doing the repairs, as the Law Commission (No. 40, at p.9) was concerned in the section to deal with 'defects of quality'.

More extensive proposals are under discussion at the EC level. In 1993 DGIII circulated a Commission Staff Discussion paper concerning possible Community action with regard to liabilities and guarantees in the construction sector, which contained a set of recommendations made by GAIPEC (Groupe des Associations InterProfessionelles Européenes de la Construction). The basic thrust of these was to make each participant in the construction process liable to the owner for the time being of the building.[23] It is interesting to note that the paper envisaged liability extending beyond the cost of repair to cover loss of rent when a binding lease was in existence when the damage was discovered (see para. D11(2) of the extracts). On the other hand the participant would only be liable for its own share of the loss (para. D9(3)). I understand that this limitation has been quite significant reason for some sectors of the British construction industry being prepared to accept the proposals. It is this which makes me think that in other contexts the manufacturer might be expected to bear the equivalent liability, ie cost of hiring a replacement.

---

21 This can happen in sales situations also: eg the defect in a new car which the dealer carelessly fails to spot when it does the pre-delivery inspection.

22 Civil Liability (Contribution) Act 1978, s.1.

23 Relevant extracts are set out in the appendix. I understand that consultation did not produce a clear response and that the proposals are being considered further by DGIII.

Conclusions on Cases 1 and 2

My conclusion is that there is a good case for making sure that the customer who has bought goods which carry the manufacturer's brand name and which are defective because of default on the part of the manufacturer has rights against the latter. There is a reasonably strong one in favour of similar liability on the part of sub-contractors who have done defective work.

Unbranded goods

What about the case of the manufacturer of unbranded goods? My argument that the customer buys in reliance on the manufacturer rather than the retailer does not work in such a case. The argument that the manufacturer only escapes by chance still holds. And if the manufacturer of unbranded goods should escape, why should not also the manufacturer who has branded its goods but with a name of which the customer has never heard? Neither the New Zealand Statute nor the regimes provisionally proposed by the DTI or the EC draw any distinction between branded and unbranded goods. I am not inclined to do so either; nor to distinguish between contractors to whom the customer has assented and those to whom he has not.

But in each case I think there may be arguments for limiting the liability to the cost of repair or replacement plus the cost of hiring a substitute (or loss of rental where the item is hired out.)

Limitation of liability clauses

What should be the effect if the manufacturer in its contract of sale, or the subcontractor in the subcontract, has inserted a clause limiting its liability; or if there is a limitation of liability clause in the contract of sale between retailer and customer or in the main building contract?

Space precludes a detailed consideration of this. I will give only a brief outline of my provisional view, using the construction contract example.

If it is to be established that subcontractors should be directly liable to clients for defective work, I am not clear why a clause in a contract to which the client is not a party should be seen as reducing the client's entitlement. I see the relevance of the clause if the liability was previously unknown; the imposition of liability might result in the imposition of wholly unlooked-for risks. But surely this would not apply to an established form of liability, any more than a clause in a manufacturer's contract with its wholesaler should affect a consumer's right to sue for damage caused by negligence on the manufacturer's part. I would accept that the customer's rights should be limited if it has expressly or impliedly consented to such a limitation of the sub's liability.[24] A fortiori I would give effect to the clause if the customer has accepted a similar clause in his own contract, as in *Norwich City Council* v. *Harvey.*[25]

If the clause is in the main contract, I would solve the problem by asking whether it was intended to benefit the sub. This will usually depend on the wording of the clause. If the clause is worded neutrally (eg a maximum liability 'for any defect') I am personally not inclined to read that as intended to benefit the subcontractor just because the parties are linked in a network.[26] I am not convinced that a party who gives up its rights against one participant in the network even presumptively intends to the same against others, of whom it may know little or nothing.[27]

CASE 3: THE CUSTOMER WHO BUYS GOODS OR CONTRACTS FOR SERVICES ON THE BASIS OF INCORRECT INFORMATION GIVEN BY THE MANUFACTURER OR SPECIALIST SUBCONTRACTOR

English law strikes me as unduly restrictive of liability when the customer buys goods or contracts for services on the basis of incorrect information given by the manufacturer or specialist subcontractor. The other party to the contract, the seller or contractor, will be liable only if in some form or other it repeats the information: for example by applying the manufacturer's description to the goods, passing on the manufacturer's product information in the form of a representation or giving an undertaking as to fitness for purpose in reliance on the manufacturer's statements. But if a customer buys goods in reliance on what it has read elsewhere (even, perhaps, if it

---

24 Cf. *Morris* v. *CW Martin & Sons Ltd.* [1966] 1 QB 716 and *The Pioneer Container* [1994] 2 AC 324, both of which were cases of sub-bailment. See further Beale, 1995

25 [1989] 1 WLR 828. In that case it was appropriate to find that there was no duty at all on the subcontractor because the employer had accepted all risks of fire; if the clause had been one merely limiting liability the technical difficulties would have been that much greater.

26 C.F. Adams and Brownsword (1990).

27 I would however accept that clauses are intended to benefit employees of the parties covered by the clause: cf the *London Drugs* case [1993] 1 WLR 1, noted by Adams and Brownsword 1993.

could have obtained the same information from the seller but did not ask for it and was not given it) the seller will not be responsible.[28]

Again, I suspect that this does not conform to the way that we often shop for goods nowadays. I select the model of printer I want to buy by reading information in a variety of places – manufacturers' advertisements made in magazines, leaflets read in shops where I go to see what the various models look like – and then I order the model I want from the discount supplier, not thinking to get the supplier to repeat the information which I may have read half a dozen times before. If it's wrong – for example, if the printer won't do anything like 700 pages of print per ink cartridge even if it's not in any other sense defective – I think I should have a remedy, but I am far from clear that I have one. Decided cases indicate that the same problem arises in construction contracts with information from suppliers and from specialist subcontractors.[29]

It is also notoriously difficult to recover directly from the maker of the statement. In the absence of fraud, recovery would have to be on the basis of either negligent misstatement or of a collateral contract. Both are limited by what strike me as essentially similar requirements. As I argued earlier, the *Caparo* case seems to mean that there must be some fairly detailed knowledge of the plaintiff's purposes, and a statement made in relation to the particular transaction. In any event it has been held that there will not normally be the necessary special relationship between manufacturer and purchaser.[30] It is not easy to state what must be shown to establish a collateral contract on the basis of information given by the manufacturer. There must be a undertaking made with intent to create contractual relations and there must be consideration. It is the intention that is problematic. Courts tend to content themselves with inscrutable statements that there is or is not such intention on the facts. However I suggest that on the present authorities[31] there must be a specific statement to the customer in relation to a particular transaction which the customer is then thinking of entering. Manufacturer's publicity does not count;[32] nor, I suspect, would information given over the phone unless the caller gave its name and stated its requirements in some detail.

---

28 See also Willett, 1993.

29 E.g. *Shanklin Pier Co v. Detel Products Ltd* [1951] 2 KB 854; *University of Warwick* v. *Sir Robert McAlpine* (1988) 42 BLR 1.

30 *Lambert* v. *Lewis* [1980] 2 WLR 299 (CA).

31 *Shanklin Pier*, above; *Wells (Mertsham) Ltd. v. Buckland Sand & Silica Co.* Ltd. [1965] 2 QB 170; *IBA* v. *EMI* (1980) 14 BLR 1; *Lambert* v. *Lewis* [1982] AC 225, 262-263.

32 *Lambert* v. *Lewis*, above.

I am not at all clear why English law is so restrictive. Statements made in the course of negotiating a direct contract between the two parties are treated as warranties provided the speaker is relatively expert[33] and the information is of obvious importance.[34] It hardly lies in the mouth of a manufacturer to say that information given out to boost sales of its product is unimportant. There must be some policy reason behind the restrictive attitude of the English courts but I am not sure what it is. The arguments used to justify restrictions on liability for negligent misstatements generally - that information is costly to produce but may be passed on, so that full liability for foreseeable losses might deter production of the information do not seem to me to apply to information deliberately produced to boost sales (Bishop 1981).

A traditional answer to the customer who has been misled in this way is that it should have safeguarded itself by getting a warranty from the manufacturer or specialist subcontractor, or by ensuring that the retailer or contractor confirmed or took responsibility for the information. But again I do not think that this is realistic in modern conditions. First, I am sure that large numbers of people buying products or services in the way that I have described do not realise the need for such safeguards and it is obvious that I do not find their ignorance inexcusable. Second, even if they realise the problem, obtaining acceptance of responsibiltiy by the manufacturer or the retailer may be very time-consuming.

I admit that this is not just a matter of welfarism to protect those not sophisticated enough to protect themselves. Rather, it is curing inefficiencies caused by the presence, in the real world, of substantial transactions costs. In the transactions costs-free world imagined by economists, the parties – presumably all the actors involved – would negotiate until the most efficient set of rights and duties had been agreed. I am at least sure that it would be agreed that either the manufacturer or the retailer would be responsible for this information, since otherwise the correct incentives to be careful in producing information will be lacking. In practice, there are negotiation costs which make it not worthwhile to negotiate such complex arrangements for anything except very major purchases. This is true however sophisticated the parties. Just as I argued at the start of the paper the law often now tries to do with exclusion clauses, the law should also here mimic what would have been agreed in the absence of transactions costs.

---

[33] *Dick Bentley Productions Ltd* v. *Harold Smith (Motors) Ltd.* [1965] 1 WLR 623.

[34] Ibid. and *Bannerman* v. *White* (1861) 10 CBNS 844.

Who should be responsible: the manufacturer, the retailer or both? This topic has not been so much discussed. Both the DTI and the EC Green Paper assume that the Manufacturer's 'commercial guarantee', as the Green Paper terms it, should be legally enforceable: but they appear to be confining their consideration to the kind of 'repair or replace' warranty considered earlier.[35] Statements such as the one about the number of pages that the printer will print per cartridge or about the suitability of paint for a particular application are unlikely to be covered.

There seem to be two possible approaches. One is to recognise that the consumer's expectations are created by the manufacturer's advertising as much as by the retailer and to hold the latter liable. Thus the Dutch BW 7:8 provides:

> In determining whether a thing pursuant to a consumer sale conforms to the contract, information regarding the thing made public by or on behalf of a previous seller of that thing, acting in the course of a profession or business, is deemed to be information from the seller, except that the latter neither knew or ought to know certain information, or that he has clearly contradicted it.

§203 of the Nordic Sale of Goods Act, now in force in Sweden, has a similar provision but not limited to consumers (see appendix). This approach has its attractions. The retailer benefits from the manufacturer's advertising; should it not be responsible for it at least subject to the safeguards mentioned?

Giving a remedy against the retailer, who will usually be closer to hand,[36] has obvious practical advantages. On the other hand, retailers will argue that this might impose a significant burden on them to check the advertising of thousands of products about which they may not know a great deal. They might have difficulties in passing the loss back to the errant advertiser, particularly if they have no direct contract with it. And I am not sure that this model fits so well with my conception of modern sales of branded goods, which is that the customer looks primarily to the manufacturer not the retailer. The latter is just a distributive outlet.

Therefore I am more attracted to making the manufacturer directly responsible. This seems to be approach taken in New Zealand. Consumer Guarantees Act 1993, section 2, defines 'express guarantee' as

---

[35] Similarly Irish Sale of Goods and Supply of Services Act 1980, s.15:
'In sections 16 to 19, 'guarantee' means any document, notice or other written statement, howsoever described, supplied by a manufacturer or other supplier, other than a retailer, in connection with the supply of goods and indication that the manufacturer or other supplier will service, repair or otherwise deal with the goods following purchase.'

[36] Except, of course, in cases on cross-border shopping when someone abroad buys something made in her home state.

> an undertaking, assertion or representation in relation to ... (a) The quality, performance or characteristics of the goods...

Section 14(1) provides:

> An express guarantee given by a manufacturer in a document in respect of goods binds the manufacturer when the document is given to a consumer with the actual or apparent authority of the manufacturer in connection with the supply by a supplier of those goods to the consumer.

This may not go far enough, because it would not cover general advertising in a newspaper or on television, but it would, I suppose, cover, promotional literature of other kinds.

The re-drafters of the U.C.C. are thinking of going further. The July 1994 draft of 2-313 would treat any description, affirmation of fact or promise made by a manufacturer to the public as a warranty which any subsequent buyer can enforce, unless the statement was made to a segment of the public of which the buyer was not a part, or resulted from a mistake upon which the buyer did not reasonably rely (see appendix).

The U.C.C. draft does not confine liability to consumer cases. Given the efficiency rationale for which I argued earlier, I also would extend it to any sale. I think it might also be extended to services operated under a franchise arrangement, if the franchisor has issued incorrect information about the services.[37] Whether it should also be extended to statements made by specialist subcontractors I am not so sure. This is likely to be a more common problem in larger construction projects where the sums involved make it less costly for the parties to enter some agreement as to responsibility.[38]

CONCLUSION

In my view, manufacturers should be made responsible for defects in goods which were their responsibility, at least to the extent of having to pay for repair, replacement or a refund of the price, and to pay for the cost of hiring a substitute while this is done. I would extend the same liability to subcontractors whose defective performance has led to defects in the work.

---

37 As I understand it, the franchisee is usually required to contract with customers as principal, not as agent for the franchisor.

38 The Contractor can agree to accept responsibility for the process even though this would not normally be imposed on it; or a collateral warranty may be given by the specialist to the customer.

I would also make manufacturers and others who put out incorrect information about their products directly responsible for it to those who purchase goods or contract for services in reliance on the information.

In consumer cases these changes could be justified in welfarist terms. They can also be justified in terms of efficiency, but I have argued that this is no longer wholly distinct from 'fairness' in a broad sense. This would support extension of the changes to non-consumer cases as well.[39]

[39] I gave an earlier version of this paper as part of the 1993 – 94 Seminars in Private Law series at the University of Cambridge. I would like to thank the partcipants in that seminar for their helpful comments.

APPENDIX

Uniform Commercial Code Revised Article 2 (Draft of 28.2.94)

2-318. EXTENSION OF WARRANTIES EXPRESS OR IMPLIED.

(a) A seller's express or implied warranty, made to an immediate buyer, extends to any person who may reasonably be expected to buy, use or be affected by the goods and who is damaged by the breach of warranty. In this section, 'seller' includes manufacturer...

(b) Except as provided in subsection (c), the rights and remedies of a protected person against a seller for breach of a warranty extended under subsection (a) are determined by the enforceable terms of the contract between the seller and the immediate buyer and this Article.

(c) A buyer's rights and remedies for breach of warranty are determined under this article, as modified by subsection (d), without regardto privity of contract or to the terms of the contract between the seller and the immediate buyer if

(1) the buyer is a consumer to whom a warranty was extended under subsection (a) and the Magnusson-Moss Warranty Act applies or the seller is a merchant under Section 2-314(a) who sold unmerchantable goods; or

(2) the buyer is a member of the public to whom an express warranty was made by the seller under Section 2-313 (c) and (d).

(d) A buyer under subsection (c) has all of the rights and remedies against a remote seller provided by this Article, except as follows:

...

(2) Upon receipt of a timely notice of rejection or revocation of acceptance, the remote seller has a reasonable time either to refund the price paid by the buyer to the immediate seller or cure the breach by supplying that conform to the warranty. If the seller complies with this paragraph, the remote buyer has no further remedy against the seller, except for incidental damages under Section2-715(a). If the remote seller fails to comply with thissubsection, the buyer may claim damages for breach of

warranty, including consequential damages under Section715(b).

(3) Except as provided in paragraph (2), a buyer has no right to consequential damages unless expressly agreed with the remote seller.

...

Recommendations of GAIPEC (Groupe des Associations InterProfessionelles Européenes de la Construction):

B4 If all or part of a Building is legally transferred by a Client to an Owner or from an Owner to a successive Owner, the rights conferred by this text on the Client shall automatically pass to each successive Owner without the need for assignment.

D7 1. Each Participant is liable for the performance of his legal and contractual obligations.

2. The duty imposed on Participants is one of due skill, care and diligence.

D9 1. Each Participant is liable only for his own acts, omissions, decisions and lack of diligence as well as for those of his employees and/or subcontractors freely chosen and/or accepted by him, even if they have been approved by the Client or by other Participants.

2. Each Participant is also responsible for any defect caused by the unsuitability of construction products he has freely chosen or accepted.

3. The liability of each Participant is always individual. In the case where more than one Participant is liable for the same Defect or Damage, the liability of each Participant will have to be established, if necessary by an independent expert evaluation involving all parties concerned.

D11 1. A Participant who is responsible for a Defect has the right and obligation to repair it in a reasonable time or pay damages according to the stipulations of the contract or of this text.

2. Such Participant is also obliged to compensate the claimant for all costs directly and necessarily incurred as a consequence of a defect, including loss of rent when a binding lease was in existence when the Damage was discovered.

Nordic Sale of Goods Act, §203:

(1) Goods are to be considered defective if they do not conform with information about their quality or use which the seller has supplied before the conclusion of the contract and which must be presumed to have influenced the buyer when making his purchase.

(2) Goods are to be considered defective if they do not conform with information about their quality or use supplied by other persons than the seller in earlier links of the sales chain or on account of the seller when marketing the goods, and which must be presumed to have influenced the buyer when making his purchase. There is, however, no defect if theseller did not know or ought not to have known of the said information.

(3) The rules in paras. (1) and (2) do not apply if the information has been corrected in time and in clear terms.

Uniform Commercial Code Revised Article 2 (Draft of 28.2.94)

2-313 EXPRESS WARRANTIES BY AFFIRMATION, PROMISE, DESCRIPTION OR SAMPLE

(a) Except as otherwise provided in subsection (b):

(1) Any affirmation of fact or promise by the seller, including a manufacturer, made directly or through a dealer to the buyer which relates to the goods presumptively becomes part of the agreement between them and creates an express warranty that the goods will conform to the affirmation or promise. To create an express warranty it is not necessary that the seller use formal words such as 'warrant' or 'guarantee', or have a specific intention to make a warranty.

...

(c) Subject to subsection (d), any description, affirmation of fact or promise made by a seller, including a manufacturer, to the public which relates to goods to be sold presumptively creates an express warranty to any buyer that the goods will conform to the description, affirmation or promise. Subject to Section 2 – 318, the buyer may enforce the express warranty directly against the seller, whether or not the express warranty is part of the contract with its immediate seller.

(d) An express warranty is not created under subsection (c) if the seller establishes that the description, affirmation of fact or promise:

(1) was not made within a reasonable time of the sale;

(2) was made to a segment of the public of which the buyer was not a part or

(3) resulted from a mistake upon which the buyer did not reasonably rely.

REFERENCES

Adams and Brownsword (1993) Privity of Contract 56 MLR 722.

Adams, J. and Brownsword, R. (1990) 'Privity and the Concept of a Network Contract', 10 L.S. 12–37.

Atiyah, P. (1989) *Introduction to the Law of Contract* (4th ed.).

Beale, H. 'Privity of Contract: Judicial and Legislative Reform' (forthcoming, JCL).

Beale, H. (1986) 'Inequality of Bargaining Power', Oxford J Legal Studies 123.

Beale, H. (1989) 'Unfair Contracts in Britain and Europe', C.L.P. 197.

Beyleveld, D. and Brownsword, R. (1991), 54 MLR 48

Bishop in Burrows, P. and Veljanovsky, C. (1981) (eds), *The Economic Approach to Law* 167-186.

Commission of the EC, (1993) *Green Paper on Guarantees for Consumer Goods and After-Sales Service* (COM(93) 509).

Commission of the EC, DG III/D, *Commission Staff Discussion paper concerning possible Comminity action with regard to liabilities and guarantees in the construction sector.*

Department of Trade and Industry, (1992) *Consumer Guarantees: a Consultation Document,* proposal 1, p.6.

Law Commission (1991) Consultation Paper No. 121, *Privity of Contract: Contracts for the Benefit of Third Parties.*

Markesinis, B. (1987), An Expanding Tort Law – 'The Price of a Rigid Contract Law', 103 LQR 354.

Posner and Rosenfield (1977) 'Impossibility and Related Doctrines in Contract Law: An Economic Analysis' 6 J.L.S. 83.

Schwartz (1974) 49 Indiana LJ 367, 370-371.

Spencer, (1974) CLJ 307,318.

Willett, C. (1993) 'The Quality of Goods and the Rights of Consumers' 44 NILQ 218, 228.

8. Repeated Games, Social Norms and Incomplete Corporate Contracts

William W. Bratton, Morten Hviid and Joseph McCahery

Recent legal theories of the firm tend to build on a foundation of economic contract. This chapter shows, first, that there are sharp differences among the economic models of contract available to lend content to these contractual firms, and, second, that the descriptive and normative implications of these differences have yet to be fully appreciated in the legal literature.

We begin with the contractarian firm, the economically-grounded description that has become standard in contemporary American corporate legal theory. We move on to describe and contrast an incomplete contracting model of the firm that follows from a very different set of economic assumptions. We then combine this model with basic points from the literature of repeated games. Taken together, they support two assertions. First, under certain conditions rational actors will not ground their firms in contracts. Second, contracts made in connection with firms are likely to be so incomplete as to render any available theory of contract inadequate as a basis for a law of the firm. We argue that this incomplete contracting model provides a more plausible basis for describing corporations than does the contractarian model. We also explore some of its normative implications.

In section 1 we draw on our incomplete contracting model to show why firm contracts do not function in the fashion predicted by the contractarian approach. There we also situate our approach within the existing range of incomplete contracts models. All of these describe contracting problems which leave parties with less than the information necessary to approximate their first-best expected utility. But they offer different conceptual techniques for dealing with these problems. Some closely resemble the contractarian theory of the firm in seeking to complete incomplete firm contracts by approximating a theoretical contract that succeeds *ex ante* in describing all future states of nature. Our model of incomplete contract draws on a different body of economic literature to insist that the very fact that parties are limited by what they can put into a contract denudes the attempt at *ex ante* approximation of feasibility. A regime in which legal decision-makers take an *ex post* perspective that supersedes the bargain of the parties becomes inevitable.

The suggestion that a legal decision-maker legitimately might supplant the parties' bargain (whether actual or hypothetical) creates a considerable problem for an economic theory of the firm. Without the bargain (actual or hypothetical) as a base point, the theory lacks an obvious source of normative content for the *ex post* gap-filling exercise. In section 2, we suggest that game theoretic models of repeated games can be drawn on to solve this problem. Here we outline the basic features of repeated game models and their implications for understanding long term production relationships. We show the robust pictures of private enforcement strategies and relational stability that have evolved in the repeated game literature. These now can help us understand how, given conflicting parties in situations where contract is not feasible, trust and co-operation can emerge to benefit the parties.

In section 3 we expand on the literature of repeated games to examine its points of influence on recent discussions of corporate contract theory. This discussion shows that the process of breaking with contractarianism already has begun, but that the full implications of the repeated game models and related principles of incomplete contracting have not yet been articulated in the corporate law context. Section 4 completes this discussion by drawing on a new line of social theory. This approach, which also draws on game theoretic models of co-operation, offers a behavioural description in which trust and rational calculation co-exist and complement one another. We argue that this description provides the basis for a theory of the firm that admits both contract and a positive law of fiduciary duty as independent elements.

1 Contractarian Theory, Incomplete Contracts and the Theory of the Firm

1.1 Contractarian theory

Under the contractarian theory dominant in American corporate law during the past fifteen years, the firm has been viewed as a set (or 'nexus') of incentive contracts (see Bratton, 1989). This theory derived from the principal-agent theory earlier developed in economics and extended it in a number of directions.[1] According to the contractarian theorists, the primacy of contract implies that corporate law should contain no mandates, only default terms. In addition, legal decision-making respecting firms should be treated as an exercise in contractual gap-filling pursuant to the 'hypothetical contract principle', a universal norm to guide decision-makers in supplying default terms and filling gaps. Under the principle, the legal system supplies the rule which both parties to the contract would have adopted had they addressed the matter *ex ante* in a costless world. Terms that follow the principle, says the theory, will be efficient for all situations. And, because the theory's operative class of 'contracts' includes any and all voluntary economic relationships, the field deemed appropriate for application of its regime of *ex ante* default rules and gap fillers is quite large.

The literature on contractarian theory begins with rational, well-informed actors and asserts that prevailing governance systems result from their efficient, equilibrium choices. The presence of competition makes this assertion plausible: We can assume that existing arrangements, whether nominally stemming from contract or positive law, result from efficient, equilibrium choices because, in the long run, only efficient choices will survive (see Johnston, 1993). Contactarian theory then shifts its time reference to future arrangements to assert that contract trumps mandate because rational, well-informed actors contracting *ex ante* can be expected to do a better job at economizing on transaction costs and devising safeguards against opportunism than can legal decision-makers intervening *ex post* (see Williamson, 1993). The legal regime's only function is to provide *ex ante* cost economies by providing pre-packaged default rules formulated under the hypothetical contract principle (see Easterbrook and Fischel, 1991). In the final contractarian picture we get a complex of contract terms that govern all future contingencies, all derived *ex ante*, either in fact or by hypothesis.[2] A normative admonition greets a party who shows a loss *ex post* caused by another's opportunism: Since you could

---

1 More specifically, contractarian theory combines two related theories (agency costs and the efficient market hypothesis), and states that managers will have an incentive to create legal rules which mimic the market. In general terms, the function of corporate law is to design an efficient set of default rules to govern the rights and duties among members of the firm. Thus conceived, corporate law, as a set of efficient default rules, reduces the costs of contracting. See, Easterbrook and Fischel, 1991.

2 A complete contract is a contract that all the relevant and foreseeable contingencies are foreseen and that the parties have agreed on efficient provisions for each state contingency. *Ex ante* completeness also assumes that the parties will implement the contract and not renegotiate *ex post* the terms of the agreement. See generally, Moore, 1992.

have contracted to protect yourself, you should have done so. The positive law of the firm serves only to open a field for self-regulation, and intervention to impose duties on corporate actors pursuant to juridical notions of responsibility should be avoided as unproductive.

But the contractarian description has a significant shortcoming. It gives us *ex ante* contracts across-the-board and thereby makes corporate governance entirely contractual without providing a description of the processes by which corporate actors make contracts (see Johnston, 1993). It avoids the necessity of a theory of bargaining with two assumptions – that bargaining is relatively cheap and that competition will force parties to bargain their way into efficient arrangements.[3]

1.2 From the Complete Contracts Firm, through the Incomplete Contracts Firm, to the Firm Without Contracts

Incomplete contract models deal with the problems that arise when contracting parties possess less information than is necessary to approximate their first-best expected utility. Most work on incomplete contracts falls into one of two basic paradigms: the transaction costs approach and a contrasting approach which derives incompleteness from first principles. The transaction costs approach already has received the complete attention of those who work on the theory of the firm, and, indeed, has been assimilated into contractarian theory. The component ideas of the first principles approach have only just begun to show up in legal commentaries.[4] We argue in this section that they suggest a thorough-going, process-based challenge to the contractarian paradigm.[5]

Under the transaction costs view, the problems which arise from attempting to write *ex ante* contracts are due to a diverse range of transaction costs. First, it is difficult for parties to anticipate all the possible state contingencies that might arise, and design the contractual provisions to deal with them. Second, even if the parties could specify all the relevant contingencies, it may be impossible for the parties adequately to specify these future states in order to forge an agreement. Third, there are too

3 The mandatory/enabling discussion in US corporate law developed on the weakness of these assumptions, concluding that information asymmetries, along with shareholder collective action and rational apathy problems, prevent effective bargaining and make certain actual contracts suspect. The apparent weakness of the contractarian approach left open a place for normative mandates in the field of corporate governance. However, mandates were subsumed in the larger complex of hypothetical contracts.

4 See e.g., Ayres, 1991.

5 In the discussion which follows, we will use the term incomplete contracts approach to cover situations where there are asymmetries of information and possibly problems of third party verification or private information.

many contingencies making it difficult for the parties to write them into a contract. Fourth, the costs of verifying the performance of the party may create disincentives to write a complete contract. Fifth, the enforcement of the contract is expensive. The transaction costs model asserts that the cumulation of these costs prevents actors from negotiating a complete *ex ante* solution to all problems. But it goes on to take on entirely ex ante perspective in dealing with the problem, asserting that actors putting capital at risk still can be expected to design *ex ante* governance structures that minimise the costs of future uncertainty. Furthermore, it insists that legal decision-makers assisting the parties by providing terms *ex post* should cast those terms from an *ex ante* time perspective in order to guard against disruption of the parties' allocation of financial risk and to minimise future transaction costs. As a result, it tends to join contractarian theory at the normative bottom line to counsel self-protection through explicit contract and impose an overwhelming presumption against legal intervention to protect dependent actors.

What we term the 'first principles' paradigm of incomplete contracts begins with the same definition of incompleteness as the transaction costs approach but goes on to make a number of contrasting claims, both substantive and procedural. The substantive claim brings the notion of incompleteness to bear on a more precise conception of 'contract'. More specifically, *ex ante* incompleteness is due to the formal nature of the contract in addition to the costs of complete specification. Thus, unlike the transaction costs approach and its inclusion of any voluntary economic relation within its notion of contract, the first principles approach usually looks to situations where a contract must be explicitly specified by its parties in order to be recognised as such and enforced. That is, to have 'contract' terms that govern future states, those contingent states must be specified and the future outcomes must be computable. Since some future states of nature clearly are not computable, transacting parties as a result lack the technology necessary to enable the negotiation and composition of a contract term *ex ante* (see Anderlini and Felli, 1994). Indeed, under certain conditions problems concerning specification of future contingencies become so intractable that rational parties in search of gains from trade may proceed to transact without writing a contract at all.[6]

The first principles approach also draws on bargaining theory to recognise the collection of process infirmities that also limit the utility of

---

6 This literature takes seriously the idea that there may be no contract. We should note that there are varying degrees of contractual incompleteness: in particular it assumes intermediate forms of incompleteness which limit transaction costs by resorting to third parties to *ex post* decide the contractual outcomes; see Tirole, 1988.

contract. Bargaining theory models the problems that come up when relational economic actors transact. It asserts that, even where parties could cost-beneficially specify a contract term, information asymmetries and strategic behaviour may prevent them from so doing. This implies that bargaining processes often shape contractual results, and in turn leads to the question whether a viable set of governance provisions for a firm can be derived through any available model of contract. Some bargaining models show co-ordination failures: Rational actors can conceivably adopt any one of a number of mutually consistent arrangements and market forces may fail to assure that only efficient patterns emerge from the range of possibilities.[7] Other models identify costs of bargaining that prevent efficient results. Consider a price negotiation over the sale of a nonfungible product. A buyer seeking a greater share of the gains of trade might invest in quality information to gain a bargaining advantage. Such an investment in a pure distributional advantage is inefficient, since only total benefits and costs matter from an efficiency standpoint (see Milgrom and Roberts, 1990). In the alternative, each bargaining party stands to benefit from the communication of information about its own preferences. The resulting informational uncertainty can result in the loss of a beneficial transaction, and induces inefficient informational investment in any event.

The first principles approach thus recognises three limitations on the zone of *ex ante* contracting-technological failure, private information and strategic behaviour. Taken together these limitations permit us to see that the contract-based vision of corporate law suffers from two fundamental limitations. First, contrary to the nexus of contracts approach, the firm cannot plausibly be described as a sum of contractual parts.[8] The reason is simple costs and technological limitations prohibit bargaining across the range of pertinent contingencies (see Milgrom and Roberts, 1992). Second, fundamental questions must be asked about the viability of the central contractarian assumption that contracting agents will bargain to optimal

---

7 The standard assumption that markets will overcome co-ordination problems given competitive supply conditions is not safe where multiple goods are involved and more than two parties must agree in order for exchange to go forward.

8 The contractarian approach relies on the principal-agent theory as a framework for analyzing governance issues which involve members of the organization. (See Easterbrook and Fischel 1991 pp. 1-39). Principal-agent theory addresses the central problems of economic organization and motivation through the design of optimal contracts which distribute incentives and risk-sharing effectively. These contracts are *ex ante* complete in that they specify for the relevant foreseeable contingencies. Hart points out, however, that the complete contracting assumption necessarily excludes a role for corporate governance in that there is no role left for a mechanism to decide residual issues of control; Hart, 1995.

arrangements if left to their own devices. It is this premise that permits the theory to complete the incomplete contracts that actors conclude in the real world by drawing on the hypothetical contract principle, and to recharacterize corporate law's set of positive instructions as contract terms (see Easterbrook and Fischel, 1991). If, as the first principles approach suggests, information asymmetries may cause the parties to fail to bargain their way to an efficient term even in a costless environment, (see Fudenberg and Tirole, 1991), then it follows that the existence of meaningful hypothetical contract terms cannot be assumed. Further, given the complexity of corporate situations, actual negotiated corporate contracts will not necessarily be optimal even where they exist in the real world the parties (and by implication the economists who write about contracts) quite simply lack the technological wherewithal to create such ideal governance arrangements. If contracting can be inefficient, then its frequent absence in the practice of real world corporate actors makes complete sense, and the choice of legal institutions, as opposed to that of contractual terms, can be the primary influence on the efficiency of the outcome (see Fudenberg and Tirole, 1991).

We note that this analysis implies a modification of contractarian theory's descriptive and normative bottom lines only to the extent that bargaining costs and effects of technological failure are nontrivial. As to bargaining costs, competition certainly will assure triviality in some cases. But the bilateral monopoly situation that accompanies firm-specific investment strongly suggests that the bargaining costs of firm governance are nontrivial (see Milgrom and Roberts, 1990). The same conclusion should follow for technological limitations if recent experiences with standard American corporate contract forms may be taken as a guide. The inadequacy of the standard terms employed in contracts governing senior securities is widely acknowledged. The inadequacy of the stock of terms governing junior equity investments is acknowledged even more widely. Here investment proceeds under contract terms and state-supplied governance structures that leave open such constant risks of opportunistic exploitation that contractarian theory, even at its high point, never quite succeeded in delegitimating American corporate law's apparatus of fiduciary protection.

Once contract's significant bargaining costs and technical limitations are acknowledged, serious questions start coming up about contractarian theory's basic assertions. How, given contract's institutional limitations, can we safely assume that rational actors ground their firms in *ex ante* contractual risk allocations? And if that assumption is unsafe, how can the law be left to follow the contractarians advice and remit actors to *ex ante* contracting, when so doing would invite them to dissipate resources?

But these questions can be countered with other questions: If not contracting, then what? How, given opportunism, can co-operative production go forward without a complete backstop of state-enforced promises, actual or hypothetical? One answer, according to non co-operative game theory, lies in reputational incentives. Game theoretic models of spontaneous order suggest that, given reputational incentives, rational actors can produce co-operatively without any contracts at all (see Boot, Greenbaum and Thankor, 1993). By providing a working description of the economics of production in the absence of contracts, these models provide us with a theoretical base point for a theory of the firm that admits an *ex post* approach to the incomplete contract – an approach pursuant to which an intervening court legitimately could supplant the parties' bargain. This approach, by recognising that the parties are limited in what they can write into a contract,[9] would invite legal decision-makers to consider a range of possible default rules as supplements for the bargaining process. Ultimately, it would even sanction the use of corporate law's inherited normative framework in the *ex post* solution of non-contractible problems.

2 Repeated Games and Folk Theorems

Sovereign enforcement is a problem for all contracting parties, at least in the absence of a mechanism that instantaneously and costlessly translates counterparty breach into a present payment of correctly calculated damages. Even given a perfect *ex ante* specification of an aggrieved party's rights, a breach may turn out to be difficult (and costly) to observe or, even if easily observed, may be difficult (and costly) to verify to a legal decision-maker. These problems tend to become more serious, and sovereign enforcement less and less feasible, as the contract becomes more incomplete. As a result, informal enforcement mechanisms such as reputation become essential components of such contracting relationships. Indeed, given a completely effective reputational enforcement mechanism, parties can dispense with the institution of sovereign-enforced contract all together. The medieval merchant guild is said to provide an historical illustration of such a mechanism: the merchant guilds were established to create a reputation mechanism in which merchants overcame rulers' commitment

---

9 Hence, central to the idea of incomplete contracts is the role of courts in interpreting gaps in contract. *Cf.* Schwartz, 1992, pp. 76-108; see also Tirole, 1992 pp. 109-113.

problems (see Grief, Milgrom and Weingast, 1994 and Milgrom, North and Weingast, 1990).

Today, game theory's models of repeated games offer theoretical descriptions of the behavioural and structural requisites for stable, informally enforced co-operative relationships. These models seek in terms to provide a formal theory of relational exchange in the absence of contract. In so doing, they have the incidental benefit of enhancing our understanding of the behavioural and structural components of incomplete contracts (see Milgrom and Roberts, 1992). They confirm the feasibility of incompletely specified relationships and also enhance our appreciation of the useful support provided to these relationships by both social norms and legal intervention grounded in noncontractual presuppositions (see Kandori, 1992).

Here in section 2 we examine some ways in which repeated game models show how trust and co-operation can emerge absent contracts and despite conflicting interests. Section 2.1 begins with an introduction to the basic elements of repeat games. Section 2.2 shows how these models' description of reputational enforcement has become more robust over time. In section 2.3 we compare the properties of finitely repeated games to those of infinitely repeated games. In sections 2.4 and 2.5 we report on the terms of some cutting edge models that make notable moves in the direction of realism as they identify strategies likely to enhance co-operation. Section 2.6 describes a repeat play theory of the firm.

2.1 The Folk Theorem and Repeated Games

We turn first to the Folk Theorem for repeated games. A repeated game is defined as a T-fold repetition of a particular (stage)game. In the simplest version, at each stage the players know the past history of the game including the past actions by all players. Loosely speaking, the Folk Theorem states that if the players are sufficiently patient and the game is repeated for a sufficient number of periods, all outcomes of the stage game which are individually rational[10] and feasible can be supported by some punishment strategy.

We can illustrate this by outlining the repeated trust game of David Kreps. The stage game, which is to be repeated, has a sequence of two moves in each round (see Kreps, 1990). Party A has to decide whether to put herself at hazard by trusting Party B. If Party A accepts the hazard and trusts Party B, Party B then has to decide whether to honour or abuse A's

---

10 An outcome is individually rational for a player, if it gives that player a pay off at least as high as its minimax payoff.

trust. The payoffs are set so that the trust/honour outcome maximises the joint gain, but that B's immediate gain is maximised through abuse of A's trust. In a one shot game the trust will be abused, and Party A, being rational, will not place herself at risk in the first place absent an enforceable contract protecting her investment. But, as noted above, high drafting and enforcement costs may preclude that alternative. Repetition of this situation increases the number of equilibria. Given enough repetition, trust will emerge and Party A's investment can be made without a contract. The repeated game scenario works as a self-enforcing trust/honour arrangement so long as there is a high probability that each round will be followed by a succeeding round: B's expected playoffs from future rounds deter defection and induce co-operation in the present round, provided that A can see what B is doing and stands ready to discontinue play, punishing B, if B ever defects from co-operation. (Note again that an important aspect of the model is that the players can observe one another's actions in each repetition, so that the deviations from equilibrium strategies are detectable.) Given an *ex ante* projection of this repeat play scenario, investment in a protective contract by the parties would be irrational.

We can sum up by abstracting a relatively simple idea from the Folk Theorem: if the game is repeated a number of times and the transaction's profitability is high, it is likely that a co-operative strategy which is an efficient equilibrium will emerge. A player will invest in his reputation and co-operate so long as that player values the returns from co-operation over time higher than the short-term gains of opportunistic behaviour. Thus the player's self-interest serves as the mechanism that overcomes the collective action problem; here self-interested rationality and co-operation are synchronised. But a couple of requisite conditions must also be noted. First, the reputational interest that makes co-operation consonant with self-interest emerges within the context of repeated transactions.[11] Second, the model presupposes credible threats and assumes that they can inform and shape current behaviour; self-enforcement will be effective only where there exists a retaliation mechanism for players who transgress.

2.2 Strategies which Support Co-operation[12]

One of the earlier approaches to the study of perfect folk theorems relied on a severe and unforgiving punishment strategy to deter each player from cheating. Following a deviation, all players revert to choosing their myopic best reply forever. In the trust model, if a deviation is observed by player

---

11 But the number of such transactions need not be infinite--reputation also emerges in short-term relationships. Tirole, 1992.

12 For a summary, see Pearce, 1992.

A, it refuses all future co-operation. The problem with this approach is that, because punishment goes on forever, there is in some sense too much punishment.

Dilip Abreu made an important contribution towards the elimination of this problem by successfully introducing the possibility of forgiveness. He constructed a simple set of punishments (the Stick) and rewards (the Carrot) that yield the maximal cooperation which can be supported given the possibility of defection (see Abreu, 1986). The theory is based on a punishment path which punishes harshly for just enough periods so as to wipe out the original gain from cheating and then forgives totally and reverts to the co-operative path. Any deviation from the punishment is met by restarting the punishment. Significantly, only a very simple informational structure is needed to sustain collusion under this strategy. All you need to do is calculate the stick, the carrot, and the length for which the stick must be wielded.

Other models introduce uncertainty and informational asymmetries and show that they mainly pose a technical challenge, with folk theorem-like results appearing despite the introduction of modifications. For instance, if a player only receives a garbled signal about what the other player has done and hence does not know this period's result is due to dishonesty or bad luck, a punishment phase will have to be initiated in some cases. Hence, we will observe sporadic bursts of punishment where information is incomplete. But this should not be interpreted as the end of co-operation, but rather as a sign that co-operation can work in less than perfect conditions.

Credible punishment strategies also have presented barriers to the development of a repeat game model with robust implications for the world of practice. The problem with the punishment strategy that supports co-operative outcomes is that in many cases both the guilty and the innocent are harmed by the punishment. The punishment phase is still credible because any failure by party A to punish results in party A being punished. But a problem remains. Punishment itself hurts party A because it entails foregoing a higher co-operative payoff. The guilty party B therefore has an incentive to seek more immediate forgiveness and party A has an incentive to give it. This (although the parties proceed here without a contract) is termed the problem of 'renegotiation' after a deviation. The possibility of forgiveness through renegotiation threatens the overall co-operative outcome – if deviations from co-operation are not punished co-operation will break down.

This analytical tension has led some researchers to look for punishment strategies which are proof to renegotiations. The resulting literature is problematic, however. A large number of possible definitions of renegotiation proof equilibria has emerged reflecting different (and conflicting) interpretations of what renegotiation proofness means. But regardless of which definition of renegotiation proofness is used, renegotiation proofness does reduce the number of possible outcomes, although in some cases not by very much and in others by too much if no renegotiation proof equilibrium exists. In effect, the jury is still out on this concept and one should proceed with care.[13]

This discussion of renegotiation mirrors a discussion familiar in the field of contract law. As is well known, even complete specification of terms and sovereign enforcement do not cure the problem of incentive to forgive breach where the victim of the breach has an economic interest in continued performance. The contract law solution is of course a rule of unenforceability for a class of suspect modifications. Such a rule permits the victim of opportunism who renegotiates to counter-defect at a convenient future time and thus deters breach *ex ante*. From the point of view of contract doctrine, then, the extent to which renegotiation proofness is a real worry depends on the courts attitude to contract modifications (see Baird, Gertner and Picker, 1994).

But it must be noted that, even assuming a successful doctrinal solution, renegotiation proofness will remain an economic problem in the world of transactions so long as contract enforcement is costly and many contracts are incomplete. An alternative theoretical suggestion, is thus worth considering: A social norm entailing punishment for cheaters would clearly support co-operation and accordingly would prove useful (see Deakin, Lane and Wilkinson, 1994). It follows that the contrary social norm of forgiveness, which is often preached but rarely followed to the letter, might be detrimental to society's ability to sustain co-operation. Note also that this social norm against cheating serves to introduce a second, alternative technique of informal enforcement (see Kandori, 1992). The first mode, employed in all the models described up to now in this part, is personal enforcement. Under this enforcement against defection is ensured by repeated interaction among the players themselves. Under the second mode, the community supplies social norms in order to achieve efficient, co-operative outcomes.

---

13 Pearce argues that the appropriate definition is case specific. Furthermore, if renegotiation is really a concern, it should be modelled explicitly, i.e. it should be part of the description of the game that at certain points in time the original agreement can be renegotiated see Pearce, 1992.

2.3 Finitely Repeated Games

Significantly, the co-operative equilibrium does not prevail for those scenarios in which the number of projected plays, however large, is finite and known (see Kreps, Milgrom Roberts and Wilson, 1982). In order to see this point, let us return to the trust game and let it be based on a finite repetition. In this case Player B's incentives revert to defection at the last round. But Player A will anticipate this and will not trust Player B in that last round. As a result, the penultimate round becomes the last round from B's point of view. Player A in turn anticipates this shift, and will not offer trust in the penultimate round. The third-to-last round then becomes the last round, and so on. Ultimately, this process of backward induction leads to the collapse of the whole scenario of co-operation, and defection becomes the dominant strategy *ex ante* (see Benoit and Krishna, 1985). Central to the idea of self-enforcement, therefore, is the insight that co-operation is not likely to emerge if the end period is known (see Baird, Gertner and Picker, 1994).

Before we go on, we should note that finitely repeated games suffer from a limitation that makes them a case that approximates only a special class of real life finite repetitions.[14] The limitation is the fact that the identity of the last play is by definition specified *ex ante*. Such advance specifications are not always present in real world finite play situations. To see this point, compare a bond and a share of publically-traded common stock issued by the same corporation. The bond, with its due date, is a real world investment that does roughly resemble a finitely repeated game. Unsurprisingly, bond investments are made under relatively complete (albeit imperfect) contracts – a legally enforceable promise to repay on the termination date must be there at a minimum. Now compare the conditions surrounding investment in the stock. No member of either of the groups of parties to the corporate equity relationship -- the shareholders and the managers -- may anticipate an infinite duration. Yet all of these parties nevertheless may operate with an indefinite, long-term time horizon lacking a fixed termination date.[15] Infinitely repeated games in which the duration of play is at any given stage stated probabilistically closely approximate these conditions.

Putting these *caveats* to one side, it is worth noting that with some restructuring of the base of assumptions, co-operation can emerge in finite play situations. There turns out to be a material difference between finite

---

[14] See for instance the discussion by Rubinstein, (1992).

[15] Special end period situation such as mergers and tender offers are exceptions. Unsurprisingly, American fiduciary law has articulated a special set of stricter rules for these situations.

play models where the stage game has a unique equilibrium, such as the trust game and more generally the Prisoner's dilemma, and models where the stage game has multiple equilibria. In the former case, co-operation does not emerge. With multiple equilibria things work differently. One can construct good and bad endgames consisting of different selections of the stage game equilibria. The best endgame then becomes the carrot and the worst endgame becomes the stick. The length of an endgame needed to wipe out any gain from deviation is independent on the actual number of repetitions. Hence by increasing the number of repetitions, we can get as close as possible to the outcome which would emerge with an infinite repetition (see Kreps 1985).

There also is another way to avoid the non-co-operative result in the finite repetition situation. Again the assumptions are changed. The model dispenses with the assumption that the players know the exact characteristics of the player they are facing.[16] To see the implications of this strategy, let us return to the finite trust game, modifying it so that players have incomplete information about who Player B really is: There is some small chance that Player B is not a rational economic actor at all, but is an irrational type who will respect trust despite self-interest. A very small probability that a given type of Playér B is an irrational type will restore the trust/honour outcome for most of the game so long as the number of repetitions are large enough. As the probability that Player B will respect trust increases, Player A's investment is more easily induced. Interestingly, in this class of games, the particular patterns of co-operative results hinge on particular assumptions about the type of 'craziness' about which the Player B is attempting to generate a reputation. Given the right type of 'craziness', a unique outcome can emerge in contrast to the folk theorems. But by choosing another type of 'craziness', the same set of equilibria can be supported as in the folk theorems.

2.4 Co-operation amongst Mortals and over Generations

We return to infinitely repeated games to take up the relaxation of another important limiting assumption. In the models we have described up to now, the cast of players always has remained the same and all players have stayed in the game forever. This rigidity as to the players' identities limits the model's potential as a source of practical learning, since the world of long-term economic relationships tends to present situations where finitely

[16] Kreps, Milgrom, Roberts and Wilson 1982 developed a model in which they introduced a one-sided asymmetric information in the finitely repeated prisoners' dilemma. They showed that if they only introduced a small amount of information about one player's type, it will have a large impact on the players tendency to cooperate.

lived agents come and go against the backdrop of an infinite time horizon. Happily, these conditions have successfully been introduced to the infinite repetition models. With these modifications, the literature begins to produce the components of a theory of the firm.

Allowing for differences in the identity of the players over time turns out to be a minor modelling problem. There is now an extensive literature on games with one long-run player and a series of short-run players (see Fudenberg, 1992). The problem to be surmounted concerns the short-run players' lack of an incentive to punish on behalf of future short-run players who later will be matched with the long-run player. The long-run player's reputational interest in attracting participation by future short-run players solves the problem: The current behaviour of the long-run player affects beliefs and hence the reputation for honesty may disappear if the long-run player takes present advantage of a short-run player.

We can employ Kreps' trust game to illustrate the point (see Kreps, 1990). The repeated trust game can admit of multiple Players A, each of whom makes a one shot transaction with Player B. So long as the As can observe B's past transactions and B has a financial incentive to co-operate with new As in future rounds, contract will be unnecessary to sustain the co-operative relationship. Player B's incentive to preserve her reputation for in future rounds provides the necessary guarantee of performance. The game can be extended to multiple Players B as well as multiple Players A by introducing the device of the firm. New Players B purchase interests in Firm B from departing Players B: Firm B's reputation induces investment by new Players A; new Players B have an incentive to continue to honour commitments to Players A because defection will ruin the firm's reputation and result in a loss of their investments. The firm emerges as an intangible reputation bearer, operating successfully so long as the actors making its decisions have a vested interest in its reputation.

Kreps notes that we can reach the same result – a sequence that admits new Bs and new As – with a conventional contract simply by having each new B post a bond to be forfeited in the event of abuse of trust reposed by a transacting A (see Kreps 1990). But that arrangement will depend on the costs of contracting and after the fact of enforcement. Even if *ex ante* contracting is cheap, *ex post* enforcement may not be. If it is not, the threat to go to court has no credibility. And information problems may make enforcement difficult. If honour and dishonour are observable but not verifiable, or are too expensive to verify, then contract will not induce investment. The self-enforcing arrangement, in contrast, depends on observability only (see Kreps, 1990).

Finally, we consider overlapping generations of players. Kandori has studied how co-operation can be obtained in an overlapping generation framework (see Kandori, 1992). In this model agents have a finite life, but at any given point in time there are several generations in the game. It turns out that here self-enforcing arrangements evolve with difficulty. Kandori resorts to the device of self enforcing contractual understanding in order to get a co-operative result. He sets this 'bond' as follows: Either the older members of society are paid off by the young (assuming that everybody has behaved co-operatively so far), or, the old want to sell on their rights (i.e. their business) to the youngest (or emerging) generation. The idea that up front bonding can solve incentive problems is well known from the franchising and efficiency wage literatures.

2.5 Co-operation and Mixed Strategies

Another type of model which allows the identity of players to change is the random matching literature. Kandori, for example, considers a situation where agents change their partner over time, (see Kandori, 1992), with players in each stage being matched two and two using some (possibly random) matching process. For co-operation to emerge in this situation the second mode of informal enforcement must be invoked and dishonest behaviour against one partner must cause sanctions by other members of society. The model thus recalls the law merchant literature: With the Law Merchant system, norms held by the group encouraged merchants dealing with strangers to behave honestly. Here the repeated game literature reaches the same result as a formal proposition.

One might predict that the information requirements necessary to co-ordinate the social sanctions are very demanding but, as shown in Kandori, co-operation can be obtained given the following simple structure. Each agent carries a label and the necessary information is transmitted by the agents' labels. After each stage, the label is updated using only the original label and the action at this stage. This is referred to as local information processing as only local information is used. That is, the labels contain information sufficient to permit the agents to act without having to use any other information they might possess. This ensures that the equilibrium does not depend on the set of information known to the broader society. Furthermore, the equilibrium should not depend on the manner in which agents are matched nor on the number of agents. Although these are demanding requirements, Kandori proves a folk theorem in which the strategies have a particularly simple structure. Four strategies are needed. The strategies include: (1) an honest agent meeting honest agent; (2) an honest agent meeting a guilty agent; (3) a guilty agent meeting another guilty agent; and (4) a guilty agent meeting an honest agent. In addition to these strategies the equilibrium requires a mechanism which updates the label. A guilty agent carries that label for T periods, and, provided that he or she does not sin again, is then restored to a label saying 'honest'.

2.6 Multiple Equilibria, Hierarchies and Focal Points

As noted above, in many cases in the world of repeated games there is a very large (possibly infinite) number of outcomes which are better than the non-co-operative outcome and which can be supported by some combination of promises and threats. These persistent multiple equilibria give rise to questions respecting the viability of the reputation effects model of co-operation (even as modified to allow for changing rosters of players) to provide the basis for a theory of the firm. Quite simply, the number of equilibria predicted vastly outnumber the number we would expect to observe in the real world. This creates the problem of predicting an outcome from these potential equilibria.

Some theorists have resorted to norms or conventions as a means of selecting equilibrium outcomes and solving the indeterminancy problem. One such approach is taken by Kreps as he goes about expanding the trust game into a theory of the firm. The first step in the expansion is Kreps' assertion that the trust game implies an hierarchical firm. To illustrate this point, he presents a fact pattern keyed to the distinction between observation and verification. The amount of B's future compensation depends on the nature of B' performance, and B's performance, while observable, is unverifiable. Given this, the practical result is that one of the parties will have to specify the payment amount *ex post*. It is the specification power that makes the transaction hierarchical. Significantly, the reputational model allows for such a transaction structure absent verifiability: one party will willingly take an hierarchically inferior position – that is, an A will extend to a B a power to make a determination respecting B's performance so long as observability can lead to punishment in the case of an opportunistic determination. The more transparent the performance the better the arrangement works; but it may go forward even with partial observability, with inefficiency creeping in as limited information makes punishment episodic.

These hierarchical arrangements, says Kreps, are also well-adapted to the treatment of unforeseen contingencies that resist contractual treatment *ex ante*: The parties may specify a procedure pursuant to which the hierarchical superior later determines a provision covering the unforeseen event, with the hierarchical inferiors relying on reputation and self-enforcement in dealing with that determination. But how will that later evaluation be evaluated, given that its character is by definition unforeseen? And how, *ex ante* can a firm communicate a commitment to later fidelity to the inferiors' interests?

Kreps at this point draws on Schelling's concept of a focal point (see Schelling, 1960) – a generally stated behavioural principle that evolves through experience on which actors can draw in reacting to new situations. Corporations, he suggests, will articulate such principles and communicate them to hierarchical inferiors *ex ante*, giving them an idea as to how the organisation will react to unforeseen contingencies. These focal point principles reduce the number of future possible equilibria by lending identity to the organisation, and even provide a means by which to measure the performance of hierarchical superiors. They constitute a 'corporate culture' that evolves over time and provide a point of friction that generates predictable outcomes. Past experience determines its shape, but its principles are redefined as unexpected events occur.

3 The Game Theoretic Models of Private Information and Their Implications for Corporate Legal Theory

Kreps' expansion of the repeated game models into a theory of the firm offers a picture in marked contrast with that of contractarianism. Since co-operation evolves over time in these models, emphasis shifts emphasis away from *ex ante* planning respecting future events about which actors know little or nothing to *ex post* adjustment conducted when the actors have the pertinent information. The producing actors, sceptical about both the efficiency of bargaining and the possibility of writing complete contingent claims contracts, place their activities under a centralised authority and thereby economise on the costs of contractual specifications.

But, as argued in Williamson, (1993) Kreps' model of production as spontaneous order is not outfitted for direct transportation to the legal context. A game theoretic exercise such as this is, by definition, a stylised, assumption-laden search for equilibria that are credibly self-enforcing, undertaken without reference to contract or direct legal mandate. In practice, actual firm contracts exist in some situations, and the game theory does not suggest that informal punishment strategies are somehow intrinsically superior to them. Moreover, game theory deploys the same rational actors as does the contractarian model, bolstering the case for their self-reliant capabilities by modelling co-operative production without any state protection at all.

However the game theoretic firm need not be transferred to legal contexts on a stand alone basis. It holds a set of basic assumptions in common with the first principles approach to incomplete contracting described in section 1. The two approaches can be combined to provide the basis for an alternative legal theory of the firm that breaks with contractarianism. Section 3.1 lays out this argument, showing how the insights of the game theoretic models can be interpolated into our understanding of real world incomplete firm contracts.

But we also acknowledge that the composition and direction of the questions prompted by the game theoretic models depend to some extent on the disposition of the questioner. There is an alternative view pursuant to which these models import scepticism respecting some contractarian assumptions and techniques, but do not imply abandonment of the overall approach. For purposes of contrast, section 3.2 describes points made in some precedent and much more incrementalist corporate law applications of points from the game theoretic models.

3.1 Fundamental Questions About the Contractarian Firm

Although, the game theoretic model does not compel a fundamental critique of the contractarian paradigm, it does provide the basis for one. The contract model builds the firm on layers of arms length bargains actual and hypothetical. Power is transferred so as to create hierarchies, but through contractually controlled delegations: The shareholder is the principal and the manager is the agent. The incomplete contracts paradigm undercuts the base of hypothetical arms length bargains with its assertion that rational economic actors may not be able to contract their way into governance structures. The game theoretic models, having assimilated that point, build firm hierarchies on open-ended, noncontractual transfers of power: Here the manager is the hierarchical superior, and (in the finitely repeated game models) production literally follows from the possibility that trust successfully may be reposed in an honourable actor. Rational self-protection is not absent; but it manifests itself in noncontractual refusals to deal rather than in contracts.[17]

Of course these models describe a framework that completely avoids reliance on legal enforcement. Any negative implications therefore appear to lie equally against the contractarian model and the traditional legal model in which trustworthiness is imposed through fiduciary responsibility. But now let us change an assumption: Although informal punishment works in the repeated game models, in practice some sort of legal enforcement is

[17] Williamson 1992 objects that Kreps' attempt to model the firm as a spontaneous organization underplays the element of intentionality that distinguishes hierarchical production from market exchange. That criticism can be accepted; in fact Kreps has accepted it.

needed. Now, given this, hypothesise that legal enforcement can be made available in only one of two forms: It can either be conditioned on actual and exhaustive contracting by the actors or can proceed under a minimal set of state-supplied legal standards. What form of legal intervention will work best, given the model?

If, as the game theoretic models assume, contracting can be neither expected nor demanded, then, as between the two, the state-supplied rules might facilitate production better (see Aghion and Hermalin, 1990). Recall that under contractarianism the law serves only to save the actors incidental costs by providing contractual provisions in advance. It assumes that absent these default provisions the actors would spend the money to create them. But if we take into account the causes of contractual incompleteness technological limitations, private information and strategic behaviour – it becomes just as easy (and perhaps easier) to assume that this might not happen. The actors, accordingly, might prefer a few state supplied standards supplemented by noncontractual reputational enforcement over contract.[18]

A functional justification for the positive law firm follows directly: Since actors will not necessarily devise thorough-going contractual structures, the law should facilitate production with a handful of backstop mandates, leaving open a field for contract to the extent that the actors can manage it. The mandates protect the extension of trust by hierarchical inferiors, thereby encouraging production. The protection stems from the transfer of the noncontractual punishment function from the firm participant to the legal decisionmaker (Milgrom, North and Weingast, 1990).[19]

The overlap between the game theoretic model and the traditional legal model, thus established, thickens with a reference to Kreps' focal points. In his model, these serve (in the absence of contract equilibria) as co-ordinating concepts on which the noncontractual firm grounds it reputation.

---

18 Arnoud Boot *et al.* show that financial contracts often exist when there is no legally binding obligations. In the context of loan commitment, banks supplement their reputational capital by honouring their contracts. The decision to honour or not will impact the guarantor's reputation. Boot *et al.* point out that it is the reputation mechanism, embodied in the form of publicly-observable formal documents, which gives banks an alternative to contract. Discretionary contracts are useful to banks in that they reveal high and low types, which offers them a basis to develop their reputation. See A. Boot, *et al.* 1993, pp. 1165-1183.

19 The transfer of the punishment function to a legal decisionmaker shores up the assumptional problem with the game theoretic model. It has been suggested that relentless forward punishment in the event of a defection is not safely assumed in repeat games--in the next stage the defecting actor will request forgiveness, and future returns may make it rational to accede to the request. See, Fudenberg and Tirole, 1991. The mandate imports renegotiation proofness even if facilitates ongoing play.

Nothing prevents them from continuing to do so when the noncontractual firm is coupled to the legal firm: To the extent that legal enforcement is costly, the firm will remain concerned about its reputation. Given a 'legal firm', the focal points serve an additional function. They provide a practice referent on which to ground the substance of the mandate. Indeed, Kreps' focal points lend themselves to recharacterization as old-fashioned legal norms.[20] Like traditional fiduciary standards, they come to bear in response to transfers of authority, they are directed to the expectations of dependent parties, and they are instantiated and reshaped through a process of *ex post* application.[21] One point of difference should be noted, however. Kreps' focal points represent a normative regime that is completely internal to the particular firm. The norms of corporate law, in contrast, look both to the firm' internal expectational picture and broader notions about appropriate conduct that circulate in the world of firms in general. That is, they combine the Kreps' focal points with the mode of social enforcement we see in Kandori's model of randomly matched players.

Recall also that Kreps introduces focal points into his model in order to support the reputation that literally holds his noncontractual firm together. The element of functional necessity, taken together with the device's resemblance to the legal norm, suggests a challenge to the contractarian assertion that the burden of proof always lies against regulation. If firms need co-ordinating norms and contract cannot be assumed to provide them, then a global deregulatory presumption is unjustified. Consider the legal problem presented when a plaintiff asks that a new legal standard be extended to cover an unforeseen development. Under Kreps' analysis the determination presumably would be left to fact specific determination either way, rather than automatically resolved in favour of refusal to extend the standard on the ground that the dependent party 'should' have made a contract.

The challenge to the contractarian burden of proof can be restated at a more fundamental level. Recall that one function of Kreps' focal points is to provide standards to guide the firm's response to changing circumstances. But, viewed from the vantage point of a dependent investor, focal point

---

20 Kreps acknowledge this point (see Kreps, 1990), pp. 143-145.

21 We reject the idea, advanced by Clayton Gillette, that the *ex post* discovery of the appropriate focal point is unrealistic ambition because of the high transaction costs involved and the fact that there may be too many equilibria for the court to analyze, (see Gillette, 1993). The problem with Gillette's analysis is that it relies on a first-best view of contract (i.e., that the parties will be able to design the appropriate majoritarian default), and does not investigate the menu of choices available to courts in selecting a focal point.

principles cannot completely solve the problem of changed circumstances. The dependent investor remains vulnerable to drastic alterations in the game's payoff structure that transform the game from an infinite play pattern to one in which the end period is immediately foreseeable. Here, as is well known, reputation matters little to a rational actor. The sudden appearance of hostile take-overs and management buyouts of the 1980s provide an example of such a sudden shift in the terms of the game.

This possibility of a change in fundamental circumstance makes necessary a reference to the finite play models. These suggest a cost economics of investment that succeeds by abandoning the assumption that all actors are purely self-interested and introducing the possibility of honourable conduct. Of course, the modification is a limited one: An A's trust of the Players B need not be thorough-going; trust is based on a probabilistic appraisal as to type and A is ready to punish defection. Even so, the model displays a conceptual tie to the traditional mode of the fiduciary relation. It invites us to divide the world of economic interaction into two broad categories. In one category, *ex ante* contracting is cost effective and sufficiently complete to solve the problem of self-interest by providing a satisfactory guaranty of legal protection. In the other, complete contractual protection *ex ante* is not cost effective because of informational asymmetries and a long list of possible future relational problems. Complex transactions, accordingly, will depend on noncontractual enforcement techniques. But, given real world informational asymmetries and changing circumstances these are unlikely to provide a complete solution to the problem of contractual incompleteness. These transactions as a result will require an extension of trust by one or both parties; and, absent a population of honourable types, these transactions may not occur.[22] Doubts about the prevalence of honour in the population can be mitigated by a backstop regime of legal protection that enforces honour.

3.2 Incrementalist Contractarian Applications: Default Rule Analysis

Contractarian theory asserts that corporate law's only function is to save costs by providing default rules in advance, with the terms for which a majority of parties would contract in a costless world leading to the greatest cost savings (see Easterbrook, and Fischel, 1991). The incomplete contracts paradigm, with its emphasis on informational asymmetries and recognition of the presence of multiple equilibria, rebuts the second part of this assertion. The literature articulating this rebuttal is well-developed. It

[22] A resemblance to Ian MacNeil's division of transactions into discrete and relational categories is noted.

moves us from a legal discourse limited to the determination of what most of parties would want in a costless world to a discourse directed to the comparative assessment of the contractual equilibria that result from alternative defaults (see Ayres, 1992). Instead of a single state-supplied corporate contract, we get menus of regulatory possibilities (see Ayres, 1992). Suppletory rules that the parties would not have chosen for themselves, called 'penalty defaults', may prove to be more efficient than majoritarian defaults because they fore parties to share information as they bargain around them.[23] Models of bargaining under asymmetric information even support unqualified legal prohibitions of certain contract terms (see Aghion and Hermalin, 1990). A third alternative, the high cost of contracting *ex ante* for unforeseen contingencies supports default rules framed along the lines of the vague standards of existing fiduciary law.

Ian Ayres, arguing the latter point, brings an openness to *ex post* consideration of the import of events to bear against contractarianism's insistence of terms based on complete allocation of risk *ex ante* (see Ayres, 1992). Since the corporation is a long-term relational contract that must cover all future states of the world, and costs prevent *ex ante* negotiation of these terms, judicial intervention *ex post* promotes efficiency by supplying the necessary terms. Fiduciary law's 'muddy' (or open ended) defaults occasion these interventions by providing for judicial determination of duties after the fact, when circumstances can be verified.[24] Furthermore, argues Ayres, such terms may be cost efficient even if a majority of firms

---

23 Ayres and Gertner suggest the 'penalty default' in corporate gap-filling contexts. Under this, the contractarian judge departs from the hypothetical contract principle to introduce a term to which the parties would not have agreed in order to prod the party with greater information into disclosure. The function of a default rule is to supply the best possible pooling equilibrium term. The choice of penalty default depends upon the features of multiple Nash equilibria in the asymmetric model design being considered. Ayres and Gertner, 1989. Ayres and Gertner also open up the distinction between tailored and untailored suppletory rules. In the former case the judge ascertains what the parties in the case would have contracted for, a particularistic exercise. In the latter case, the judge constructs a single off the rack standard for all legal contracts. Ayres and Gertner suggest that in the particular case, the selection of the particular suppletory rules will be complex, depending on the contract cost picture and the effects of the different possible supplementing rules. Ayres' claim that penalty defaults can be extended to corporate contracts is challenged by Klausner, who argues that, due to network externalities, contracting parties may reach suboptimal bargains. Because penalty defaults may produce a wide range of responses, firms are less likely to co-ordinate their actions so as to capture network benefits. (See, Klausner, 1995, pp. 757-852).

24 Ayres states that 'Muddy defaults make contractual obligations contingent on circumstances ("states of the world") that are verifiable by courts *ex post*, but prohibitively costly to identify *ex ante*.

would prefer clear rules that explicitly permit or prohibit stated conduct. Muddy rules of reasonableness are prohibitively expensive *ex ante* because they can be articulated only over time through judicial treatment of particular situations. Clear rules, in contrast can be stated cheaply in advance because information about the state-of-the-art file of clear legal forms is cheaply available. Forcing the majority to opt into the clear rules as it reacts to the body of judicial precedents thus saves costs overall.[25]

Ayres' treatment is incremental and stays well clear of the traditional doctrinal theories that justify fiduciary intervention. It validates fiduciary methodology within a framework that stays with contract at the bottom line: Here *ex post* judicial intervention is legitimated only on the basis of an *ex ante* default rule that has been justified on a contractual cost-benefit analysis.[26] The penalty default concept works similarly. Under it, the legal rule gets its substance by reference to its effect on an assumed bargaining process insofar as it leaves terms open until relevant information is available.

Game theoretic exercises in this incrementalist mode have an indeterminate aspect. Here, game theoretic techniques work together with contractarian assumptions, and the latter can come to dominate the mix. The penalty default concept, although generally assumed to import support for protective rules, can be deployed to the opposite effect. Jason Johnston's model of close corporation bargaining brings this possibility into view (see Johnston, 1992). Johnston's analysis leads to a default recommendation that cuts against a protective standard that has evolved in American close corporation cases.

Johnston takes up a two party problem that recurs in disputes over fiduciary duties in close corporations.[27] An entrepreneur provides the financial capital and controls the corporation through majority stock ownership; a manager contributes human capital and owns a minority of the

---

25 Carrying Ayres' point a step further, it can be argued that 'muddy' fiduciary determinations provide a useful positive law base point for the articulation of private per se rules over time. Situational judicial precedent provides information respecting changing relational contingencies. Absent this experimental data, information costs could loom larger in the drafting of clear prohibitions.

26 Klausner contends that the muddy default analysis is for the most part consistent with a network externalities perspective. Muddy defaults are preferable to untailored default in that they are more likely to reduce the probability of a suboptimal uniformity. Indeed, the *ex post* tailoring of defaults is more likely to reduce network externalities for heterogeneous firms. Moreover, muddy defaults may, to the extent that new information is fed back into the customizing process, promote optimal contract networks for homogenous firms (see Klausner, 1995).

27 See *Jordan* v. *Duff and Phelps Inc.*, 815 F. 2d 429 (7th Cir. 1987).

stock. If the two co-operate, returns will be maximal. But both are in positions of exposure to the other's opportunism. A bad entrepreneur will fire the manager after the manager has made a firm specific investment of labour. A bad manager will shirk and, when justifiably fired, bring a bad faith lawsuit alleging breach of fiduciary duty. The parties have to decide whether to include a term providing that the manager can be terminated only in good faith at the time of corporate organisation. The outcome of this negotiation will bear on the firm's later operation, affecting the entrepreneur's decision whether to divert firm specific assets and the manager's decision whether to make firm specific investments.

The situation, thus outlined, presents a variant of the prisoners' dilemma combined with an *ex ante* signalling game. Here both the information asymmetry and exposure to opportunism are double sided each party has an opportunity to defect and each lacks knowledge as to whether the other is an honourable or dishonourable person. The bad entrepreneur will divert the manager's investment, the good manager will make specific investments. A good faith termination term plays out differently depending on the probabilities as to type. The good faith term or fiduciary duty encourages investment by the good manager, but provides a basis for the bad manager's bad faith lawsuit. Bargaining over the term signals as to type.

Johnston's detailed analysis concludes that fiduciary protection is not efficient on most fact patterns.[28] Even so, bargaining should result in a protective term in many cases – a good entrepreneur can be expected to propose it as a way of signalling a trustworthy character to the manager whenever the risk of the bad faith lawsuit is tolerable. Strict limits on the implied in law duty, says Johnston, thus help good managers find good entrepreneurs. They also increase the chance that bad people will reveal their type, destabilising comparative ventures that should not get past the formation stage.

These conclusions are reached despite the recognition that an implied in law duty would reduce rewards to bad people *ex post*. Significantly, Johnston reaches this result only after making a pair of contractarian assumptions. First, he assumes that actors are well-informed and rational and will attempt to bargain into such responsibilities as suit them at the formation stage. Second, he assumes that courts acting in litigation

28 In his view the situation in which a hypothetical contract case for a duty can be made out is narrow. Three factors must combine: A bad faith managerial law suit must be unlikely, managerial investment must be very sensitive to levels of legal protection, and firm specific investment by the entrepreneur must be unimportant. In all other cases the parties should be left to bargain for their own term. Johnston, 1992, p. 323.

contexts do a bad job of determining what the parties would have wanted *ex ante*. Johnston contrasts and rejects an alternative assumption under which the parties simply trust rather than treat trustworthiness as an information problem for solution through bargaining. In such a world of probabilistic 'degenerate beliefs' in the certainty of trustworthiness, says Johnston, a legal regime with broad fiduciary duties is 'simply a shorthand for what the parties actually believed and expected'. *Ex post* interpolation of duties has no effect on *ex ante* incentives of parties modelled in this trusting mould because they do not bargain in the first place.

Thus, Johnston withholds *ex post* protection on a penalty default basis even while recognising that most parties may be trusting.[29] He thereby brings the penalty default device into alignment with the contractarian norm of forced bargaining. His approach must be questioned in a number of respects, however.

First, references to the incomplete contract paradigm and to the evolution of practice respecting close corporations make it possible to reverse Johnston's penalty default. Consider his assumption that parties will be rational and disposed towards contract. This does not exclude the possibility that an exhaustive contract may be prohibitively costly, even given a strategic legal stick. Nor, given past legal patterns, does a disposition to bargain by itself support a penalty default. Historically, corporate law placed the burden of protection on close corporation actors themselves. It learned to intervene on behalf of those injured in dependent positions at the same time that it learned to broaden the field for self-protective contracting. An extensive file of protective contract forms became available as a result. This evolutionary pattern makes it hard to argue that a penalty default is needed to prompt reference to the form file by actors already disposed to do so. The judicial good faith duty seems unlikely to remove their incentive to contract, given the high cost and uncertainty of enforcement.

Second, Johnston's assertion that courts do a bad job at reconstructing *ex ante* bargains should be compared with Ayres' defence of muddy defaults. Following Ayres, it becomes possible to assert that the value of the courts' contribution does not turn on their relative ability to reconstruct non-existent *ex ante* bargains. Their job instead is to apply general principles to the performance pattern that emerges in history, so as to facilitate adjustments in subsequent generations of contracts.

29 A determining contractarian norm is implicit. Presumably, in an evolutionary context determined by the survival of the fittest, the trusting 'degenerates' will perish in time. Then, with a legal regime keyed to *ex ante* strategic problems, we will have an ideal population of good people who are also well informed two-fisted bargainers.

Finally, it seems unsafe to assume that forced contracting will prompt beneficial informational exchanges as good actors seek out other good actors at the formation stage. It could be that the honourable dispositions that enhance productivity are not easily flicked off for purposes of negotiation and then flicked back on when performance starts later on. Just as a good entrepreneur signals trustworthiness by proposing a fiduciary duty, so may a good manager signal trustworthiness by waiving the opportunity to enter into a two-fisted negotiation. Moreover, the contractual matching of good types leaves unsolved the problem of unforeseen events. Fidelity to a joint and productive project is not a permanent given. Good types in long-run performance situations can stumble into misunderstandings; objectively opportunistic actions may follow, even as both actors remain sure of their own goodness. Their reciprocal commitment needs periodic modification and reconfirmation as the commercial situation changes in a dynamic environment. The more stable the environment, the better its chances for sustenance (see Frank, 1988). The legal backstop imports stability for contracting actors even as it protects more trusting types.[30]

4 Contrarian Possibilities: Trust, Social Norms, and A Complex Model of the Actor

Game theoretic models of co-operation have inspired a new line of social theory. This offers a behavioural description of co-operative production in which trust and rational calculation coexist and complement one another. This description, having included trust as an independent motivation, goes on to recognise that normative constraints play a role in the formation of economic institutions. And it claims to achieve this result while respecting the self-interest incentive and the power of rational expectations analysis. Thus framed, this approach inadvertently tracks the traditional model of fiduciary law.

---

[30] An implied in law duty does not change the *ex ante* bargaining context. The parties must contract to opt out rather than opt in, and strategic barriers make this difficult. Presumably, the bad entrepreneur would be signalling his or her type by suggesting opting out. The good entrepreneur might be afraid of a bad type lawsuit and wish to pare down an implied duty, but be chary of sending a wrong signal as to type. But since the legal duty promotes investment, there is a compensating benefit under Johnston's model. Indeed but for the problem of the bad faith lawsuit, legal protection is an unalloyed positive. To the extent that Johnston overstates the disincentive properties of the lawsuit, there is every reason to resolve doubts in favour of fiduciary protection so long as the parties remain free to opt out.

This socio-economic theory of the firm begins with the game theoretic model of co-operation, but shifts its emphasis so as to bring the extension of trust into the centre of the description. In the retold story, one actor in the co-operative venture ends up in a dependent position, necessitating assurances against defection on the dominant actor's part (see Williams, 1988). The dominant actor' reputation, which grows from behaviour over time that reveals the actor's honourable disposition, provides this assurance. The reputation gives rise to trusting expectations respecting the dominant actor's future conduct (see Dasgupta, 1988). The trust compensates for the dependent actor's informational advantage. Without it there will be no producing relationship. But, following game theory, trust will be insufficient taken alone. Since information is incomplete and the dominant party's reputational incentives will be subject to change over time, trust will be a fragile commodity. Thus, credible sanctions for defection also must be present (see Dasgupta, 1988). Sanctions push the utility of the self-interested dominant party toward ongoing co-operation, further assuring the dependent party (see Williams 1988). As the coercive backstop becomes stronger, trust diminishes; but, with a stronger backstop, less trust will be required to sustain the relationship (see Gambetta, 1988). Given the absence of perfect coercive arrangements, trust emerges as a social lubricant that makes production and exchange possible. Since neither rationality nor contract by themselves can assure the emergence of co-operative arrangements, we should design our institutions so as to bank on trust.

The socio-economic theory then turns to the other side of the trust/honour outcome, looking to game theory to ground an assertion that social norms must be included in the description of co-operative production. Norms solve the problem presented by the repeated games' multiple equilibrium outcomes. As already noted, multiple equilibria limit game theory's explanatory power since it predicts many more equilibria than we find in the real world (see Dasgupta 1988). Contractarian theory avoids this problem by assuming that competition pushes actors into first best equilibria. But that approach does not satisfy theorists who accept the point that rational norm free negotiations cannot resolve the uncertainties of bargaining (see Elster, 1989). Game theoretic models do address the problem they produce thin co-ordinating norms, such as truth-telling and promise keeping in tit-for-tat patterns. Kreps, as we have seen, goes farther and suggests that focal points evolve to support equilibrium strategies in co-operative situations. But the focal point concept is problematic in Kreps' account since it neither shows us how a significant group of players comes to follow the focal point as a norm, nor explains what motivates the players to adhere to it (see Pettit, 1990). The social theorists jump in at this point. They expand on the 'focal point', using social norms and moral codes to fill in the missing elements in the description. Norms of reciprocity equality, and co-operation, like focal points, are points of friction that generate predictable outcomes. Since they evolve in history, the matter of derivation is dealt with exogenously (see Biccheiri, 1990).

More importantly, the norms sustain trust by lending credibility to the commitments of dominant actors. The credibility lies in the response of disapproval that follows upon deviance from the norm (see Pettit, 1990). The social threat can prove to be a stronger reputational incentive than the economic threat of refusal to deal. As the game theoretic models show us, refusal to deal has serious limitations whenever the aggrieved party's economic interests lie in favour of more deals and against punishment. If continued co-operation looks profitable, they might as well forgive (see Pettit, 1990). Social disapproval, in contrast, occurs automatically, without reference to the alignment of the money, and involves a wider audience.

At the bottom line, the socio-economic approach offers a picture of production in which actors draw on a range of devices to import credibility to commitments to cooperage. Some of the devices, such as precommitment, investment in bargaining, and investment in reputation, are consonant with a rational expectations description. On the other hand, there are constraints that gain their credibility from social norms (see Elster 1989). The norms often coincide with self-interest as they shape actors' conduct, but they never fully reduce to explanation in self-interested terms (see Elster 1989).

With this last point, the social-economic theory asks us to reconsider the rational actor itself. Given the need for trust and the stabilising role of norms of self-abnegation, it follows that an exclusively egoistic model of the actor suffices as a basis for explanation no better than does an exclusively altruistic model. Only a mixed model of the actor works well, a model allowing for counterpreferential choices to commit to alternatives that make actors worse off but benefit a project (see Sen, 1982).

This complex actor still may be conceived as a utility maximiser: She may derive satisfaction from counterpreferential choices, a satisfaction stemming from a balance of self-interested and social motivations. But, as Frank has argued, she has disruptive characteristics when considered in the narrower framework of economic utility. In Frank's view, the project to reconstruct co-operative behaviour in rational, self-maximising terms runs afoul of its own assumption. In reaches an immovable emotional bloc in relational situations where actors solve contracting problems by committing themselves to future behaviour that could turn out to be against self-interest.

A paradox arises in these situations: the conscious pursuit of self-interest is incompatible with its attainment. Frank proposes a 'commitment model' to solve these problems: Co-operative contracting solutions have to be experienced as noninstrumental in order to work. Significantly, those directly motivated to pursue self-interest will be less successful as contracting actors than those emotionally disposed to adhere to commitments in good faith. The honourable actor offers a more credible commitment and therefore makes a more advantageous contract (see Frank, 1988). Therein lies the paradox. For the model to work, satisfaction from doing the right thing must not be premised on the fact that material gains may later follow; it must be intrinsic to the act itself. If an actor lacks the necessary motivation, material gains will not follow.

4.1 Conclusion: The Trust-Based Firm and the Traditional Legal Model

The incomplete contracts paradigm and the theory of repeated games together suggest a fundamental critique of the contractarian firm. With multiple equilibria and bargaining costs, they undermine the assumption that market constrains a first best equilibrium. By identifying significant bargaining costs, they counsel scepticism of global contractarian penalty defaults that seek to force contracting by denuding dependent actors of legal protection. Their alternative co-ordinating device, the noncontractual focal point, suggests that protective default rules may work well after all. Finally, their division of the world into honourable and dishonourable types invites us to drop the assumption that self-interested behaviour is inevitable.

The socio-economic gloss takes us beyond critique to an alternative model. Here the game theoretic firm is restated with emphases on a base of trust, the complexity of the actor it deploys, and the co-ordinating role of social norms. This trust-based firm has a predictive capacity it the legal context that manifestly outstrips that of the contractarian firm. In the trust-based firm, as in the legal model, self-interest and honour interplay, even though each has an aspect that negates the other. As in the legal model, neither behavioural characteristic subsumes the other so as to reach a fusion that provides a clear base for *ex ante* arrangements. With the trust-based model, we can account for the evolution of a legal system in which the same conflicts come up again and again over extended periods, and in which the decision maker serves as an *ex post* mediator. The trust-based firm's thicker description also leads to an explanation of positive law with it we can side-step the contractarian conjuring trick that turns positive law into contract and protective norms into *ex ante* bargains.

The trust-based firm thus implies a new endorsement of traditional fiduciary theory. Business relationships that balance self-interest with honour will have a potential for instability over time. This cannot be avoided through contract, because *ex ante* welfare calculations will never adequately identify *ex post* problems of unreciprocal treatment. Given this, normative interventions under the fiduciary rubric that enforce commitment to honour another's interests play a co-ordinating role. Fiduciary moralism confirms the norms' presence in the positive law construct. The norm's transfer from business practice to the law facilitates its communication to the large numbers of actors involved in production in firms. Enforcement of the legal norm supplements the informal sanctions of social disapproval and economic refusal to deal. The functional significance of legal enforcement increases as the numbers of actors become larger and collective action problems make informal enforcement less effective. Finally, the exercise of legal enforcement will be mediative, tending towards less precise determinations based on a complex behavioural model rather than attempts to formulate more precise *ex ante* calculations. Judges will always lack information necessary for the latter exercise. Moreover, the decision as to the norm's violation may be non instrumental an attitudal response of approval or disapproval of conduct that occurs at the moment of judgement.

Social theory and microeconomics influence the trust-based firm equally. As a result, it remains open to a range of strategies for dealing with firm hierarchies. Legal intervention is one of these. But the need to trust and rely on norms is obviated to the extent that contract succeeds. In the alternative, punishment through refusal to contract may suffice in some situations. But, in any event, the deregulatory presumption of contractarianism has no place. The trust-based model invites us to apply the inherited legal framework in new situations without the assistance of a global presumption either way.

REFERENCES

Abreu, D., (1986), External Equilibria of Oligopolistic Supergames, *Journal of Economic Theory, Vol. 39* pp. 191-225.

Aghion, P., and Hermalin, B., (1990), Legal Restrictions on Private Contracts Can Increase Efficiency, *Journal of Law, Economics and Organisation,* Vol. 6, pp. 381-409.

Anderlini, L., and Felli, L., (1994), Incomplete Written Contracts: Undescrible States of Nature, *Quarterly Journal of Economics,* Vol. 109, pp. 1085-1124.

Ayres, I., (1991), 'The Possibility of Inefficient Corporate Contracts', *University of Cincinnati Law Review,* Vol. 60 pp. 387-404.

Ayres, I., (1992), Making a Difference: The Contractual Contributions of Easterbrook and Fischel, *The University of Chicago Law Review,* Vol. 59, pp. 1391-1420.

Ayres, I., and Gertner, R., (1989), Filling Gaps in Incomplete Contracts: An Economic Theory of Default Rules, *Yale Law Journal,* Vol. 99, pp. 87-130.

Baird, D., Gertner, R., and Picker, R. (1994), *Game Theory and the Law,* Cambridge, Mass.: Harvard University Press.

Benoit, J. and Krishna, V., (1985), Finitely Repeated Games, *Econometrica,* Vol. 17, pp. 317-20.

Bicchieri, C., (1990), Norms of co-operation, *Ethics,* Vol. 100, pp. 838-861.

Binmore, K., (1994), *Playing Fair, Game Theory and the Social Contract, Volume 1.,* Cambridge, Mass.: MIT Press.

Boot, A., Greenbaum, S., and Thakor, A., (1993), Reputation and Discretion in Financial Contracting, *American Economic Review,* Vol. 83, pp. 1165-83.

Bratton, W., (1989), The "Nexus of Contracts" Corporation: A Critical Appraisal, *Cornell Law Review,* Vol. 74, pp. 407-465.

Dasgupta, P., (1988), Trust as a Commodity, in D. Gambeta, (ed.) *Trust, Making and Breaking Co-operative Relation* pp. 49-72.

Deakin, S., Lane, S. and Wilkinson, F., (1994), Trust or Law? Towards an Integrated Theory of Contractual Relations Between Firms, *Journal of Law and Society,* Vol. 21, pp. 329-349.

Easterbrook, F., and Fischel, D., (1991), *The Economic Structure of Corporate Law,* Cambridge, Mass.: Harvard University Press.

Elster, J., (1989), *The Cement of Society, A Study of Social Order,* Cambridge: Cambridge University Press.

Frank, R., (1988), *Passions within Reason,* New York: Norton Press.

Fudenberg, D., (1992), Explaining Co-operation and commitment in repeated games, in J.J. Laffont (ed.) *Advances in Economic Theory, Sixth World Congress,* Cambridge: Cambridge University Press pp. 89-131.

Fudenberg, D., and Maskin, E., (1986), The Folk Theorem in repeated games with discounting or with incomplete information *Econometrica* Vol. 54, pp. 533-54.

Fudenberg, D., and Tirole, J., (1992), *Game Theory,* Cambridge, Mass.: MIT Press.

Gambetta, E., (1988), Can We Trust Trust? in D. Gambetta (ed.) *Trust, Making and Breaking Co-operative Relations,* Oxford: Basil Blackwell pp. 213-237.

Gillette, C., (1993), Co-operation and Convention in Contractual Defaults, *S. Cal. Interdis. L.J.,* Vol. 3, pp. 167-187.

Grief, A., Milgrom, P., and Weingast, B., (1994), Co-ordination, Commitment and Enforcement: The Case of the Merchant Guild, *Journal of Political Economy,* Vol. 94, pp. 745-76.

Haddock, D.D., and McChesney, F.S.,(1991), Bargaining costs, bargaining benefits, and compulsory nonbargaining rules, *Journal of Law, Economics and Organisation,*Vol. 7, pp. 334-354.

Harsanyi, J., (1969), Rational Choice Models of Behaviour versus Functionalist and Conformist Theories, *World Politics,* Vol. 22, pp. 513-38.

Hart, O.D., (1995), *Firms, Contracts, and Financial Structure,* Oxford: Clarendon Press.

Johnston, J., (1993), 'The Influence of *The Nature of the Firm* on the Theory of Corporate Law', *Journal of Corporations Law,* Vol. 18, p 244.

Johnston, J., (1992), Opting In and Opting Out, Bargaining for Fiduciary Duties in Co-operative Ventures, *Washington University Law Quarterly,* Vol. 70, pp. 291-352.

Kandori, M., (1992a), Social Norms and Community Enforcement, *Review of Economic Studies,* Vol. 59, pp. 63-80.

Kandori, M., (1992b), Repeated Games Played by Overlapping Generations of Players, *Review of Economic Studies* Vol. 59, pp. 81-92.

Klausner, M., (1995), Corporations, Corporate Law and Networks of Contracts, Vol. 81, *Virginia Law Review,* pp. 757-852.

Kreps, D., (1990), Corporate Culture and Economic Theory, in J. Alt and K. Shepsle (eds) *Perspectives on Positive Political Economy,* Cambridge: Cambridge University Press pp. 90-143.

Kreps, D., Milgrom, P., Roberts, J., and Wilson, R., (1982), Rational cooperation in the finitley repeated prisoners dilemma, *Journal of Economic Theory,* Vol. 27, pp. 245-252.

Kreps, D., and Wilson, R., (1982), Reputation and Imperfect Information, *Journal of Economic Theory,* Vol. 27, pp. 253-279.

Milgrom, P., North, D., and Weingast, B., (1990), The Role of Institutions in the Revival of Trade: The Medieval Law Merchant, Private Judges, and the Champagne Fairs *Economics and Politics,* Vol. 2, pp. 1-23.

Milgrom, P., and Roberts, J., (1992), *Economics, organisation and management,* Englewood *Cliffs:* Prentice Hall.

Milgrom, P., and Roberts, J., (1990), Bargaining Costs, Influence Costs, and the Organisation of Economic Activity in James Alt and Kenneth Shepsle (eds.) Perspectives on Positive Political Economy, Cambridge: Cambridge University Press pp. 57-89.

Moore, J.H., (1992), Implementation, contracts and renegotiation in environments with complete information, in Jean-Jacques Laffont (ed.) *Advances in Economic Theory, Sixth World Congress,* Vol. 1, Cambridge: Cambridge University Press pp. 182-282.

Pearce, D., (1992), Repeated Games: Co-operation and Rationality, in J.J. Laffont (ed.) *Advances in Economic Theory, Sixth World Congress,* Vol. 1, Cambridge: Cambridge University Press pp. 132-174.

Pettit, P., (1990), *Virtus Normativa*: Rational Choice Perspectives, *Ethics,* Vol. 100, pp. 725-755.

Rubinstein, A., (1992), Comments on the interpretation of repeated games theory, in J.J. Laffont (ed.) *Advances in Economic Theory, Sixth World Congress,* Vol. 1, Cambridge: Cambridge University Press pp. 175-181.

Schwartz, A., (1992), Legal Contract Theories and Incomplete Contracts, in Lars Werin and Hans Wijkander (eds.) *Contract Economics,* Oxford, Blackwell pp. 76-108.

Sen, A., (1982), Rational Fools: A Critique of the Behavioural Foundations of Economic Theory, *Philosophy and Public Affairs,* Vol. 6, pp. 317-344.

Schelling, T., (1960), *The Strategy of Conflict,* Cambridge, Mass.: Harvard University Press.

Tirole, J., (1988), *The Theory of Industrial Organisation,* Cambridge, Mass: MIT Press.

Tirole, J., (1992), Comment, in Lars Werin and Hans Wijkander' (eds.) *Contract Economics,* Oxford: Blackwell pp. 109-113.

Tirole, J., (1992), Collusion and the Theory of Organisations, in Jean-Jacques Laffont (ed.) *Advances in Economic Theory, Sixth World Congress,* Vol. 2, Cambridge: Cambridge University Press pp. 151-214.

Williams, B., (1988), Formal Structures and Social Reality, in D. Gambetta (ed.) *Trust, Making and Breaking Co-operative Relations,* Oxford: Basil Blackwell pp. 3-13.

Williamson, O., (1993), Calculativeness, Trust and Economic Organisation, *Journal of Law and Economics,* Vol. 36, pp. 453-486.

APPENDIX: DIRECTIVE ON UNFAIR TERMS IN CONSUMER CONTRACTS – TERMS REFERRED TO IN ARTICLE 3 (3) AS BEING INDICATIVELY UNFAIR

---

1. Terms which have the object or effect of:

(a) excluding or limiting the legal liability of a seller or supplier in the event of the death of a consumer or personal injury to the latter resulting from an act or omission of that seller or supplier;

(b) inappropriately excluding or limiting the legal rights of the consumer *vis-a-vis* the seller or supplier or another party in the event of total or partial non-performance or inadequate performance by the seller or supplier of any of the contractual obligations, including the option of offsetting a debt owed to the seller or supplier against any claim which the consumer may have against him;

(c) making an agreement binding on the consumer whereas provision of services by the seller or supplier is subject to a condition whose realisation depends on his own will alone;

(d) permitting the seller or supplier to retain sums paid by the consumer where the latter decides not to conclude or perform the contract, without providing for the consumer to receive compensation of an equivalent amount from the seller or supplier where the latter is the party cancelling the contract;

(e) requiring any consumer who fails to fulfil his obligation to pay a disproportionately high sum in compensation;

(f) authorising the seller or supplier to dissolve the contract on a discretionary basis where the same facility is not granted to the consumer, or permitting the seller or supplier to retain the sums paid for services not yet supplied by him where it is the seller or supplier himself who dissolves the contract;

(g) enabling the seller or supplier to terminate a contract of indeterminate duration without reasonable notice except where there are serious grounds for doing so;

(h) automatically extending a contract of fixed duration where the consumer does not indicate otherwise, when the deadline fixed for the consumer to express this desire not to extend the contract is unreasonably early;

(i) irrevocably binding the consumer to terms with which he had no real opportunity of becoming acquainted before the conclusion of the contract;

(j) enabling the seller or supplier to alter the terms of the contract unilaterally without a valid reason which is specified in the contract;

(k) enabling the seller or supplier to alter unilaterally without a valid reason any characteristics of the product or service to be provided;

(l) providing for the price of goods to be determined at the time of delivery or allowing a seller of goods or supplier of services to increase their price without in both cases giving the consumer the corresponding right to cancel the contract if the final price is too high in relation to the price agreed when the contract was concluded;

(m) giving the seller or supplier the right to determine whether the goods or services supplied are in conformity with the contract, or giving him the exclusive right to interpret any term of the contract;

(n) limiting the seller's or supplier's obligation to respect commitments undertaken by his agents or making his commitments subject to compliance with a particular formality;

(o) obliging the consumer to fulfil all his obligations where the seller or supplier does not perform his;

(p) giving the seller or supplier the possibility of transferring his rights and obligations under the contract, where this may serve to reduce the guarantees for the consumer, without the latter's agreement;

(q) excluding or hindering the consumer's right to take legal action or exercise any other legal remedy, particularly by requiring the consumer to take disputes exclusively to arbitration not covered by legal provisions, unduly restricting the evidence available to him or imposing on him a burden of proof which, according to the applicable law, should lie with another party to the contract.

2. Scope of subparagraphs (g), (j) and (l)

(a) Subparagraph (g) is without hindrance to terms by which a supplier of financial services reserves the right to terminate unilaterally a contract of indeterminate duration without notice where there is a valid reason, provided that the supplier is required to inform the other contracting party or parties thereof immediately;

(b) Subparagraph (j) is without hindrance to terms under which a supplier of financial services reserves the right to alter the rate of interest payable by the consumer or due to the latter, or the amount of other charges for financial services without notice where there is a valid reason, provided that the supplier is required to inform the other contracting party or parties thereof at the earliest opportunity and that the latter are free to dissolve the contract immediately.

(c) Subparagraphs (g), (j) and (l) do not apply to:

– transactions in transferable securities, financial instruments and other products or services where the price is linked to fluctuations in a stock exchange quotation or index or a financial market rate that the seller or supplier does not control;

– contracts for the purchase or sale of foreign currency, traveller's cheques or international money orders denominated in foreign currency;

(d) Subparagraph (1) is without hindrance to price indexation clauses, where lawful, provided that the method by which prices vary is explicitly described.

Index